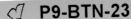

SQL
FOR
DUMMIES®

Allen G. Taylor

IDG Books Worldwide, Inc.
An International Data Group Company

Foster City, CA ◆ Chicago, IL ◆ Indianapolis, IN ◆ Braintree, MA ◆ Southlake, TX

For More Information...

For general information on IDG Books Worldwide's books in the U.S., please call our Consumer Customer Service department at 800-762-2974. For reseller information, including discounts and premium sales, please call our Reseller Customer Service department at 800-434-3422.

For information on where to purchase IDG Books Worldwide's books outside the U.S., contact IDG Books Worldwide at 415-655-3021 or fax 415-655-3295.

For information on translations, contact Marc Jeffrey Mikulich, Director, Foreign & Subsidiary Rights, at IDG Books Worldwide, 415-655-3018 or fax 415-655-3295.

For sales inquiries and special prices for bulk quantities, write to the address at top of the facing page or call IDG Books Worldwide at 415-655-3200.

For authorization to photocopy items for corporate, personal, or educational use, please contact Copyright Clearance Center, 222 Rosewood Drive, Danvers, MA 01923, or fax 508-750-4470.

SQL For Dummies is distributed by Macmillan Canada for Canada; by Computer and Technical Books for the Caribbean Basin; by Contemporanea de Ediciones for Venezuela; by Distribuidora Cuspide for Argentina; by CITEC for Brazil; by Ediciones ZETA S.C.R. Ltda. for Peru; by Editorial Limusa SA for Mexico; by Transworld Publishers Limited in the United Kingdom and Europe; by Al-Maiman Publishers & Distributors for Saudi Arabia; by Simron Pty. Ltd. for South Africa; by IDG Communications (HK) Ltd. for Hong Kong; by Toppan Company Ltd. for Japan; by Addison Wesley Publishing Company for Korea; by Longman Singapore Publishers Ltd. for Singapore, Malaysia, Thailand, and Indonesia; by Unalis Corporation for Taiwan; by WS Computer Publishing Company, Inc. for the Philippines; by WoodsLane Pty. Ltd. for Australia; by WoodsLane Enterprises Ltd. for New Zealand.

Welcome to the world of IDG Books Worldwide.

IDG Books Worldwide, Inc., is a subsidiary of International Data Group, the world's largest publisher of computer-related information and the leading global provider of information services on information technology. IDG was founded more than 25 years ago and now employs more than 7,700 people worldwide. IDG publishes more than 250 computer publications in 67 countries (see listing below). More than 70 million people read one or more IDG publications each month.

Launched in 1990, IDG Books Worldwide is today the #1 publisher of best-selling computer books in the United States. We are proud to have received 8 awards from the Computer Press Association in recognition of editorial excellence and three from Computer Currents' First Annual Readers' Choice Awards, and our best-selling ...*For Dummies*® series has more than 19 million copies in print with translations in 28 languages. IDG Books Worldwide, through a joint venture with IDG's Hi-Tech Beijing, became the first U.S. publisher to publish a computer book in the People's Republic of China. In record time, IDG Books Worldwide has become the first choice for millions of readers around the world who want to learn how to better manage their businesses.

Our mission is simple: Every one of our books is designed to bring extra value and skill-building instructions to the reader. Our books are written by experts who understand and care about our readers. The knowledge base of our editorial staff comes from years of experience in publishing, education, and journalism — experience which we use to produce books for the '90s. In short, we care about books, so we attract the best people. We devote special attention to details such as audience, interior design, use of icons, and illustrations. And because we use an efficient process of authoring, editing, and desktop publishing our books electronically, we can spend more time ensuring superior content and spend less time on the technicalities of making books.

You can count on our commitment to deliver high-quality books at competitive prices on topics you want to read about. At IDG Books Worldwide, we continue in the IDG tradition of delivering quality for more than 25 years. You'll find no better book on a subject than one from IDG Books Worldwide.

John J. Kilcullen

John Kilcullen
President and CEO
IDG Books Worldwide, Inc.

About the Author

Allen G. Taylor is a 20-year veteran of the computer industry and the author of 14 computer-related books, including *dBASE for Windows Solutions*, *Teach Yourself Paradox*, *Voodoo OS/2*, and *Unix Guide for DOS Users*. He is an industry consultant and seminar leader in database design and application development, and speaks nationally on improving quality and productivity through the appropriate application of technology. Allen lives with his family on a small farm outside of Oregon City, Oregon.

Credits

**Senior Vice President
and Publisher**
Milissa L. Koloski

Associate Publisher
Diane Graves Steele

Brand Manager
Judith A. Taylor

Editorial Managers
Kristin A. Cocks
Mary Corder

Product Development Manager
Mary Bednarek

Editorial Executive Assistant
Richard Graves

Editorial Assistants
Constance Carlisle
Chris Collins
Kevin Spencer

Production Director
Beth Jenkins

Production Assistant
Jacalyn L. Pennywell

**Supervisor of
Project Coordination**
Cindy L. Phipps

Supervisor of Page Layout
Kathie S. Schnorr

**Supervisor of Graphics
and Design**
Shelley Lea

Production Systems Specialist
Steve Peake

Reprint/Blueline Coordination
Tony Augsburger
Patricia R. Reynolds
Theresa Sánchez-Baker
Elizabeth Cárdenas-Nelson

Media/Archive Coordination
Leslie Popplewell
Melissa Stauffer
Michael Wilkey

Project/Manuscript Editor
Madhu Prasher

Technical Editor
Phil Shaw

Graphics Coordination
Gina Scott
Angela F. Hunckler
Carla Radzikinas

Proofreaders
Deb Kaufmann
Dwight Ramsey

Indexer
Liz Cunningham

Cover Design
Kavish + Kavish

Dedication

This book is dedicated to Georgina A. Taylor, who introduced me to the magic of reading, and enriched my life immeasurably in the process.

Acknowledgments

Many people have contributed to help improve the quality and content of this book. I would especially like to thank David Kalman and Chris Date for their helpful advice. I am deeply indebted to Phil Shaw for his careful scrutiny of the manuscript and many valuable suggestions. It has been a joy to work with my editor, Madhu Prasher, as well as with Amy Pedersen, Anne Marie Walker, Chris Williams, and all the other folks at IDG Books.

I very much appreciate the support I have received from vendors, especially Nan Borreson and Karen Giles of Borland International, as well as helpful people at Microrim and Oracle Corporation. I want to thank all the members of my database program development course at Linfield College, who have "beta-tested" much of the material in this book.

Thanks to my agent Matt Wagner, for his ongoing assistance in furthering my career, and to my brother David Taylor, who, as far as I know, is the only person in the world who has bought a copy of every one of my books, including foreign translations.

My biggest thanks go to my wife Joyce, for encouraging me to be myself.

The publisher would like to give special thanks to Patrick McGovern, without whom this book would not have been possible.

Contents at a Glance

Cartoons at a Glance

By Rich Tennant

page 71

page 19

page 1

page 30

page 239

page 117

page 269

page 323

page 330

page 46

Table of Contents

· ·

Introduction

•••

*W*elcome to database development using the industry standard query language(SQL). There are many different database management system (DBMS) tools on the market, running on many different hardware platforms. The differences among them can be great indeed, but all serious products have one thing in common: They all support SQL data access and manipulation. It doesn't matter what DBMS you are using, or what operating system or hardware the DBMS is running on. If you know SQL, you can build relational databases and get useful information out of them.

About This Book

Relational database management systems are vitally important to many organizations. The creation and maintenance of these systems are often viewed as extremely complex activities—the domain of database gurus possessing a degree of enlightenment beyond that of ordinary mortals. This book sweeps away the database mystique. Database design and use are really straightforward activities that you can definitely do, and do well. In this book you will learn:

- What a database is
- How a DBMS is structured
- The major functional components of SQL
- How to build a database
- How to protect a database from harm
- How to operate on database data
- How to get the information you want out of a database

The purpose of this book is to show you how to build relational databases, and how to get valuable information out of them, using SQL.

What Is SQL?

SQL is an industry standard data sublanguage, specifically designed for creating, manipulating, and controlling relational databases. Since most organizations keep their important information in relational databases, knowing SQL is important to anyone who wants to understand what's in their databases, and how to get the information they want out of their databases.

Who Should Read This Book?

If you need to store data or retrieve information from a DBMS, you will be able to do a much better job if you have a working knowledge of SQL. You don't need to be a programmer to use SQL, and you don't need to be conversant in any programming languages, such as COBOL, Fortran, C, or Basic. SQL's syntax is very much like English.

If you are a programmer, you can incorporate SQL into your programs. SQL adds powerful data manipulation and retrieval capability to conventional languages. This book tells you what you need to know if you want to take advantage of SQL's rich assortment of tools and features from inside your programs.

How This Book Is Organized

This book contains six major parts. Each part contains several chapters. The book is designed to be read in order the first time through. After that, it becomes a handy reference guide. You can turn directly to whatever section is appropriate to answer your current question.

Part I: Basic Concepts

Part I introduces the concept of a database and distinguishes relational databases from other types. It describes the most popular database architectures, as well as the major components of SQL.

Part II: Using SQL to Build Databases

You don't need SQL to build a database. This part shows an example of how to build a database using an interactive Rapid Application Development

(RAD) tool, then shows you how to build the same database using SQL. In addition to the essential step of defining database tables, this part covers a variety of other important database features: domains, character sets, collations, translations, keys, and indexes.

Throughout this part I place major emphasis on protecting your database from corruption—which is a bad thing that can happen in a number of ways. SQL gives you the tools, but you must use them to prevent problems caused by bad database design, harmful interactions, operator error, and equipment failure.

Part III: Retrieving Information

Once you have some data in your database, you'll want to do things with it. You may want to add to it, change it, or delete it. Ultimately, you will want to retrieve useful information from the database. SQL provides tools that enable you to accomplish all these objectives. These tools give you low-level, detailed control over your data. If you can conceive of something you want to do with your data, you'll probably be able to do it with SQL.

Part IV: Controlling Operations

A big part of database management is protecting the data from harm. Harm can come in a variety of shapes and forms. People may accidentally or intentionally put erroneous data into database tables. You can protect yourself against this kind of threat by controlling who can access your database and what they can do with it. Another threat to data comes from unintended interaction of the operations of concurrent users. SQL provides powerful tools to prevent this kind of problem too. SQL provides much of the protection automatically, but it's important to understand how the protection mechanisms work to assure that you are getting all the protection you need.

Part V: Using SQL Within Applications

SQL is different from most other computer languages in that it operates on a whole set of data items at once, rather than dealing with them one at a time. This difference in operational modes makes it a challenge to combine SQL with other languages, but it is a challenge that you can easily face, using the information in this book. You'll learn how to include set-oriented SQL statements in your programs, and also how to get SQL to deal with data one item at a time. You'll also find out how to include SQL statements in your programs even when you don't know what tables or columns the statements will be operating on.

Part V also covers error handling. SQL provides you with a lot of information whenever something goes wrong in the execution of an SQL statement. You'll learn how to retrieve and interpret that information.

Part VI: The Part of Tens

This section provides some important tips on what to do, and what not to do, when designing, building, and using a database.

Icons Used in This Book

Tips will save you a lot of time, and keep you out of trouble. ▪

Pay attention to the information marked by this icon. You will very probably need it later. ▪

This icon will help you keep track of the special terms you'll need to know to understand SQL and relational databases. ▪

Heeding the advice pointed to by this icon can save you from major grief. Ignore it at your peril. ▪

This icon marks helpful information that supplements the main text. ▪

This icon alerts you to the presence of technical details that are interesting, but not absolutely essential to an understanding of the topic being discussed. ▪

Let's Get Started

Now for the fun part! Databases are the best tools ever invented for keeping track of the things you care about. Once you understand databases and can use SQL to make them do your bidding, you will wield tremendous power. Co-workers will come to you when they need critical information. Managers will seek your advice. Youngsters will ask for your autograph. But most important, you will know, at a very deep level, how your organization *really* works.

Part I
Basic Concepts

In This Part...

In Part I I'll present the big picture. Before talking about SQL itself, I'll explain what databases really are, and how they're different from data stored in unstructured files. I'll go over the most popular database models, and discuss the physical systems that the databases run on. Then I'll move on to SQL itself. We'll take a brief look at what SQL is and how it came about, then identify and discuss its major components.

Chapter 1

Relational Database Fundamentals

SQL is an industry-standard language specifically designed to let people create databases, add new data to databases, maintain the data, and retrieve selected parts of the data. There are a number of different kinds of databases, each adhering to a different conceptual model. SQL was developed to operate on data in databases that follow the relational model. In this chapter I will discuss data storage, the major database models, how the relational model compares with the others, and the important features of relational databases.

Before we talk about SQL, let's make sure we agree on what we mean by the term *database*. In fact, let's go back one step further and talk about the way computers have changed the way we record and maintain information.

Keeping Track of Things

Today we use computers to do a lot of things that we used to do with other tools. Computers have replaced typewriters as the primary means of creating and modifying documents. They've replaced electromechanical calculators as the best way to do math. They've also replaced millions of pieces of paper, file folders, and file cabinets as the principal storage medium for important information. Compared to the old tools, computers do a lot more a lot faster, and with greater accuracy. However, these benefits are achieved at a cost: Computer users no longer have direct physical access to their data.

When computers aren't working as expected, office workers sometimes wonder if computerization really improved anything at all. In the old days, a file folder rarely "crashed." When it did, you merely knelt down, picked up the papers, and put them back in the folder. A disk crash is another matter entirely. You can't "pick up" the lost bits and bytes. Barring earthquakes or other major disasters, file cabinets never "go down," and they never give you an error message. Computers, on the other hand, are sensitive to mechanical, electrical, and human failures that can make your data permanently unavailable.

Even so, computers really *are* an improvement over the old tools. By taking proper precautions, you can protect yourself from accidental data loss. Once protected, you can start cashing in on the greater speed and accuracy that computers provide.

When you are storing important data, you have four main concerns:

- ✔ Storing data should be quick and easy, since you will probably be doing it often.
- ✔ The storage medium must be reliable. You don't want to come back later and find that some or all of your data is missing.
- ✔ Data retrieval should be quick and easy, regardless of the number of items you have stored.
- ✔ You should be able to sift the exact information you want from the tons of data you don't want.

Small is beautiful

Computers really shine when it comes to data storage. They can store all kinds of things — text, numbers, sounds, graphic images, TV programs, animations — as binary data. The data can be stored at very high densities, allowing large quantities of information to be kept in a very small space. As technology continues to advance, more and more data will occupy smaller and smaller spaces. This trend has caused computers to be used in ways that once seemed quite improbable. Today the gas pumps at your neighborhood filling station contain computers. Your car probably has several computers. How long can it be before we see computerized shoes that alter the resilience of their soles depending on whether you are walking, running, or taking a jump shot?

State-of-the-art computer databases satisfy these four criteria. If you are storing more than a dozen or so data items, you probably want to store them in a database.

What Is a Database?

In recent years the term "database" has been used rather loosely, and as a result, has lost some of its usefulness. To some people, a database is any collection of data items. Other people define the term more strictly.

In this book I will define a *database* as a self-describing collection of integrated records. ∎

A *record* is a representation of some physical or conceptual object. For example, say you want to keep track of a businesses' customers. You would assign a record for each customer. Each record would have multiple *attributes*, such as name, address, and telephone number.

A database is *self-describing* in that it contains a description of its own structure. This description is called *meta-data*. The database is *integrated* in that it includes the relationships among data items as well as the data items themselves.

A database is made up of both data and meta-data. *Meta-data* is data about the structure of the data in a database.

This meta-data is stored in a part of the database called the *data dictionary,* which describes the tables, columns, indexes, constraints, and other items that make up the database. ∎

Since a flat file system has no meta-data, applications written to work with flat files must contain the equivalent of the meta-data as part of the application program.

Database Size and Complexity

Databases come in all sizes, from a simple collection of a few records to millions of records.

A *personal database* is designed for use by a single person on a single computer. It tends to be rather simple in structure and small in size. A *departmental* or *workgroup database* is used by the members of a single department or workgroup within an organization. It is generally larger than a personal data-

The value is not in the data; it's in the structure

Years ago some overly clever person calculated that if you reduced a human being to his component carbon, hydrogen, oxygen, and nitrogen atoms (plus traces of others), the person would be worth 97 cents. This clearly misleading assessment did grave damage to people's self images around the world. People aren't composed of collections of atoms. Our atoms are combined into enzymes, proteins, hormones, and many other substances that cost millions of dollars per ounce on the pharmaceutical market. It is the *structure* of the combinations of atoms that give them value.

Database structure makes it possible to interpret seemingly meaningless data. The structure brings to the surface patterns, trends, and tendencies in the data. Unstructured data, like uncombined atoms, has little or no value.

base, and it is necessarily more complex, since it must handle multiple users trying to access the same data at the same time. An *organizational database* can be huge. It may model the critical information flow of an entire large organization. ■

What Is a Database Management System?

A *database management system (DBMS)* is a set of programs used to define, administer, and process databases and their associated applications. A database is a structure you build to hold data that is valuable to you or your organization. A DBMS is the tool you use to build that structure and operate on the data contained within it. ■

There are many DBMSs on the market today. Some run only on mainframe computers, some only on minicomputers, and some only on personal computers. There is a strong trend, however, for such products to work on multiple platforms or on networks that contain all three classes of machines.

A DBMS that runs on platforms of multiple classes is said to be *scaleable*. ■

Regardless of the size of the computer that hosts the database, and regardless of whether it is connected to a network, the flow of information between the database and the user is the same. Figure 1-1 shows that the user communicates with the database through the DBMS. The DBMS masks the physical details of the database storage, so that the application only has to know about the logical characteristics of the data, not how it is stored.

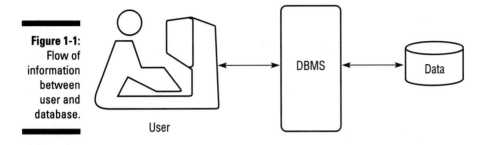

Figure 1-1:
Flow of
information
between
user and
database.

User

DBMS

Data

Flat Files

Flat files got their name from the fact that they are nothing more than a collection of data records. They have minimal structure. These files contain one data record after another in a format specified when the file is designed. Flat files contain the data, the whole data, and nothing but the data. Since structural information (meta-data) is not stored in the file, overhead is minimal.

Say you wanted to keep track of the names and addresses of your company's customers in a flat file system. It might be structured something like this:

```
Harold Percival26262 S. Howards Mill RdWestminster CA92683
Jerry Appel    32323 S. River Lane Rd  Santa Ana   CA92705
Adrian Hansen  232   Glenwood Court     Anaheim     CA92640
John Baker     2222  Lafayette St       Garden GroveCA92643
Michael Pens   77730 S. New Era Rd      Irvine      CA92715
Bob Michimoto  25252 S. Kelmsley Dr     Stanton     CA92610
Linda Smith    444   S.E. Seventh St    Costa Mesa  CA92635
Robert Funnell 2424  Sheri Court        Anaheim     CA92640
Bill Checkal   9595  Curry Dr           Stanton     CA92610
Jed Style      3535  Randall St         Santa Ana   CA92705
```

As you can see, the file contains nothing but data. Each field is of a fixed length (the name field, for example, is always exactly 15 characters long), and there is no structure to separate one field from another. Any program using this data must "know" which character positions have been assigned to each field.

On the plus side, operating on flat files can be very fast, since they contain nothing but data. On the minus side, application programs must include logic that manipulates the data in the file at a very low level. The application must know exactly where and how the data is stored. For small systems, flat files work fine. The larger a system is, however, the more cumbersome a flat file system becomes. Using a database rather than a flat file system eliminates duplication of effort and makes applications more portable across various hardware and operating system platforms. It also makes it easier to write application programs, because the programmer doesn't need to know the physical details of where and how the data is stored.

Databases eliminate duplication of effort because the DBMS handles the details of data manipulation. Applications written to operate on flat files must include those details in the application code. If multiple applications all access the same flat file data, they must all (redundantly) include that data manipulation code. With a DBMS, the applications do not need to include such code at all.

Clearly, if an application includes data manipulation code that is specific to a particular hardware platform, it will not be easy to migrate the application to a new platform. All the hardware-specific code will have to be changed. As a result, it is *much* harder to migrate a flat file-based application to another platform than it is to migrate a similar DBMS-based application.

Database Models

Different as databases may be in size, they are generally always structured according to one of three database models: hierarchical, network, and relational. The first databases to be widely used were large organizational databases built according to either the hierarchical or the network model. Systems built according to the relational model followed.

Hierarchical model

A *hierarchical* database assigns different types of data to different levels of a data structure. The links between a data item on one level and data items on a different level are simple and direct. A major advantage of the hierarchical model is the simplicity of the relationships among data items. However, its rigid structure is a major disadvantage. (Network databases also suffer from structural rigidity.) ■

Dave's Auto Parts uses a simple hierarchical database structure (Figure 1-2) to maintain the names of customers, the products they have purchased, and their method of payment. The relationships between data items are easy to follow, which is one of the great strengths of the hierarchical model.

A disadvantage of the model is that a single data item can appear multiple times in the database. This data redundancy can cause problems when the database is updated. If all redundant data elements are not updated in exactly the same way, errors could be introduced, resulting in a progressive

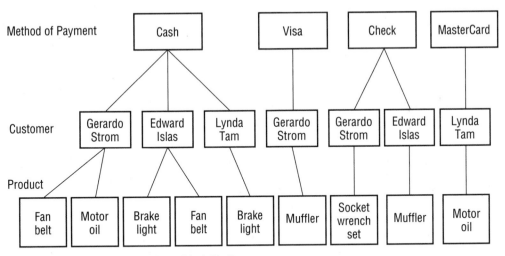

Figure 1-2: Dave's Auto Parts hierarchical database.

corruption of the database. Another disadvantage of a hierarchical database is that it is difficult to alter its structure once you have added data to it.

Network model

The opposite of a hierarchical structure is one in which any node has direct access to any other. There is no need to duplicate nodes, since they are all universally accessible. The *network model* is based on this concept. ■

Is "efficient government" an oxymoron?

Modern government bureaucracies, whether they are in capitalist, socialist, or communist countries, all function in the same way. They have a rigid hierarchical structure where the person in charge has subordinates, who in turn, have subordinates of their own, and so on down to the individual contributor (peon) level. The rigid nature of the structure makes it difficult for new ideas to gain acceptance. The tendency is to continue to do things the way they have always been done in the past. Hierarchical databases have a similar structure, and consequently a similar inability to accommodate change.

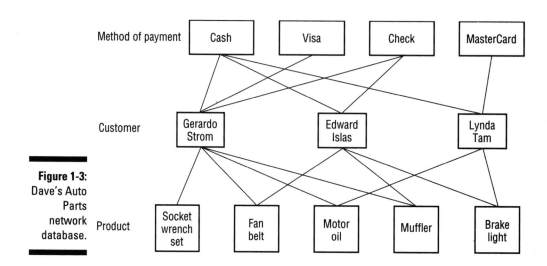

Figure 1-3:
Dave's Auto
Parts
network
database.

This seemed like a great idea to the members of the Conference on Data Systems Languages Data Base Task Group (CODASYL DTBG). CODASYL gained fame as the committee that developed the COBOL language.

CODASYL formulated the network database model in 1969 to eliminate the data redundancy inherent in the hierarchical model. The network model avoids data redundancy, but in doing so it makes the relationships between data items more complicated. Figure 1-3 shows the database for Dave's Auto Parts, this time structured according to the network database model.

The network (CODASYL) database model was designed to eliminate the data item duplication inherent in the hierarchical model. It does so, but at the cost of making the relationships among data items more complex. One disadvantage is traded for another. You won't see too many new installations of network DBMSs for the same reason people today aren't buying new hierarchical systems. There is a better alternative.

Relational model

The relational database model was first formulated by E. F. Codd of IBM in 1970, and started appearing in products about a decade later. Figure 1-4 shows how the Dave's Auto Parts database would appear if it were structured according to the relational model. It contains three structurally related tables.

Relational databases have attributes that distinguish them from databases built according to other models. Probably the most important of these is that

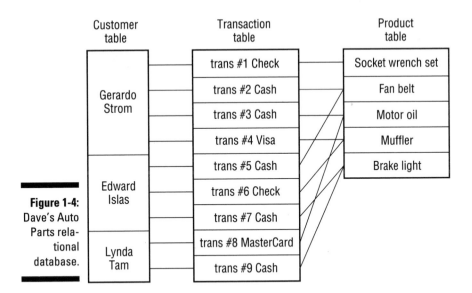

| Customer table | Transaction table | Product table |

Figure 1-4:
Dave's Auto
Parts rela-
tional
database.

in a relational database the database structure can be changed without requiring changes to applications that were based on the earlier structure. For example, suppose you add one or more new columns to a database table. Older applications that processed that table won't need to be changed, because the columns they deal with are unaltered. (Of course, if you remove a column that an existing application refers to, you will have problems no matter what database model you are following. One of the best ways to make a DBMS crash is to ask it to retrieve something that isn't there.)

Why relational is better

In applications written with DBMSs that follow the hierarchical or the network model, database structure is "hard-coded" into the application. If you add a new attribute to the database, you will have to change your application to accommodate the change, whether the application uses the new attribute or not.

Because of the structural flexibility of relational databases, applications written for them are easier to maintain than applications written to work with other kinds of databases. Furthermore, the same structural flexibility allows you to retrieve combinations of data that you had not anticipated needing at the time the database was designed.

If you organize either a hierarchical or a network database to optimize it for one class of applications, it will inevitably be dreadful for other classes of applications. For example, in a hierarchical system, you might design a

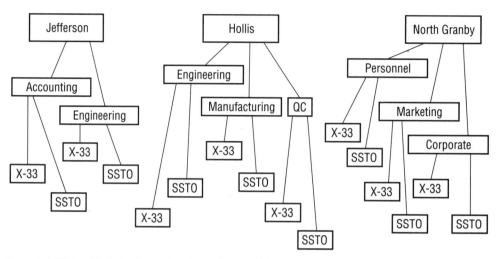

Figure 1-5: Hierarchical database, showing projects within departments within locations.

database with PROJECT records nested within DEPARTMENT records, and those DEPARTMENT records nested within LOCATION records.

Figure 1-5 shows the projects X-33 and SSTO nested within the departments (accounting, engineering, manufacturing, QC, personnel, marketing, and corporate), which are in turn nested within locations (Jefferson, Hollis, and North Granby). Notice that there is considerable redundancy in this structure.

This organization is fine for some applications. However, sooner or later, you will need another application that wants to see data organized by project, with the related departments nested within projects, and the location nested (redundantly) under each department.

The hierarchical organization of the database makes it difficult to write such an application, and once the application is written, it runs very inefficiently. With a relational database, on the other hand, you merely define a "view" of the data for the application. This view "inverts" the data into a different logical structure that the application can operate on efficiently. A similar flexibility is characteristic of innovative organizations that are more focused on producing the desired results than they are on maintaining the status quo.

Historical perspective

In the early 1980s personal databases appeared for the first time on personal computers. The earliest products were based on flat file systems, but some early products attempted to follow the relational model. As they have evolved, the most popular PC DBMSs have come progressively closer to being truly relational.

Starting in the latter part of the 1980s, more and more PCs in organizations have been hooked together into workgroups or departmental networks. To fill this new market niche, relational DBMSs that originated on large mainframe computers have migrated down, and relational PC DBMSs have migrated up from standalone personal computers.

Products adhering to the hierarchical, the network, and the relational model all have large installed bases. The owners of these systems will continue to use and expand upon what they are now using. New installations, however, that have no obligation to retain compatibility to "legacy" systems are overwhelmingly being built according to the relational model.

Components of a Relational Database

Relational databases gain their flexibility from the fact that their data resides in tables that are largely independent of each other. You can add, delete, or change tables without affecting the data in the other tables. In this section we will see what the tables consist of, and how they relate to the other parts of a relational database.

Guess who's coming to dinner?

At holiday time, lots of my relations come to my house and sit down at my table. Databases have relations also, but each relation has its own table. A relational database is made up of one or more relations.

A *relation* is a two-dimensional array of rows and columns, containing single-valued entries and no duplicate rows. Each cell in the array can have only one value, and no two rows may be identical. ■

Most people are familiar with two-dimensional arrays of rows and columns, in the form of electronic spreadsheets such as Microsoft Excel or Lotus 1-2-3. The offensive statistics listed on the back of a major league baseball player's baseball card is another example of such an array. On the baseball card,

Player	Year	Team	Game	At Bat	Hits	Runs	RBI	2B	3B	HR	Walk	Steals	Bat. Avg.
Roberts	1988	Padres	5	9	3	1	0	0	0	0	1	0	.333
Roberts	1989	Padres	117	329	99	81	25	15	8	3	49	21	.301
Roberts	1990	Padres	149	556	172	104	44	36	3	9	55	46	.309

Figure 1-6: Table of a baseball player's offensive statistics.

there are columns for year, team, games played, at-bats, hits, runs scored, runs batted in, doubles, triples, home runs, bases on balls, steals, and batting average. There is a row for each year that the player has played in the major leagues. This data could be stored in a relation (table), which has the same basic structure. Figure 1-6 shows a relational database table holding the offensive statistics for a single major league player.

Columns in the array are *self consistent*, in that a column has the same meaning in every row. If a column contains a player last name in one row, it must contain a player last name in all rows. The order in which the rows and columns appear in the array has no significance. This means that as far as the DBMS is concerned, it does not matter which column is first, which is next, and which is last. The table will be processed the same way, regardless of the order of the columns. The same is true of rows. It does not matter what order they are in.

Relations are commonly called *tables* by the development community. Academics and theoreticians prefer the term "relation," but both terms mean the same thing. In this book, I will call them tables. ■

Every *column* in a database table embodies a single *attribute* of the table. The meaning of a column is the same for every row of the table. A table may, for example, contain the names, addresses, and telephone numbers of all of an organization's customers. Each *row* (also called a *record* or a *tuple*) in the table holds the data on a single customer. Each column holds a single attribute, such as customer number, customer name, customer street, customer city, customer state, customer postal code, or customer telephone number. Figure 1-7 shows some of the rows and columns of such a table.

Enjoy the view

One of my favorite views is the view of the Yosemite Valley as seen from the mouth of the Wawona tunnel, late on a spring afternoon. The sheer face of El Capitan is bathed in golden light, Half Dome glistens in the distance, Bridal Veil Falls forms a silver cascade of sparkling water, while a trace of wispy

Columns

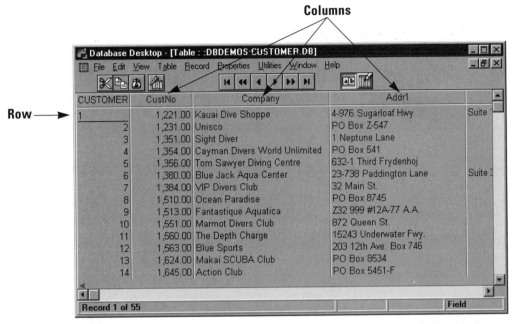

Row ────▶

Figure 1-7: Each database row contains a record; each database column holds a single attribute.

clouds weaves a tapestry across the sky. Databases have views also. They may not be quite as beautiful, but can be very useful.

Tables can contain many columns and rows. Sometimes you are interested in all of that data and sometimes you are not. You may be interested in only some of the columns of a table, or in only rows that satisfy a certain condition. You may be interested in some columns of one table and some other columns of a related table. A *view* is a subset of a database that can be processed by an application. It may contain parts of one or more tables.

NOTE
Views are sometimes called *virtual tables*. To the application or the user they behave exactly like tables. However, they have no independent existence. They are a way of looking at data; they are not the data itself. ■

Say you are working with a database that has a CUSTOMER table and an INVOICE table. The CUSTOMER table has columns CUSTOMER_ID, FIRST_NAME, LAST_NAME, STREET, CITY, STATE, ZIPCODE, and PHONE. The INVOICE table has columns INVOICE_NUMBER, CUSTOMER_ID, DATE, TOTAL_SALE, TOTAL_REMITTED, and FORM_OF_PAYMENT.

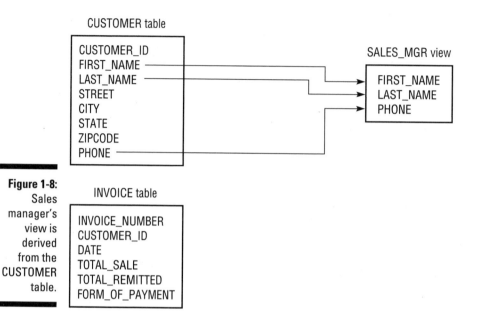

CUSTOMER table

| CUSTOMER_ID |
| FIRST_NAME |
| LAST_NAME |
| STREET |
| CITY |
| STATE |
| ZIPCODE |
| PHONE |

SALES_MGR view

| FIRST_NAME |
| LAST_NAME |
| PHONE |

Figure 1-8:
Sales manager's view is derived from the CUSTOMER table.

INVOICE table

| INVOICE_NUMBER |
| CUSTOMER_ID |
| DATE |
| TOTAL_SALE |
| TOTAL_REMITTED |
| FORM_OF_PAYMENT |

A national sales manager would like to look at a screen that contains only the customer first name, last name, and telephone number. Creating a view that contains only those three columns from the CUSTOMER table makes available all needed information, without the distraction of the data in the unwanted columns. Figure 1-8 shows the derivation of the national sales manager's view.

A branch manager might want to look at the names and phone numbers of all customers whose ZIP code falls between 90000 and 93999 (Southern and Central California). A view that places a restriction on the rows retrieved as well as the columns displayed will do the job. Figure 1-9 shows where the branch manager's view's columns come from.

The accounts payable manager might want to look at customer names from the CUSTOMER table and TOTAL_SALE and TOTAL_REMITTED from the INVOICE table, where TOTAL_REMITTED is less than TOTAL_SALE. This requires a view that draws from both tables. Figure 1-10 shows data flowing into the accounts payable manager's view from both CUSTOMER and INVOICE tables.

Views are useful because they allow you to extract and format database data without physically altering the stored data. In Chapter 7 I will show how to create a view using SQL.

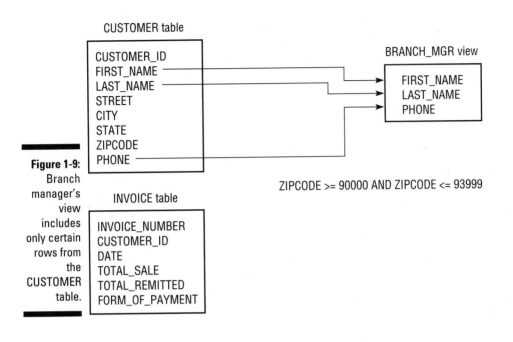

Figure 1-9:
Branch manager's view includes only certain rows from the CUSTOMER table.

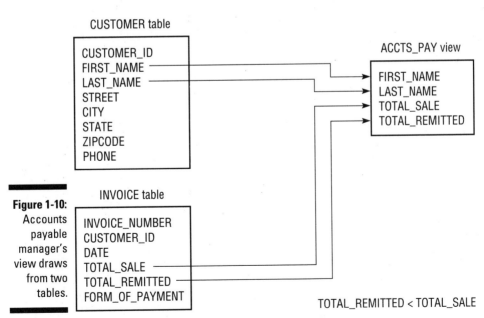

Figure 1-10:
Accounts payable manager's view draws from two tables.

Schemas, domains, and constraints

A database is more than a collection of tables. Additional structures, on several levels, help to maintain the integrity of the data. A database's *schema* provides an overall organization to the tables. The *domain* of a table column tells us what values may be stored in the column. You can apply *constraints* to a database table to prevent invalid data from being stored in it.

Schemas

The structure of an entire database is called the *schema* or conceptual view. It is sometimes also called the complete logical view of the database. The schema is meta-data, and as such it is a part of the database. The meta-data, which describes the structure of the database, is itself stored in tables that are just like the tables that store the regular data. ■

Domains

An attribute of a relation (that is, a column of a table) can assume some finite number of values. The set of all such values is the *domain* of the attribute. ■

As an example, say you are an automobile dealer who handles the newly introduced Curarri GT 4000 sports coupe. You keep track of the cars you have in stock in a database table named INVENTORY. One of the columns of that table is named COLOR, which holds the color of the exterior of each car. The GT 4000 comes in only four colors, blazing crimson, midnight black, milk white, and metallic gray. Those four colors are the domain of the COLOR attribute.

Constraints

Constraints are an important, although often overlooked component of a database. They are rules that determine what values the attributes of a table can assume. ■

By applying tight constraints to a column, you can prevent erroneous data from being entered into that column. Of course, every value that is legitimately in the domain of the column must satisfy all the column's constraints. As I mentioned above, the domain of a column is the set of all values that the column can contain. A constraint is a restriction on what a column may contain. The characteristics of a table column, plus the constraints that apply to that column, determine the column's domain. By applying constraints, you can prevent the entry of data into a column that falls outside of the column's domain.

In the auto dealership example, you could constrain the database to accept only one of four values in the COLOR column. If a data entry operator tried to enter a value of, for instance, forest green in the COLOR column, the system would not accept the entry. Data entry could not proceed until a valid value was entered into the COLOR field.

Database Design Considerations

A database is a representation of a physical or conceptual structure, such as an organization, an automobile assembly, or the performance statistics of all the major league baseball clubs. The accuracy of the representation depends on the level of detail of the database design. The amount of effort you put into database design should depend on the type of information you want to get out of the database. Too much detail is a waste of effort, time, and disk space. Too little detail may render the database worthless. Decide how much detail is needed now and how much will be needed in the future, then provide that level of detail in your design: no more and no less.

Today's database management systems, complete with attractive graphical user interfaces and intuitive design tools, can give the would-be database

The 5th Wave   By Rich Tennant

I'll tell you this—retraining for client/server isn't going to be easy. Do you know how old some of these dogs are?

designer a false sense of security. They can make it seem that designing a database is comparable to building a spreadsheet, or some other relatively straightforward task. No such luck. Database design is difficult. If you do it improperly, you get a database that becomes gradually more corrupt as time goes on. Often the problem does not become visible until a great deal of effort has gone into data entry. By the time you know you have a problem, it's already serious. In many cases the only solution is to completely redesign the database and reenter all the data.

This book doesn't tell you how to design a database. It assumes that you or somebody else has already created a proper design, and tells you how to implement that design with SQL. If you suspect that you don't have a good database design, by all means fix it before you try to build the database. The earlier you detect and correct problems in a development project, the cheaper the corrections will be. ■

Chapter 2

Client/Server Architecture

- -

In This Chapter

▶ Multiuser database architectures

▶ Advantages of client/server architecture

▶ SQL in client/server systems

▶ What the server does

▶ What the client does

- -

Database Architecture

Just as the *logical* structure of one database can differ markedly from the structure of another database, (depending on which model they follow), there can be major differences in the *physical* structure of database systems. Mainframe computers differ markedly from minicomputers, and even more so from personal computers. Yet they all can run database systems. The architecture of these systems depends on hardware and on the type of access to data that is desired.

There are a number of ways you can structure a computer system to give you access to a database, but they all fall into one of two categories, standalone and multiuser. In a standalone system there is only one computer, which hosts both the database and the one and only user. In a multiuser system, multiple people may access the database simultaneously. The database may be on one computer or spread over several computers.

Standalone database systems

A standalone database system involves only one computer, usually a personal computer. The data resides in the computer's memory and the user sits in front of its screen, tapping on its keyboard. The database management system is a single integrated piece of software. Since such a system can serve only one person at a time, standalone databases and their associated applications tend to be relatively small.

This mode of operation is generally an extravagant waste of computer power. In the time it takes for a human finger poised above a keyboard key to descend and make a keypress, the computer could have executed a million instructions. Standalone computers dealing with small databases spend the overwhelming majority of their time waiting for their operator to do something. Luckily, computers don't suffer from boredom or the feeling that their talents are going to waste. If they did, I'm afraid many standalone computers would be depressed, and probably in need of therapy.

Multiuser database systems

You can tell by its name that a multiuser database system (in contrast to a standalone system) can be used by more than one person at a time. This is great from an efficiency standpoint, because the system can respond to the request of one user while waiting for input from others.

Four distinct configurations provide multiuser capability. They are teleprocessing, client/server, resource sharing, and distributed data processing.

Teleprocessing

The classical approach is the *teleprocessing* system, in which a powerful central processor is connected to multiple "dumb terminals" (that is, terminals with no standalone computing capability). Users interact with the database through the dumb terminals. This method, illustrated in Figure 2-1, has serious drawbacks. Because one processor is doing all the work, performance can degrade significantly as users are added. Performance depends on the bandwidth (information carrying capacity) of the channels that connect the processor to the users. The lower the bandwidth, the less information the channel can carry per second. As you add users the available bandwidth becomes clogged up with more and more traffic. Furthermore, computers powerful enough to support a large number of users tend to be very expensive mainframes.

Client/server

A second type of multiuser configuration is the *client/server* architecture. In a client/server system a central processor called the *server* is connected to multiple computers called *clients*. Users sit at the client machines, which run applications that operate on a database residing on the server. Since the

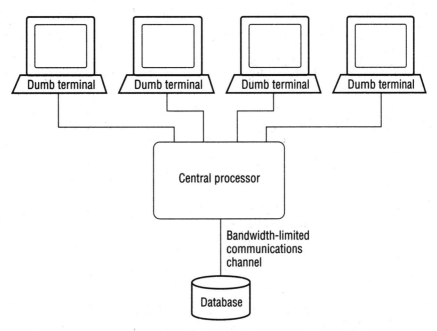

Figure 2-1:   A teleprocessing system supports multiple users with a single processor, a single database, and a single channel between them.

client machines handle a significant part of the processing load (the application), the server, running the DBMS's database engine, can concentrate on data manipulation.

A *database engine* is that part of a DBMS that directly interacts with the data. ■

The intelligent server in a client/server system is called a *database server*. The database server can be an inexpensive personal computer, rather than an expensive mainframe, because its processing load is much lower than the one placed on a central processor in a teleprocessing system with the same number of users. A client/server system can have multiple servers, but if it does, each server will hold different database files. Figure 2-2 shows a typical client/server arrangement.

Resource sharing

A third approach to multiuser computing is *resource sharing*. This architecture is similar to client/server in that one or more servers are connected to multiple personal computers, each of which provides an interface for a single user. However the division of labor between the users' machines and the

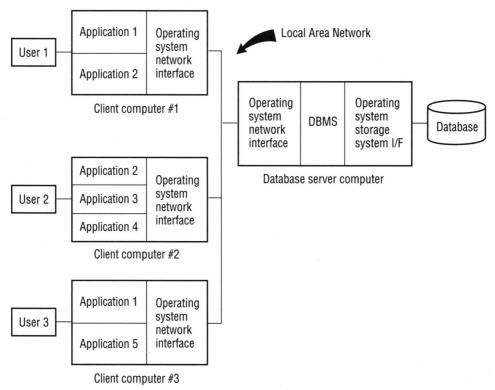

Figure 2-2: In a client/server system, the processing load is divided between user interface functions on the client machines and data access functions on the server.

servers is different. A resource sharing system has *file servers* rather than database servers. The file server is relatively "dumb." It holds the data, but not the database management system. It does no database processing. The DBMS resides on the users' machines and it accesses the data on the server over a local area network (LAN). Figure 2-3 shows a resource sharing configuration. Note that there is no DBMS on the server. Essentially all the processing takes place on the client machines.

The resource sharing arrangement is older and less efficient than the client/server arrangement. Because the database and the DBMS are physically separated and connected only by the local area network, the LAN must carry very heavy traffic as entire data files are shuttled back and forth. Furthermore, when one user is operating on a file, all other users must be locked out of it to prevent possible file corruption. This can introduce significant processing delays.

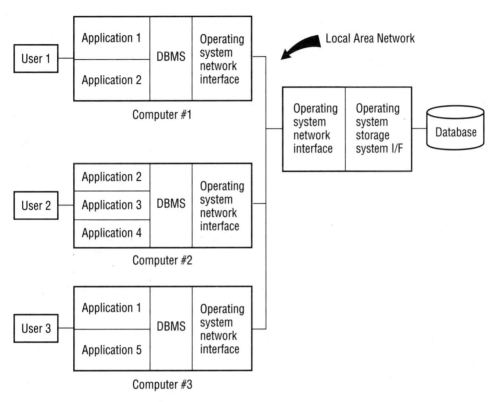

Figure 2-3: In a resource sharing system, the client machines carry most of the processing load while the file server merely responds to client requests for data operations.

Distributed data processing

A fourth approach is *distributed data processing*. This type of system uses multiple servers as well as multiple clients. As distinct from a multiuser client/server system, however, multiple servers may simultaneously be host to the *same* database tables. Having the data available on multiple servers reduces contention for server time, resulting in a big boost in performance. However, such systems must be very carefully controlled to assure that the data on one server does not become desynchronized from the corresponding data on the other servers. All copies of the same database must remain the same at all times or system integrity will be lost. Figure 2-4 shows an example distributed database system.

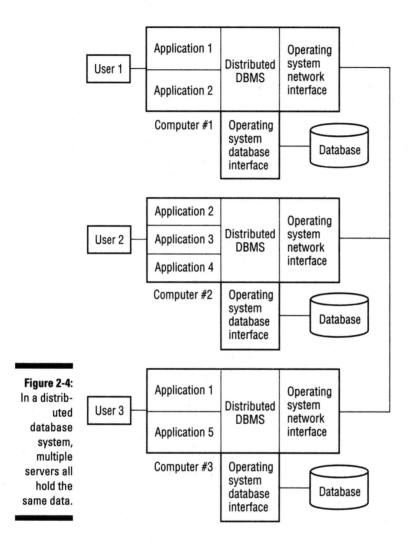

Figure 2-4:
In a distributed database system, multiple servers all hold the same data.

Why Client/Server?

The client/server architecture has emerged as the dominant type of multiuser configuration. There are several good reasons for this.

- ✔ *Hardware cost*. Both the server and the client can be inexpensive personal computers. Teleprocessing requires expensive mainframes.

- ✔ *Software cost*. Personal computer software is much less expensive than comparable software that runs on mainframes or minicomputers.

    ✔ *Network cost.* Client/server systems need less bandwidth to get the same level of performance as resource sharing installations.

    ✔ *Performance.* Client computers preprocess data, which reduces the demand for network bandwidth and ensures that no time is wasted sending extra data between server and client. Because tasks are distributed between the client and the server, parallel operation reduces processing time even further. Distributed data processing systems have the potential for higher performance, but redundancy and complexity can make them much more expensive.

    ✔ *Ease of use.* Vendors of application development systems have invested heavily in making their client/server products as easy to use as possible.

Using SQL in a Client/Server System

SQL is a data sublanguage that will work on a standalone system or on any of the multiuser systems mentioned in the preceding sections. It works particularly well in a client/server system. The application program on a client machine contains SQL data manipulation commands. The DBMS sends these commands to the server over the communications channel that connects the server to the client. At the server, the server portion of the DBMS interprets and executes the SQL command, then sends the results back to the client over the communication channel. Very complex operations can be encoded into SQL at the client, and then decoded and performed at the server. This means that the bandwidth of the communication channel is used effectively.

When you retrieve data using SQL on a client/server system, only the data you want is transmitted from the server, over the communication channel, to the client. In contrast, a resource sharing system, with minimal intelligence at the server, would send huge blocks of data over the channel in order to give you the small piece of data that you want. Needless to say, this can slow operations considerably. The client/server architecture complements the characteristics of SQL to provide good performance at a moderate cost on small, medium, as well as large networks.

The Server

Unless it receives a request from a client, the server does nothing. It just stands around and waits. However, if multiple clients require service at the same time, servers need to respond quickly. Servers generally differ from client machines in that they have large amounts of very fast disk storage. They are optimized for fast data access and retrieval. And because they must handle traffic coming in simultaneously from multiple client machines, servers need a fast processor.

What the server is

The server (short for database server) is the part of a client/server system that holds the database. It also holds the server portion of a database management system. This part of the DBMS interprets commands coming in from the clients and translates these commands into operations in the database. The server software also formats the results of retrieval requests and sends them back to the requesting client.

What the server does

The job of the server is relatively simple and straightforward. All it has to do is read, interpret, and execute commands that come to it over the network from clients. Those commands will be in one of several data sublanguages. A *sublanguage* does not qualify as a complete language — it implements only part of a language. A *data sublanguage* deals only with data handling. It has operations for inserting, updating, deleting, and selecting data, but does not have flow control structures such as DO loops, local variables, functions, procedures, or I/O to printers. SQL is the most common data sublanguage in use today, and has become an industry standard. Proprietary data sublanguages are gradually being supplanted by SQL on machines in all performance classes.

Attributes of the ideal server

An ideal database server would have the following attributes:

- ✔ Executes incoming commands and returns responses in zero time
- ✔ Never returns incorrect answers to queries
- ✔ Provides truly helpful error messages in response to invalid or inappropriate commands
- ✔ Protects the database from accidental or malicious damage
- ✔ Assures that access is provided only to authorized users
- ✔ Prevents actions of one client from damaging the data of another client
- ✔ Warns you when the data retrieval command you have written does not accurately reflect the retrieval you have pictured in your mind

Alas, the ideal database server does not exist, and probably never will. Many servers today do have a number of the attributes of an ideal server, and at least approach other attributes. It will probably be quite a while, however, before mind-reading becomes a standard feature of database servers. Until that day, we will have to get along with systems based on SQL or something like it.

The Client

The client part of a client/server system consists of a hardware and a software component. The hardware is the client computer and its interface to the local area network. This hardware may be very similar to, or even identical to, the server hardware. The software is the distinguishing component.

What the client is

The primary job of the client is to provide a user interface. As far as the user is concerned, the client machine *is* the computer and the user interface *is* the application. The user may not even realize that there is a server involved in the process. It is usually out of sight — even in another room. Aside from the user interface, the client also contains the application program and the client part of the DBMS. The application program performs the specific task to be done, such as accounts receivable or order entry. The client part of the DBMS executes the application program commands and exchanges data and SQL data manipulation commands with the server part of the DBMS.

What the client does

The client part of a DBMS displays information on the screen and responds to user input transmitted via the keyboard, mouse, or other input device. The client may also process data coming in from a telecommunications link or from other stations on the network. All of the application-specific "thinking" is done by the client part of the DBMS. To a developer, the client part of a DBMS is the interesting part. The server part just handles the requests of the client part, and does so in a repetitive, mechanical fashion.

Attributes of the ideal client

An ideal database client would have the following attributes:

- ✔ Displays a screen that is immediately understandable to anyone using the system
- ✔ Displays all the information needed to perform the current task
- ✔ Displays no extraneous information
- ✔ Presents an interface that is easy on the eyes and brain
- ✔ Makes all response options that are available to the user intuitively obvious and easy to perform
- ✔ Requires no more than two keystrokes or mouse clicks to perform any function
- ✔ Requires that any action which irreversibly changes data be verified by a confirming action

The ideal database client is a goal that application designers can strive for, but will probably never reach. By keeping the characteristics of the ideal client in mind, however, they will be able to produce clients that closely approach the ideal.

The 5th Wave   **By Rich Tennant**

"OH SURE! LEAVE IT TO THE FORESTRY SERVICE TO START TALKING DISTRIBUTED COMPUTING ENVIRONMENT JUST WHEN I GET THE MAINFRAME UP AND RUNNING."

Chapter 3

SQL Fundamentals

SQL is the most widely used tool for communicating with a relational database. It is a flexible tool, that can be used in a variety of ways. In this chapter we'll talk about what SQL is and what it isn't — specifically, about what distinguishes it from other types of computer languages. We'll go briefly into the history of SQL, revealing some little-known facts, and recount the evolution of a universally recognized SQL standard. Then we'll introduce the commands and data types supported by standard SQL, and explain a couple of key concepts: null values and constraints.

What SQL Is and Isn't

The first thing you need to understand about SQL is that it isn't a procedural language like FORTRAN, BASIC, C, COBOL, Pascal, or Ada. To solve a problem in one of those languages, you write a *procedure* that performs one operation after another until the task is complete. The procedure may be a linear sequence, or it may loop back on itself, but in either case the programmer specifies the order of execution. SQL is *nonprocedural*. To solve a problem with SQL, instead of telling the system how to get you what you want, you simply tell it what you want. The DBMS decides the best way to get you what you asked for.

The next version of SQL, currently code-named SQL3, *will* incorporate procedural language facilities such as BEGIN blocks, IF statements, functions, and procedures. These facilities are being added so that you can store programs at the server, where they can be optimized and used repeatedly by multiple clients. ▪

To illustrate what I mean by "tell the system what you want," suppose you have an EMPLOYEE table and you want to retrieve from it the rows corresponding to all your "senior" people. You want to define a senior person as anyone over age 40, or anyone earning more than $50,000 per year. You could do so with the following query:

```
SELECT * FROM EMPLOYEE WHERE AGE>40 OR SALARY>50000 ;
```

This statement will retrieve all rows from the EMPLOYEE table where either the value in the AGE column is greater than 40 or the value in the SALARY column is greater than 50000. With SQL, you are not responsible for specifying *how* to retrieve the information. The database engine examines the database and decides for itself how to fulfill your request. You only need to specify *what* data you want to retrieve.

A *query* is a question you ask the database. If any of the data in the database satisfies the conditions of your query, that data will be retrieved. ▪

SQL lacks many of the basic programming constructs that are fundamental to most other languages. Real-world applications usually require at least some of these programming constructs. That is why SQL is a data *sub*language. You need to use it in combination with one of the procedural languages to create a complete application. The next release of the ANSI standard SQL specification (SQL3) will include some of the flow control constructs, making SQL a more complete language. When those constructs are included in commonly available implementations of SQL, there will be less need to use another language along with SQL.

There are two ways to extract information from a database. The first is to make an *ad hoc* query from a computer console. The second is to execute a program that collects information from the database and then reports on the information. You can use SQL in both ways.

Queries from the console are appropriate when you want a quick answer to a specific question. To meet an immediate need you may require information that you never needed before from a database. You will probably never need it again either, but you need it now. Enter the appropriate SQL query statement from the console, and in due time the result will appear on your screen.

On the other hand, it makes sense to incorporate an SQL query into a program if the query is somewhat complex, and if you are likely to need to run it again in the future. That way you only have to formulate the query once.

A (Very) Little History

Like relational database theory, SQL originated in one of IBM's research laboratories. In the early 1970s, when IBM researchers were performing early development on relational DBMS (RDBMS) systems, they created a data sublanguage named SEQUEL (Structured English QUEry Language) to operate on them. Unfortunately, the IBM folks had not done a thorough trademark search on the name "SEQUEL," and ran into a conflict. When the product was finally released, they couldn't call it SEQUEL, so they named it SQL instead.

Impress your friends with your knowledge of these little-known facts

There are a couple of common misconceptions surrounding SQL. Many database books perpetuate these misconceptions, and even experienced programmers are largely misinformed. You can probably make some good money by betting database guru wannabees that they do not know the answer to the following two simple questions:

- ✔ What do the letters SQL stand for?
- ✔ How do you pronounce SQL?

To answer the first question, many otherwise well educated people say that SQL stands for Structured Query Language. Actually, the letters SQL don't stand for anything. They are just a name in the same way that "Clyde" is just a name. PL/I is another example of a computer language name composed of letters that don't stand for anything (although some people think they stand for "Programming Language One"). It's true that after the "SEQUEL" name was abandoned there was some thought of calling the language "Structured Query Language," but that idea never gained official support. Structured Query Language, like SEQUEL, was just another unofficial name for a precursor of SQL. A precursor is not the same thing as a finished product.

Some early precursors to humans were known as Neanderthals. If you were to call someone a Neanderthal, he would doubtless be offended. He might punch you in the nose. To call today's SQL Structured Query Language would be just as inaccurate, if not quite as dangerous. SQL isn't particularly structured, and it's misleading to imply that it is.

In fact, properly trained structured programmers will probably recoil in horror to learn that SQL-92 includes a GOTO command. Hackers, however, who want to write unintelligible spaghetti code, can rejoice. With SQL, it is possible. The ultimate in job security is to have written mission-critical code that nobody but you can understand. Just kidding. ■

As to the second question, many people pronounce SQL "sequel." This oddity is a carryover from the pre-release version of IBM's first SQL implementation. Because of the trademark difficulty, IBM can't endorse the "sequel" pronunciation, and neither can the American National Standards Institute (ANSI). So when you say the name of the released product and today's standard, don't slur the letters together that way. Each letter is pronounced distinctly (ess cue ell).

The SQL standards

IBM's work with relational databases and SQL were well known in the industry even before IBM's SQL/DS was introduced in 1981. By that time, Relational Software, Inc. (now Oracle Corporation) had already released its first RDBMS. These early products immediately set the standard for a new class of database management systems. They incorporated SQL, which became the *de facto* standard for data sublanguages. Vendors of other relational database management systems came out with their own versions of SQL. These other implementations typically contained all the core functionality of the IBM products, but were extended in ways that took advantage of the particular strengths of the underlying RDBMS. As a result, although nearly all vendors were using some form of SQL, compatibility across platforms was poor.

An *implementation* is a particular RDBMS running on a specific hardware platform. ■

Soon a movement began whose aim was to create a universally recognized SQL standard, that everyone would adhere to. In 1986, ANSI released a formal standard named SQL-86. The standard was updated in 1989 to SQL-89. As DBMS vendors have proceeded through new releases of their products, they have tried to bring their implementations ever closer to the standard. This effort has brought true SQL portability much closer to reality.

The most recent version of the SQL standard is SQL-92 (ANSI Document No. X3.135-1992). It is a major revision of SQL-89. In this book, I describe SQL as defined by SQL-92. Any specific implementation of SQL will differ from the standard to a certain extent. Since the full SQL-92 standard is very comprehensive, it will be a long time before available implementations support it

fully. In the meantime, however, DBMS vendors are working to support a low
and an intermediate subset of the standard SQL language. Appendix B lists
the features provided by the low and intermediate subsets. ANSI document
No. X3.135-1992 is available from the American National Standards Institute.

SQL Commands

The SQL command language is comprised of a limited number of commands
that specifically relate to data handling. Some of these commands perform
data definition functions, some perform data manipulation functions, and
others perform data control functions. The data definition commands are
covered in Chapter 4, the data manipulation commands in Chapter 7, and the
data control commands in Chapters 13 and 14. Table 3-1 is a complete list of
SQL-92 commands. It is doubtful that you will find an implementation that
includes all of them, with the capabilities defined in the SQL-92 specification.
Actual implementations have a much better chance of complying with the
low and intermediate subsets outlined in Appendix B. An implementation's
documentation should disclose its level of compliance.

Reserved Words

In addition to the commands, there are a number of other words that have a
special significance within SQL. These words, along with the commands, have
been reserved for specific uses and may not be used as variable names or in
any other way that differs from their intended use. It's easy to see why tables,
columns, and variables shouldn't be given names that appear on the reserved
word list. Confusion would abound if statements like this were possible:

```
SELECT SELECT FROM SELECT WHERE SELECT = WHERE ;
```

A complete list of SQL-92 reserved words appears in Appendix A.

Data Types

Depending on their histories, different SQL implementations support a variety of data types. The SQL-92 specification, however, recognizes only six general types: exact numerics, approximate numerics, character strings, bit
strings, datetimes, and intervals. Within each of these general types there
may be several subtypes.

Table 3-1: SQL Statements

ADD	ALLOCATE DESCRIPTOR
ALTER	ALTER DOMAIN
ALTER TABLE	AUTHORIZATION
AVG	BEGIN
CHECK	CLOSE
COMMIT	CONNECT
CONTINUE	COUNT
COUNT(*)	CREATE ASSERTION
CREATE CHARACTER SET	CREATE COLLATION
CREATE DOMAIN	CREATE SCHEMA
CREATE TABLE	CREATE TRANSLATION
CREATE VIEW	DEALLOCATE DESCRIPTOR
DEALLOCATE PREPARE	DECLARE CURSOR
DECLARE CURSOR FOR	DEFAULT
DELETE	DELETE FROM
DESCRIBE	DESCRIBE INPUT
DROP	ESCAPE
EXECUTE	EXECUTE IMMEDIATE
FETCH	FOREIGN KEY
GET	GET DESCRIPTOR
GET DIAGNOSTICS	GO
GOTO	GRANT
HAVING	INSERT INTO
MAX	MIN
OPEN	ORDER BY
PREPARE	REFERENCES
REVOKE	ROLLBACK
SELECT	SET
SUM	UPDATE

If you are using an SQL implementation that supports one or more data types that are not described in the SQL-92 specification, you can keep your database more portable by avoiding these undescribed data types. By using a nonstandard data type, you are making a conscious decision that your database will never need to be migrated to another RDBMS. ∎

Exact numerics

As you can probably deduce from the name, the *exact numeric* data types allow you to express the value of a number exactly. There are four data types that fall into this category, INTEGER, SMALLINT, NUMERIC, and DECIMAL.

INTEGER data type

Data of INTEGER type has no fractional part, and its *precision* depends on the specific SQL implementation. The database developer can't specify the precision.

The *precision* of a number is the maximum number of digits allowed. ∎

SMALLINT data type

The SMALLINT type is also for integers, but the precision of a SMALLINT in a specific implementation cannot be any larger than the precision of an INTEGER on the same implementation. Implementations on IBM System/370 computers commonly represent SMALLINT and INTEGER with 16-bit and 32-bit binary numbers, respectively. In many implementations SMALLINT and INTEGER are the same.

If you are defining a database table column that will hold integer data, and you know that the range of values in the column will never exceed the precision of SMALLINT data on your implementation, assign it the SMALLINT type rather than the INTEGER type. This allows your DBMS to conserve storage space. ∎

NUMERIC data type

NUMERIC data can have a fractional component in addition to its integer component. You can specify both the precision and the scale of NUMERIC data. Precision, remember, is the maximum number of digits allowed.

The *scale* of a number is the number of digits in its fractional part. The scale cannot be negative or larger than the precision. ■

When you specify the NUMERIC data type, your SQL implementation will give you exactly the precision and scale that you request. You may specify NUMERIC and get a default precision and scale, or NUMERIC (*p*) and get your specified precision and the default scale, or NUMERIC (*p,s*) and get both your specified precision and your specified scale.

Say, for example, that the NUMERIC data type's default precision for your implementation of SQL is 12 and the default scale is 6. If you specify a database column as having a data type of NUMERIC, the column will be able to hold numbers up to 999,999.999999. If, on the other hand, you specify a data type of NUMERIC (10) for a column, it will be able to hold numbers with a maximum value of 9,999.999999. The parameter (10) specifies the maximum number of digits allowed. If you specify a data type of NUMERIC (10,2) for a column, it will be able to hold numbers with a maximum value of 99,999,999.99. In this case you may still have ten total digits, but only two of them can be to the right of the decimal point.

NUMERIC data is for values such as 595.72. That value has a precision of 5 (the number of digits), and a scale of 2 (the number of digits to the right of the decimal point). A data type of NUMERIC (5,2) is appropriate for such numbers.

DECIMAL data type is similar to NUMERIC. It can have a fractional component, and you can specify its precision and scale. The difference is that the precision your implementation supplies may be greater than what you specify, and if it is, the greater precision is used. If you do not specify precision or scale, the implementation will use default values, as it does with the NUMERIC type.

An item specified as NUMERIC (5,2) can never contain a number that has an absolute value greater than 999.99. An item specified as DECIMAL (5,2) can always hold values up to 999.99, but, if the implementation permits larger values, they will not be rejected.

Use the NUMERIC or DECIMAL type if your data has fractional positions, and the INTEGER or SMALLINT type if your data is always composed of whole numbers. Use the NUMERIC type if you want to maximize portability, since a value defined as (for example) NUMERIC (5,2) will hold exactly the same range of values on all systems. ■

Approximate numerics

Some quantities have a range of possible values so large (many orders of magnitude) that the values cannot all be represented exactly by a computer with a given register size. (32 bits, 64 bits, and 128 bits are all examples of register sizes.) Usually in such cases exactness is not required, and a close approximation is acceptable. SQL-92 defines three approximate numeric data types to handle this kind of data.

REAL data type

The REAL data type gives you a single-precision floating point number, the precision of which depends on the implementation. In general, the hardware you are running on determines precision. A 64-bit machine, for example, will give you more precision than a 32-bit machine.

DOUBLE PRECISION data type

The DOUBLE PRECISION data type gives you a double-precision floating point number, the precision of which once again depends on the implementation. Surprisingly, the meaning of the word DOUBLE is also implementation dependent. Double precision arithmetic is primarily employed by scientific users. Different scientific disciplines have different needs in the area of precision. Some implementations of SQL cater to one category of user and other implementations cater to other categories of user.

In some systems the DOUBLE PRECISION type has exactly twice the capacity of the REAL data type for both mantissa and exponent. Any number, in case you have forgotten, can be represented as a mantissa multiplied by ten raised to the power given by an exponent. For example, 1,995 can also be written as 1.995E3. 1.995 is the mantissa, which is multiplied by ten raised to the third power (3 is the exponent). For numbers fairly close to one (such as 1,995) there is no benefit to representing them with an approximate numeric data type. Exact numeric types work just as well and take up less space in memory. However, for numbers that are either much smaller or much larger than one, such as 6.023E-23 (a very small number), you must use an approximate numeric type. The exact numeric types are not able to hold such numbers. On other systems the DOUBLE PRECISION type gives you somewhat more than twice the mantissa capacity and somewhat less than twice the exponent capacity as the REAL type. On yet another type of system the DOUBLE PRECISION type gives double the mantissa capacity but the same exponent capacity as the REAL type. In this case accuracy is doubled, but range is not.

The SQL-92 specification does not try to arbitrate or establish by fiat what DOUBLE PRECISION means. It only requires that the precision of a DOUBLE PRECISION number be greater than the precision of a REAL number. This is a rather weak constraint, but perhaps the best that can be done in light of the great differences in hardware.

FLOAT data type

The FLOAT data type is most useful if you think your database might some-day migrate to a hardware platform with different register sizes than the one on which you originally designed it. With the FLOAT data type you can spec-ify a precision, for example FLOAT (5). If your hardware supports the speci-fied precision with its single-precision circuitry, that is what it will use. If the specified precision requires double-precision arithmetic, then the system will use double-precision arithmetic.

Using FLOAT rather than REAL or DOUBLE PRECISION will make it easier to port your databases to other hardware, since the FLOAT data type allows you to specify precision. The precision of REAL and DOUBLE PRECISION numbers is hardware dependent. ■

If you aren't sure whether to use the exact numeric data types (NUMERIC/DECIMAL) or the approximate numeric data types (FLOAT/REAL), use the exact numeric types. The exact data types are less demanding of sys-tem resources and, of course, give exact rather than approximate results. If the range of possible values of your data is large enough to require the use of the approximate data types, you will probably know this in advance. ■

Character strings

These days databases store many different types of data, including graphic images, sounds, and animations. I expect odors to be next. Can you imagine a 1024 x 768 24-bit color image of a large slice of pepperoni pizza on your screen while an odor sample taken at DiFilippi's Pizza Grotto is replayed through your super-multimedia card? It might get frustrating — until you can afford to add taste type data to your system as well. Alas, it will be a long time indeed before odor and taste become standard SQL data types. These days, the next most commonly used data types after the numeric types are the character string types.

There are two main types of character data: fixed character (CHARACTER or CHAR) and varying character (CHARACTER VARYING or VARCHAR). There are also two variants of these types, named NATIONAL CHARACTER and NATIONAL CHARACTER VARYING.

CHARACTER data type

When you define the data type of a column as CHARACTER or CHAR, you can specify the number of characters the column will hold, using the syntax CHARACTER (x), where x is the number of characters. For example, if you specify a column's data type as CHARACTER (16), then the maximum length of any data entered in the column will be 16 characters. If you don't specify an argument (that is, if you don't provide a value in place of the x), SQL assumes a field length of one character. When you enter data into a CHARACTER field of a specified length, if you enter fewer characters than the specified number, the remaining character spaces will be filled with blanks.

The CHARACTER VARYING data type is useful when entries in a column can vary in length, but you do *not* want the field to be padded with blanks. It allows you to store exactly the number of characters that the user enters. There is no default value for this data type. To specify this data type, use the form CHARACTER VARYING (x) or VARCHAR (x), where x is the maximum number of characters permitted.

The NATIONAL CHARACTER and NATIONAL CHARACTER VARYING data types are the same as the CHARACTER and CHARACTER VARYING data types except the character set being specified is different from the default character set. You can specify character set when you define a table column. If you wish, each column could use a different character set. An example table creation statement using multiple character sets follows:

```
CREATE TABLE XLATE (
    LANGUAGE_1    CHARACTER (40),
    LANGUAGE_2    CHARACTER VARYING (40)  CHARACTER SET GREEK,
    LANGUAGE 3    NATIONAL CHARACTER (40),
    LANGUAGE 4    CHARACTER (40)          CHARACTER SET KANJI
    )
```

The LANGUAGE_1 column will contain characters in the implementation's default character set. The LANGUAGE_3 column will contain characters in the implementation's national character set. The LANGUAGE_2 column will contain Greek characters, and the LANGUAGE_4 column will contain Kanji characters.

Bit strings

SQL-92 has a data type that provides for strings of bits that do not represent alphanumeric characters or numbers. The BIT and BIT VARYING data types accept any arbitrary bit string. You specify fixed-length binary data with the BIT (x) format, where x is the number of bits. BIT without an argument defaults to one bit. If you want to accommodate data that sometimes is one length and sometimes another, use BIT VARYING (x), where x denotes the maximum number of bits that the data field will accept. The BIT and BIT VARYING data types may be used to hold binary or hexadecimal data. They may also be used to hold flags that indicate whether individual logical switches are on or off.

Datetimes

The SQL-92 standard defines five different data types that deal with dates and times. These are called *datetime* data types, or simply *datetimes*. There is considerable overlap among these data types, so it is quite possible that an implementation you encounter will not support all five.

 Implementations that do not fully support all five data types for dates and times may have problems with databases that you are trying to migrate from another implementation. If you have trouble with a migration, check how dates and times are represented in both the source and the destination implementations. ∎

DATE data type

The DATE type stores year, month, and day values of a date. The year value is four digits long, and the month and day values are both two digits long. A DATE value can represent any date from the year 0001 to the year 9999. The length of a DATE is ten positions, as in 1957-08-14.

TIME data type

The TIME data type stores hour, minute, and second values of time. The hours and minutes occupy exactly two digits. The seconds value is also two digits, but may in addition include an optional fractional part. For example, a time of 32 minutes and 58.436 seconds past 9 o'clock in the morning would be represented as 09:32:58.436.

The precision of the fractional part is implementation-dependent, but at least six digits. A TIME value takes up eight positions if it has no fractional part, or nine positions plus the number of fractional digits if it does have a fractional part. The ninth position holds the decimal point. Specify TIME type data either as TIME or as TIME (p), where p is the number of positions. The default assumption is that there are zero fractional digits. The example in the preceding paragraph has a data type of TIME (12).

TIMESTAMP data type

TIMESTAMP data includes both date and time information. The lengths and the restrictions on the values of the components of TIMESTAMP data are the same as they are for DATE and TIME data, except for one difference: The default length of the fractional part of the time component of a TIMESTAMP is six digits rather than zero. If there are no fractional digits, the length of a TIMESTAMP is 19 positions. If there are fractional digits, the length is 20 positions plus the number of fractional digits. The twentieth position is for the decimal point. Specify a field as of TIMESTAMP type either with TIME-STAMP or with TIMESTAMP (p), where p is the number of digit positions. The value of p cannot be negative, and its maximum value is determined by the implementation.

TIME WITH TIME ZONE data type

The TIME WITH TIME ZONE data type is exactly the same as the TIME data type except that it adds information about the offset from Universal time (formerly known as Greenwich Mean Time or GMT). The value of the offset may range anywhere from -12:59 to +13:00. This additional information takes up additional digit positions. A TIME WITH TIME ZONE that has no fractional part is 14 positions long. If you specify a fractional part, the field length will be 15 positions plus the number of fractional digits.

TIMESTAMP WITH TIME ZONE data type

The TIMESTAMP WITH TIME ZONE data type is exactly like the TIMESTAMP data type except that it adds information about the offset from Universal time. The additional information takes up 6 additional digit positions, giving 25 for a field with no fractional part, and 26 positions plus the number of fractional digits for fields that do have a fractional part.

Intervals

The interval data types are closely related to the datetime data types. An interval is the difference between two datetime values. In many applications that deal with dates, times, or both, you sometimes need to determine the interval between two dates or two times. SQL-92 recognizes two distinct types of intervals, the year-month interval and the day-time interval. A year-month interval is the number of years and months between two dates. A day-time interval is the number of days, hours, minutes, and seconds between two instants within a month. Calculations involving a year-month interval cannot be mixed with calculations involving a day-time interval, because months come in varying lengths (28, 29, 30, or 31 days long).

Data type summary

Table 3-2 enumerates the various data types and displays literals that conform to each type.

Table 3-2: Data Types

Data Type	Example Value
CHARACTER (20)	'Amateur Radio
VARCHAR (20)	'Amateur Radio'
SMALLINT or INTEGER	7500
NUMERIC or DECIMAL	3425.432
REAL, FLOAT, or DOUBLE PRECISION	6.023E-23
BIT (5)	B'11011'
BIT (16)	X'3FD0'
DATE	DATE '1995-04-03'
TIME (2) (argument specifies number of fractional digits)	TIME '12:46:02.43'
TIME (3) WITH TIME ZONE	TIME '12:46:02.432-08:00'
TIMESTAMP (0)	TIMESTAMP '04-03-1995 12:46:02'
INTERVAL DAY	INTERVAL '4' DAY

Remember that your specific implementation of SQL may not support all the data types described here. Furthermore, it may support nonstandard data types that are not described here. It may be a while before SQL-92 data types that were not included in SQL-89 show up in many of the products on the market. ■

Null Values

If a database field contains a data item, it has a specific value. A field that does not contain a data item is said to have a *null value*. In a numeric field a null value is not the same as a value of zero. In a character field, a null value is not the same as a blank. Both a numeric zero and a blank character are definite values. A null value means that a field's value is undefined. Its value is not known. ■

There are a number of situations in which a field might have a null value. Here are a few:

- ✔ The value exists, but you don't know what it is yet: You set MASS to null in the "Top" row of the QUARK table, because the mass of the top quark has not yet been accurately determined.

- ✔ The value does not exist yet: You set TOTAL_SOLD to null in the "SQL For Dummies" row of the BOOKS table, because the first set of quarterly sales figures has not been reported yet.

- ✔ The field is not applicable for this particular row: You set SALARY to null in the "Joe Girard" row of the EMPLOYEE table, because Joe is a salesperson who works on straight commission.

- ✔ The value is out of range: You set SALARY to null in the "Bill Cosby" row of the EMPLOYEE table, because you designed the SALARY column to be of type NUMERIC (7,2) and Bill's contract calls for pay in excess of $99,999.99.

A field could have a null value for many different reasons. Don't jump to any hasty conclusions about what it means. ■

Constraints

Constraints are restrictions you apply to the data that can be entered into a database table. For example, you may know that entries in a particular numeric column must fall within a certain range. If any entry is made that falls outside that range, it must be an error. By applying a range constraint to the column, you prevent this type of error.

Traditionally, constraints to a database have been applied by the application program that uses the database. However, the most recent DBMS products allow you to apply constraints directly to the database. This has several advantages. If multiple applications all use the same database, the constraints need be applied only once rather than multiple times. In addition, it is usually simpler to add constraints at the database level. In many cases, you need only to tack a clause onto your CREATE statement.

Constraints, and assertions, which are constraints that apply to more than one table, are discussed in detail in Chapter 6 in the section on integrity.

The 5th Wave

By Rich Tennant

AFTER DISCOVERING **THE LAND OF LOST FILES,** BILL AND IRWIN RUN INTO A TRIBE OF SQL INDIANS.

THIS IS GONNA BE TRICKY. THEY PROBABLY ALL SPEAK A DIFFERENT LANGUAGE.

Chapter 4

The Components of SQL

● ●

In This Chapter

▶ Creating databases

▶ Tables, views, schemas, and catalogs

▶ Manipulating data

▶ Protecting databases

● ●

SQL is a special-purpose language, specifically designed for the creation and maintenance of data in relational databases. It is defined and controlled by an ANSI standard that was most recently revised in 1992. Vendors of relational database management systems all have their own implementations of SQL. Those implementations differ from the standard to a greater or lesser degree. Close adherence to the standard is most important to people who may want to run their database and its associated applications on more than one platform.

Although SQL is not a general-purpose programming language, it does contain everything you need to create, maintain, and provide security for a relational database. The part of SQL used to create databases is called the *Data Definition Language* (DDL). Database maintenance is performed with the *Data Manipulation Language* (DML), and security is provided by the *Data Control Language* (DCL). This chapter introduces the DDL, DML, and DCL.

SQL's Data Definition Language provides you with everything you will need to completely define a database, modify its structure after it has been created, and destroy it after it is no longer needed. The Data Manipulation Language is a powerful tool for entering data into, changing, or extracting data from a database. Its richness allows you to specify exactly what you want to do. The Data Control Language provides you with the armor you need to protect your database from harm. There are many ways that a database can become corrupted. The tools provided by the DCL, if properly used, will prevent many of those problems. The amount of protection the DCL provides may vary from one implementation to another. If sufficient protection is not provided by your implementation, you will have to add it into your application program.

Data Definition Language (DDL)

The Data Definition Language is the part of SQL you use to create, change, or destroy the basic elements of a relational database. Basic elements include tables, views, schemas, catalogs, and possibly other things as well. In this section I'll discuss the containment hierarchy that relates these elements to each other, and look at the commands that operate on these elements.

In Chapter 1 I mentioned tables and schemas, noting that a schema was an overall structure that included tables within it. Tables and schemas are two elements of a relational database's *containment hierarchy*. Columns and rows are contained within tables. Tables and views are contained within schemas. Schemas are contained within catalogs. And catalogs are contained within a database.

Creating tables

A database table is a two-dimensional array made up of rows and columns. You can create one with SQL's CREATE TABLE command. Within the command, you specify the name and data type of each column.

Once you have created a table, you can start loading it with data. (Loading data would be a DML, not a DDL function.) If requirements change, you can change a table's structure after it has been created, with the ALTER TABLE command. Eventually, a table may outlive its usefulness or in some other way become obsolete. When that day arrives, you can eliminate it with the DROP command. The various forms of the CREATE and ALTER commands, together with the DROP command, make up SQL's DDL.

Say you are a database designer and you don't want your database tables to gradually turn to guacamole as updates are made over time. You decide to structure your database tables according to the best normalized form to ensure maintenance of data integrity. Normalization, which is an extensive field of study in its own right, is a way of structuring database tables so that updates do not introduce anomalies. Each table you create will contain columns that correspond to attributes that are tightly linked to each other.

For example, you might create a CUSTOMER table with the attributes CUS-TOMER.CUSTOMER_ID, CUSTOMER.FIRST_NAME, CUSTOMER.LAST_NAME, CUSTOMER.STREET, CUSTOMER.CITY, CUSTOMER.STATE, CUSTOMER.ZIP-CODE, and CUSTOMER.PHONE. All of these attributes are more closely related to the customer entity than they are to any other entity in a database that may contain many tables. They contain all of the relatively permanent information that your organization keeps on its customers.

Most database management systems provide a graphical tool for creating database tables. However, you can also do it with an SQL command. Here is a command that will create your CUSTOMER table:

```
CREATE TABLE CUSTOMER (
    CUSTOMER_ID             INTEGER              NOT NULL,
    FIRST_NAME              CHARACTER (15),
    LAST_NAME               CHARACTER (20)       NOT NULL,
    STREET                  CHARACTER (25),
    CITY                    CHARACTER (20),
    STATE                   CHARACTER (2),
    ZIPCODE                 INTEGER,
    PHONE                   CHARACTER (13) ) ;
```

For each column, you specify its name (for example, CUSTOMER_ID), its data type (for example, INTEGER), and possibly one or more constraints (for example, NOT NULL).

Figure 4-1 shows a portion of the CUSTOMER table, with some sample data in it.

CUSTOMER_ID	FIRST_NAME	LAST_NAME	STREET	CITY	STAT	ZIPCODE
1	Harold	Percival	26262 S. Howards Mill Rd.	Westminster	CA	92683
2	Jerry	Appel	32323 S. River Lane Rd.	Santa Ana	CA	92705
3	Adrian	Hansen	232 Glenwood Ct.	Hollis	NH	3049
4	John	Baker	2222 Lafayette St.	Garden Grove	CA	92643
5	Michael	Pens	730 S. New Era Rd.	Irvine	CA	92715
6	Bob	Michimoto	25252 S. Kelmsley Dr.	Stanton	CA	92610
7	Linda	Smith	444 S.E. Seventh St.	Hudson	NH	3051
8	Robert	Funnell	2424 Sheri Ct.	Anaheim	CA	92640
9	Bill	Checkal	9595 Curry Dr.	Stanton	CA	92610
10	Jed	Style	3535 Randall St.	Santa Ana	CA	92705

Figure 4-1: CUSTOMER table created by the CREATE TABLE command.

If the SQL implementation you are using complies with SQL-89, but does not fully implement SQL-92, the syntax you will need to use may differ from the syntax given in this book. ■

Imagine you have been given the task of creating a database for your organization. Excited by the prospect of building a useful, valuable, and totally righteous structure that will be very important to the future of your company, you sit right down at your computer and start entering SQL CREATE commands. Right?

Well, no. Not quite. In fact, that would be a prescription for disaster. Many database development projects go awry at the very start, when excitement and enthusiasm overtake careful planning. Even if you are sure you have a clear idea in your mind of how to structure your database, write it all out on paper before touching your keyboard. Some points to remember:

✔ Identify all tables.

✔ Define the columns that each table will contain.

✔ Give each table a primary key that is guaranteed to be unique.

✔ Make sure every table in the database has at least one column in common with one other table in the database. These shared columns serve as logical links that allow information in one table to be related to corresponding information in another table.

✔ Put each table in third normal form (3NF) or better, to assure the prevention of insertion, deletion, and update anomalies. Database normalization is discussed in Chapter 6. ■

Once you have completed the design on paper, and have verified that it is sound, you are ready to transfer it to the computer, using SQL CREATE commands.

A room with a view

There will be times when you want to retrieve some specific information from the CUSTOMER table. You don't want to look at everything, only some specific columns and rows. What you need is a view.

A *view* is a virtual table. In most implementations it does not have any independent physical existence. Its definition exists in the database's meta-data, but the actual data is pulled from the table or tables from which the view is derived. The view's data is not physically duplicated somewhere else in online disk storage. Some views zero in on specific columns and rows of a single table. Others, known as multitable views, draw from two or more tables.

Single-table view

Sometimes when you have a question, the data that will give you the answer resides in a single table in your database. If all of the information you want to see exists on a single table, you can create a single-table view of the data. Say, for example, that you want to look at the names and telephone numbers of all customers that live in the state of New Hampshire. You can create a view from the CUSTOMER table that contains only the data you want. The following SQL command creates the view:

```
CREATE VIEW NH_CUST AS
        SELECT CUSTOMER.FIRST_NAME,
            CUSTOMER.LAST_NAME,
            CUSTOMER.PHONE
    FROM CUSTOMER
        WHERE
            CUSTOMER.STATE = 'NH';
```

Figure 4-2 diagrams how the view is derived from the CUSTOMER table.

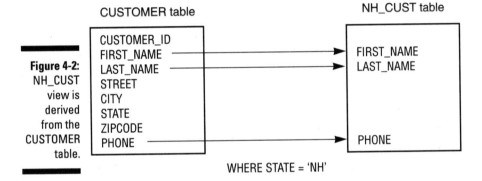

Figure 4-2:
NH_CUST view is derived from the CUSTOMER table.

This code is rigorously correct, but a little on the wordy side. You can accomplish the same thing with less typing if the SQL implementation you are using assumes all table references are the same as the ones in the FROM clause. If your system makes that reasonable default assumption, you can reduce the command to:

```
CREATE VIEW NH_CUST AS
        SELECT FIRST_NAME,
            LAST_NAME,
            PHONE
    FROM CUSTOMER
        WHERE
            STATE = 'NH';
```

Although the second version is easier to write and read, it is also more vulnerable to disruption from later ALTER TABLEs. This isn't a problem with this view that has no JOIN, but views with JOINs are much more "robust" if they use fully qualified names. JOINs are covered in Chapter 11. ■

Multitable view

More often than not, you will need to pull data from two or more tables to answer your question. For example, say you work for a sporting goods store, and you want a list of all customers who have bought ski equipment in the last year, so you can send them a promotional mailing. You will probably need information from the CUSTOMER table, the PRODUCT table, the INVOICE table, and the INVOICE_LINE table. You can create a multitable view that shows the data you need to answer your question. Once the view has been created, you can use it again and again. Each time you use it, it will reflect the changes that have occurred in the underlying tables since the last time you used it.

The sporting goods store database has four tables: CUSTOMER, PRODUCT, INVOICE and INVOICE_LINE. The tables are structured as shown in Table 4-1.

Table 4-1: Sporting Goods Store Database Tables

Table	Column	Data Type	Constraint
CUSTOMER			
	CUSTOMER_ID	INTEGER	NOT NULL
	FIRST_NAME	CHARACTER (15)	
	LAST_NAME	CHARACTER (20)	NOT NULL
	STREET	CHARACTER (25)	
	CITY	CHARACTER (20)	
	STATE	CHARACTER (2)	
	ZIPCODE	INTEGER	
	PHONE	CHARACTER (13)	
PRODUCT			
	PRODUCT_ID	INTEGER	NOT NULL
	NAME	CHARACTER (25)	
	DESCRIPTION	CHARACTER (30)	
	CATEGORY	CHARACTER (15)	
	VENDOR_ID	INTEGER	
	VENDOR_NAME	CHARACTER (30)	
INVOICE			
	INVOICE_NUMBER	INTEGER	NOT NULL
	CUSTOMER_ID	INTEGER	
	DATE	DATE	
	TOTAL_SALE	NUMERIC (9,2)	
	TOTAL_REMITTED	NUMERIC (9,2)	
	FORM_OF_PAYMENT	CHARACTER (10)	
INVOICE_LINE			
	LINE_NUMBER	INTEGER	NOT NULL
	INVOICE_NUMBER	INTEGER	
	PRODUCT_ID	INTEGER	
	QUANTITY	INTEGER	
	SALE_PRICE	NUMERIC (9,2)	

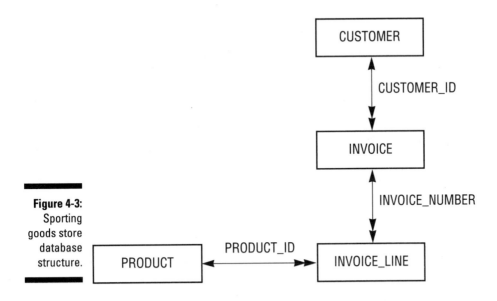

Figure 4-3:
Sporting
goods store
database
structure.

Notice that some of the columns have the constraint NOT NULL. These columns are either the primary keys of their respective tables or are columns that you for some other reason have decided must contain a value. A table's primary key must uniquely identify each row. It must contain a non-null value in every row. I will discuss keys in detail in Chapter 6.

The tables are related to each other by columns that they have in common. Figure 4-3 shows the relationships.

The CUSTOMER table bears a one-to-many relationship to the INVOICE table. One customer can make multiple purchases, generating multiple invoices. Each invoice, however, deals with one and only one customer. The INVOICE table bears a one-to-many relationship to the INVOICE_LINE table. An invoice may have multiple lines, but each line appears on one and only one invoice. The PRODUCT table also bears a one-to-many relationship to the INVOICE_LINE table. A product may appear on more than one line on one or more invoices. Each line, however, deals with one and only one product.

The CUSTOMER table is linked to the INVOICE table by the common CUS-TOMER_ID column. The INVOICE table is linked to the INVOICE_LINE table by the common INVOICE_NUMBER column. The PRODUCT table is linked to the INVOICE_LINE table by the common PRODUCT_ID column. These links are the essence of what makes this database a *relational* database.

To give you the information you want about customers who have bought ski equipment, you will need FIRST_NAME, LAST_NAME, STREET, CITY, STATE, and ZIPCODE from the CUSTOMER table, CATEGORY from the PRODUCT table, INVOICE_NUMBER from the INVOICE table, and LINE_NUMBER from the INVOICE_LINE table. You could create the view you want in stages, using the following commands:

```
CREATE VIEW SKI_CUST1 AS
    SELECT FIRST_NAME,
        LAST_NAME,
        STREET,
        CITY,
        STATE,
        ZIPCODE,
        INVOICE_NUMBER
    FROM CUSTOMER JOIN INVOICE
USING (CUSTOMER_ID) ;

CREATE VIEW SKI_CUST2 AS
    SELECT  FIRST_NAME,
        LAST_NAME,
        STREET,
        CITY,
        STATE,
        ZIPCODE,
        PRODUCT_ID
    FROM SKI_CUST1 JOIN INVOICE_LINE
    USING (INVOICE_NUMBER) ;

CREATE VIEW SKI_CUST3 AS
    SELECT FIRST_NAME,
        LAST_NAME,
        STREET,
        CITY,
        STATE,
        ZIPCODE,
        CATEGORY
    FROM SKI_CUST2 JOIN PRODUCT
    USING (PRODUCT_ID) ;

CREATE VIEW SKI_CUST AS
    SELECT DISTINCT FIRST_NAME,
        LAST_NAME,
        STREET,
        CITY,
        STATE,
        ZIPCODE
    FROM SKI_CUST3
    WHERE CATEGORY = 'Ski' ;
```

CUSTOMER table   SKI_CUST1 view   SKI_CUST2 view   SKI_CUST3 view   SKI_CUST view

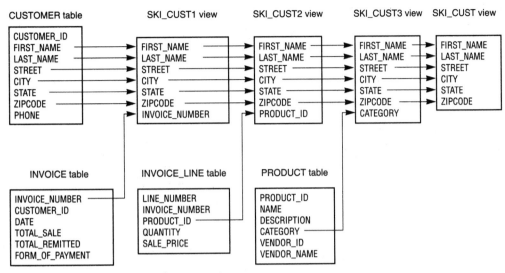

Figure 4-4: Creating a multitable view using JOINs.

These CREATE VIEW statements combine data from multiple tables using the JOIN operator. Figure 4-4 diagrams the process.

The first CREATE VIEW statement combines columns from the CUSTOMER table with a column of the INVOICE table to create the SKI_CUST1 view. The second CREATE VIEW statement combines SKI_CUST1 with a column from the INVOICE_LINE table to create the SKI_CUST2 view. The third CREATE VIEW statement combines SKI_CUST2 with a column from the PRODUCT table to create the SKI_CUST3 view. The fourth CREATE VIEW statement filters out all rows that do not have a CATEGORY of 'Ski'. The end result is a view (SKI_CUST) that contains the names and addresses of all customers who have bought at least one product in the 'Ski' category. The DISTINCT keyword in the fourth CREATE VIEW's SELECT clause assures that there will be only one entry for each customer, even if they have made multiple purchases of ski items. JOINs are covered in detail in Chapter 11.

Collecting tables into schemas

A table is composed of rows and columns. It normally deals with a specific type of entity, such as customers, products, or invoices. Useful work generally requires information about several (or many) related entities. Organizationally, the tables associated with these entities are collected together in a schema.

A *schema* is a collection of related tables. ■

On a system where several unrelated projects may co-reside, assign all tables that are related to one another to one schema. Other groups of tables can be collected into schemas of their own.

By naming schemas, you can assure that tables from one project are not accidentally mixed in with tables of another. Each project would have its own associated schema, which could be distinguished from other schemas by name. It is not uncommon for certain table names (such as CUSTOMER, PRODUCT, and so on) to appear in multiple projects. If there is a chance of a naming ambiguity, qualify your table name with its schema name (SCHEMA_NAME.TABLE_NAME). If you do not qualify a table name, SQL will assign it to the default schema.

Ordering by catalog

For really large database systems, even multiple schemas might not be enough. In a large distributed database environment with many users, there might even be duplication of a schema name. To prevent this from happening, SQL-92 has added one more level to the containment hierarchy, the catalog.

A *catalog* is a named collection of schemas. ■

You can qualify a table name with a catalog name as well as a schema name to assure that it is not confused with a table of the same name in a schema with the same schema name. The qualified name would be of the form CATALOG_NAME.SCHEMA_NAME.TABLE_NAME.

A database's *containment hierarchy* has catalogs at the highest level. A catalog contains schemas, and a schema contains tables and views. Tables and views contain columns and rows.

A catalog contains the schemas that contain user tables, but it also contains the *information schema*. The information schema contains the system tables. The system tables hold the meta-data associated with the other schemas. In Chapter 1 I defined a database as a self-describing collection of integrated records. It is the meta-data contained in the system tables that makes the database self-describing.

Since catalogs are distinguished by their names, you can have multiple catalogs in a database. Each catalog can have multiple schemas, and each schema can have multiple tables. Of course, each table can have multiple columns and rows. The hierarchical relationships are shown in Figure 4-5.

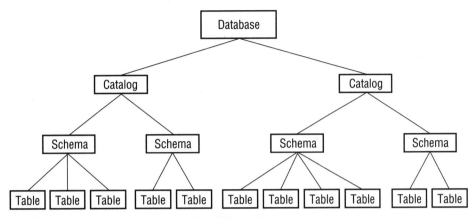

Figure 4-5: The hierarchical structure of an SQL database.

The DDL commands

SQL's Data Definition Language consists of the CREATE, ALTER, and DROP commands. The DDL deals with the structure of a database, while the Data Manipulation Language deals with the data contained within that structure. Use the various forms of the CREATE command to build the essential structures of the database. Use the ALTER command to change structures that you create. The DROP command, when applied to a table, destroys not just the table's data, but its structure as well. In the following sections I will give brief descriptions of the DDL commands. In Chapters 5 and 6 I will use them in examples.

CREATE

THE SQL CREATE command can be applied to several SQL objects, including schemas, domains, tables, and views. With the CREATE SCHEMA statement, you can create a schema, identify its owner, and specify a default character set. An example would be:

```
CREATE SCHEMA SALES
    AUTHORIZATION SALES_MGR
    DEFAULT CHARACTER SET ASCII ;
```

Use the CREATE DOMAIN statement to apply constraints to column values or to specify a collation order. The constraints you apply to a domain determine what objects can be in the domain and what objects cannot. You can create domains once you have established a schema. For example:

```
CREATE DOMAIN AGES AS INTEGER
   CHECK (AGE > 20) ;
```

Create tables with the CREATE TABLE statement, and create views with the CREATE VIEW statement. You have already seen examples of the CREATE TABLE and the CREATE VIEW statements. When you use CREATE TABLE to create a new table, you can specify constraints on its columns at the same time. Sometimes, however, you may want to specify constraints that are not specifically attached to a table, but that apply to an entire schema. You can use the CREATE ASSERTION statement to specify such constraints. There are also CREATE CHARACTER SET, CREATE COLLATION, and CREATE TRANSLATION statements, which give you the flexibility of creating new character sets, collation sequences, or translation tables.

Collation sequences define the order in which sorts are done. *Translation tables* control the conversion of character strings from one character set to another. ∎

ALTER

Once you have created a table, you are not necessarily stuck with it forever. As you start to use it, you may discover that it is not everything that you hoped it would be. Use the ALTER TABLE command to change it by adding, changing, or deleting a column in the table. Besides tables, you can also ALTER columns and domains.

DROP

It's easy to remove a table from a database schema. Just issue a DROP <table-name> command. All the table's data will be erased, as will the meta-data that defines the table in the data dictionary. It will be as if the table never existed.

Data Manipulation Language (DML)

As you have seen, the DDL is that part of SQL that creates, modifies, or destroys database structures. It does not deal with data. The Data Manipulation Language (DML) is the part of SQL that operates on the data. Some DML statements read like ordinary English-language sentences, and are easy to understand. However, since SQL allows very fine control of the data, DML statements can also be very complex. When a DML statement includes multiple expressions, clauses, predicates, or subqueries, understanding what it is trying to do can be a real challenge. It might even cause you to consider switching to an easier line of work, such as brain surgery or quantum electrodynamics. Such drastic action is probably not necessary however, since you can come to understand SQL statements by breaking them down in your mind into their basic components, and analyzing them one chunk at a time.

The DML statements are INSERT, UPDATE, DELETE, and SELECT. They can be made up of a variety of parts, including multiple clauses. Each clause may incorporate value expressions, logical connectives, predicates, aggregate functions, and subqueries. You can make fine discriminations among database records, and extract more information from your data by including these clauses in your statements. In Chapter 7, we will discuss the operation of the DML commands, and in Chapters 8 through 12 we will delve into the details.

Value expressions

Use value expressions to combine two or more values. There are five different kinds of value expressions: numeric, string, datetime, interval, and conditional.

Numeric value expressions

To combine numeric values, use the addition (+), subtraction (-), multiplication (*), and division (/) operators. Following are a few examples of numeric value expressions.

```
12-7
15/3-4
6*(8+2)
```

The values in these examples are numeric literals. They could also be column names, parameters, host variables, or subqueries — provided those column names, parameters, host variables, or subqueries evaluate to a numeric value. Here are some examples:

```
SUBTOTAL+TAX+SHIPPING
6*MILES/HOURS
:months/12
```

The colon in the last example is a signal that the following term (months) is either a parameter or a host variable.

String value expressions

String value expressions may include the concatenation operator (||). Use concatenation to join two text strings together, as shown in Table 4-2.

Table 4-2: Examples of String Concatenation

Expression	Result
'military' || 'intelligence'	'military intelligence'
'oxy' || 'moron'	'oxymoron'
CITY|| ' ' ||STATE|| ' '||ZIP	a single string with city, state, and ZIP code, each separated by a single space

Some implementations of SQL use + as the concatenation operator rather than ||. ■

Some implementations may include string operators other than concatenation, but such operators are not supported by SQL-92.

Datetime and interval value expressions

Datetime value expressions (surprise!) deal with dates and times. Data of DATE, TIME, TIMESTAMP, and INTERVAL types may appear in datetime value expressions. The result of a datetime value expression is always another datetime. You can add or subtract an interval from a datetime, and specify time zone information.

One example of a datetime value expression is:

```
DUE_DATE + INTERVAL '7' DAY
```

A library might use such an expression to determine when to send a late notice. Another example, specifying a time rather than a date is:

```
TIME '18:55:48' AT LOCAL
```

The AT LOCAL keywords indicate that the time is referenced to the local time zone.

Interval value expressions deal with the difference (how much time has passed) between one datetime and another. There are two kinds of intervals: year-month and day-time. The two cannot be mixed in an expression.

As an example of an interval, say a library book is returned after the due date. With an interval value expression like the following example, you can calculate how many days late the book was returned and assess a fine accordingly:

```
(DATE_RETURNED-DATE_DUE) DAY
```

Since an interval may be of either the year-month or the day-time variety, you should specify which kind to use. In this case I have specified DAY.

Conditional value expressions

CASE, NULLIF, and COALESCE are conditional value expressions, which are discussed extensively in Chapter 9. (Actually, NULLIF and COALESCE are macro expansions that provide a shorthand way of writing certain commonly needed CASE expressions.) The conditional value expressions give SQL the ability to take different actions, depending on which of several conditions happens to be true. The conditional value expressions in SQL-92 makes it a much more powerful language than SQL-89, which lacked them.

Predicates

Predicates are the SQL equivalents of logical propositions. An example of a proposition would be:

"The student is a senior."

In a table containing information about students, the domain of the CLASS column might be SENIOR, JUNIOR, SOPHOMORE, FRESHMAN, or NULL. You could use the predicate CLASS = SENIOR to filter out rows for which the predicate is false, retaining only those for which the predicate is true. Sometimes the value of a predicate in a row is unknown (NULL). In those cases you may choose either to discard the row or to retain it. (After all, the student *might* be a senior.) The correct course depends on the specific situation.

CLASS = SENIOR is an example of a *comparison predicate*. There are six comparison operators. A simple comparison predicate will use one of them. Table 4-3 shows the comparison predicates and examples of their use.

Table 4-3: Comparison Operators and Comparison Predicates

Operator	Comparison	Expression
=	equal to	CLASS = SENIOR
<>	not equal to	CLASS <> SENIOR
<	less than	CLASS < SENIOR
>	greater than	CLASS > SENIOR
<=	less than or equal to	CLASS <= SENIOR
>=	greater than or equal to	CLASS >= SENIOR

In this example, only the first two entries (CLASS=SENIOR and CLASS< >SENIOR) make sense, since SOPHOMORE would be considered greater than SENIOR, since SO comes after SE in the default collation sequence. This is probably not the interpretation you want.

Logical connectives

Logical connectives allow you to build complex predicates out of simple ones. For instance, say you wanted to identify all the child prodigies in a database of high school students. Two propositions that could identify them might be:

"The student is a senior."

"The student's age is less than 14 years."

You can use the logical connective AND to create a compound predicate that will isolate the student records that you want.

```
CLASS = SENIOR AND AGE < 14
```

When you use the AND connective, both of the component predicates must be true for the compound predicate to be true. Use the OR connective when you want the compound predicate to evaluate to true if either of the component predicates is true. NOT is the third logical connective. Strictly speaking, it does not connect two predicates, but instead reverses the truth value of the single predicate to which it is applied. For example the expression:

```
NOT (CLASS = SENIOR)
```

is true only if CLASS is in fact not equal to SENIOR.

Set functions

Sometimes the information you want to extract from a table does not relate to what is contained in the individual rows, but has to do with the data in the entire table taken as a set. SQL-92 provides five set (or aggregate) functions to deal with such situations. They are COUNT, MAX, MIN, SUM, and AVG. Each of these functions performs an action that draws data from a set of rows rather than from only a single row.

COUNT

The COUNT function returns the number of rows in the specified table. To count the number of precocious students in our high school database, use following statement:

```
SELECT COUNT (*)
    FROM STUDENT
     WHERE GRADE = 12 and AGE < 14 ;
```

MAX

Use the MAX function to return the maximum value that occurs in the specified column. Say you wanted to find the oldest student enrolled in your school. A statement such as the following will return the appropriate row:

```
SELECT FIRST_NAME, LAST_NAME, AGE
    FROM STUDENT
    WHERE AGE = (SELECT MAX(AGE) FROM STUDENT);
```

This will return all students whose age is equal to the maximum age. That is, if the age of the oldest student is 23, then this will return the first and last names and the age of all students that are 23.

This query makes use of a *subquery*. The subquery (SELECT MAX(AGE) FROM STUDENT) is embedded within the main query.

MIN

The MIN function works just like MAX, except it looks for the minimum value in the specified column, rather than the maximum. To find the youngest student enrolled, you could use the following query:

```
SELECT FIRST_NAME, LAST_NAME, AGE
    FROM STUDENT
    WHERE AGE = (SELECT MIN(AGE) FROM STUDENT);
```

This query returns all students whose age is equal to the age of the youngest student.

SUM

The SUM function adds up the values in a specified column. The column must be one of the numeric data types, and the value of the sum must be within the range of that type. Thus, if the column is of type SMALLINT, the resulting sum must be no larger than the upper limit of the SMALLINT data type. In the retail database created earlier in this chapter, the INVOICE table contains a record of all sales. To find the total dollar value of all sales recorded in the database, use the SUM function as follows:

```
SELECT SUM(TOTAL_SALE) FROM INVOICE
```

AVG

The AVG function returns the average of all the values in the specified column. Like the SUM function, AVG applies only to columns with a numeric data type. To find the value of the average sale, considering all transactions in the database, use the AVG function in the following way:

```
SELECT AVG(TOTAL_SALE) FROM INVOICE
```

Nulls, remember, have no value, so if any of the rows in the TOTAL_SALE column contain null values, those rows will be ignored in the computation of the value of the average sale.

Subqueries

Subqueries, as we saw in the section on set functions, are queries within a query. Any place in an SQL statement where an expression is allowed, a subquery is also allowed. Subqueries provide a powerful tool for relating information in one table to information in another table. This is because a query into one table can be embedded within a query into another table. By nesting one subquery within another, you allow information from two or more tables to be accessed to generate a final result. If you understand how to use subqueries correctly, you should be able to retrieve any information you want from a database.

SQL-89 had limited support of subqueries in that only one side of a comparison could be a subquery. Implementations that adhere to SQL-89, but not fully to SQL-92, may restrict the places where subqueries can be used. ▪

Data Control Language (DCL)

The Data Control Language has four commands, COMMIT, ROLLBACK, GRANT, and REVOKE. These commands all have to do with protecting the database from harm, either accidental or intentional.

Transactions

Your database is most vulnerable to damage while it is in the process of being changed. Even with a single-user system, the act of making a change can be dangerous to a database. A software or hardware failure while the change is in progress could leave the database in an indeterminate state that is not what it was before the change started, and not what it would have been if the change had been completed.

SQL protects your database by restricting operations that can change it so that they occur only within transactions. During a transaction, SQL acts on temporary copies of the data. Only at the conclusion of the transaction, when you issue the COMMIT statement, is the database affected. If the transaction is interrupted before the COMMIT, you can restore the system to its original state by issuing a ROLLBACK statement. Once you have rolled back the database to its state before the transaction began, you can clear up whatever caused the problem, then attempt the transaction again.

As long as a hardware or software problem is possible, your database is susceptible to damage. To minimize the chance of damage, close the window of vulnerability as much as possible. Do this by performing all operations that affect the database within a transaction, then committing them all at once. When you issue the COMMIT statement, all the actions in the transaction are executed as quickly as possible. To damage data, a failure would have to occur during that brief period while the transaction is actually being committed. ■

In a multiuser system, database corruption or incorrect results are possible even if there are no hardware or software failures. Interactions between two or more users who are accessing the same table at the same time can cause serious problems. By restricting changes so that they occur only within transactions SQL addresses these problems as well.

By putting all operations that affect the database into transactions, it is possible to isolate the actions of one user from those of another user. Such isolation is critical if you want to be sure the results you obtain from the database are accurate.

You may be wondering how the interaction of two users can produce inaccurate results. Say user one reads a record in a database table. An instant later (more or less), user two changes the value of a numeric field in that record. Now user one writes a value back into that field, based on the value that she read initially. Since user one is unaware of user two's change, the value after user one's write is incorrect.

Another problem can result when user one writes to a record, then user two reads that record. If user one rolls back her transaction, user two will be unaware of the rollback and will base his actions on the value that he read, which does not reflect the value that is actually in the database after the rollback. ■

Users and privileges

Aside from data corruption due to hardware and software problems or the unintentional interaction of two users, another major threat to data integrity is the users themselves. Some people should not be granted access to the data at all. Others should be granted restricted access to some of the data, but no access to the rest. Some should be granted unlimited access to everything. There needs to be a system for classifying users and for assigning access privileges to the users in different categories.

The creator of a schema is considered to be its owner. As the owner of a schema, you can grant access privileges to the users you specify. Any privileges that you do not explicitly grant are withheld. You can also revoke privileges that have already been granted. A user must pass an authentication procedure to prove his identity before he's allowed to access the files he's been authorized to use. That procedure is implementation dependent.

SQL gives you the ability to protect the following database objects:

- ✔ Tables
- ✔ Columns
- ✔ Views
- ✔ Domains
- ✔ Character sets
- ✔ Collations
- ✔ Translations

I'll discuss character sets, collations, and translations in Chapter 6.

SQL-92 supports six kinds of protection: seeing, adding, modifying, deleting, referencing, and using.

Access is permitted using the GRANT statement, and removed using the REVOKE statement. By controlling the use of the SELECT command, the DCL controls who can see a database object such as a table, column, or view. Controlling the INSERT command determines who can add new rows in a table. Restricting the use of the UPDATE command to authorized users controls who can modify table rows, and restricting the DELETE command controls who can delete table rows.

When one table in a database contains as a foreign key a column that is a primary key in another table in the database, you can add a constraint to the first table such that it *references* the second table. When one table references another, it is possible for the owner of the first table to deduce information about the contents of the second. As the owner of the second table you may want to prevent such snooping. SQL-92's GRANT REFERENCES statement gives you that power. The next section discusses the problem of a renegade reference and how the GRANT REFERENCES statement prevents it. With the GRANT USAGE statement you can control who can use, or even see the contents of a domain, character set, collation, or translation. This issue is covered in Chapter 13.

Table 4-4 summarizes the SQL statements used to grant and revoke privileges.

You can give different levels of access to different people, depending on their needs. Below are a few examples.

```
GRANT SELECT
    ON customer
    TO SALES_MANAGER;
```

This allows one person, the sales manager, to see the customer table.

```
GRANT SELECT
    ON RETAIL_PRICE_LIST
    TO PUBLIC;
```

This allows anyone with access to the system to see the retail price list.

```
GRANT UPDATE
    ON RETAIL_PRICE_LIST
    TO SALES_MANAGER;
```

This allows the sales manager to modify the price list. She can change the contents of existing rows, but she cannot add or delete rows.

```
GRANT INSERT
    ON RETAIL_PRICE_LIST
    TO SALES_MANAGER;
```

Now she can add new rows to the retail price list.

```
GRANT DELETE
    ON RETAIL_PRICE_LIST
    TO SALES MANAGER;
```

Now she can delete unwanted rows from it too.

Table 4-4: Types of Protection

Protection operation	Statement
Allow to see a table	GRANT SELECT
Prevent from seeing a table	REVOKE SELECT
Allow to add rows to a table	GRANT INSERT
Prevent from adding rows to a table	REVOKE INSERT
Allow to change data in table rows	GRANT UPDATE
Prevent from changing data in table rows	REVOKE UPDATE
Allow to delete table rows	GRANT DELETE
Prevent from deleting table rows	REVOKE DELETE
Allow to reference a table	GRANT REFERENCES
Prevent from referencing a table	REVOKE REFERENCES
Allow to use a domain, character set, collation, or translation	GRANT USAGE ON DOMAIN, GRANT USAGE ON CHARACTER SET, GRANT USAGE ON COLLATION, GRANT USAGE ON TRANSLATION
Prevent the use of a domain, character set, collation, or translation	REVOKE USAGE ON DOMAIN, REVOKE USAGE ON CHARACTER SET, REVOKE USAGE ON COLLATION, REVOKE USAGE ON TRANSLATION

Referential integrity constraints can jeopardize your data

You might think that if you can control the seeing, creating, modifying, and deleting functions on a table, that you are well protected. Against most threats you would be. However a knowledgeable hacker could still ransack the house using an indirect method.

A properly designed relational database has *referential integrity*. This means that the data in one table in the database is consistent with the data in all the other tables. To assure referential integrity, database designers apply constraints to tables that restrict what can be entered into them. If you had a database that included referential integrity constraints, a user could possibly create a new table that used a column in a confidential table as a foreign key. That column would serve as a link through which confidential information could be stolen.

For example, say you are a famous Wall Street stock analyst. Many people believe in the accuracy of your stock picks, so whenever you recommend a stock to your subscribers, a lot of people buy it and the stock goes up. You keep your analysis in a database, which has a table named FOUR_STAR. Your top recommendations for your next newsletter are in that table. Naturally, you restrict access to FOUR_STAR so that word does not leak out to the investing public before your paying subscribers receive it.

You are still vulnerable, however, if anyone besides yourself has the ability to create a new table that uses the stock name field of FOUR_STAR as a foreign key, as in the following command.

```
CREATE TABLE HOT_STOCKS (
   stock CHARACTER (30) REFERENCES FOUR_STAR
   );
```

The hacker could now try to insert the name of every stock on the New York Stock Exchange into the table. Those inserts that succeeded would match the stocks named in your confidential table. At computer speeds, it would not take long to extract your entire list of stocks.

You can protect yourself from the hack described above by being very careful about statements similar to the following:

```
GRANT REFERENCES (stock)
   ON FOUR_STAR
   TO HACKER;
```

Avoid granting privileges to people who might abuse them.

This is a good example of one reason for the REFERENCES privilege.

There are two other reasons:

- ✔ If the other person specifies the constraint in HOT STOCKS with a RESTRICT option, then when you go to delete a row from your table you will be told that you cannot, because it would violate a referential constraint.
- ✔ When you decide you want to DROP your table, you will find that you must either get the other person to first drop his constraint (or his table), or you must simply specify CASCADE, and destroy his table along with yours.

The bottom line is that allowing another person to specify integrity constraints on your table not only introduces a potential security breach, it also means that he will sometimes get in your way.

Delegating responsibility for security

If you want to keep your system secure, you will severely restrict the access privileges you grant and the people to whom you grant them. However, you will probably be constantly hassled by people who can't do their work due to lack of access. To preserve your sanity, you will probably have to delegate some of the responsibility for maintaining the security of your database. SQL provides for such delegation with the WITH GRANT OPTION clause. Consider the following example:

```
GRANT UPDATE
    ON RETAIL_PRICE_LIST
    TO SALES_MANAGER WITH GRANT OPTION;
```

This statement is similar to the previous GRANT UPDATE example in that it allows the sales manager to update the retail price list. However, it also gives her the right to grant the update privilege to anyone she wants. If you use this form of the GRANT statement, you must not only trust the grantee to use the privilege wisely, you must also trust her to choose wisely in granting the privilege to others.

The ultimate in trust, and therefore the ultimate in vulnerability, is to execute a statement like this:

```
GRANT ALL PRIVILEGES
    ON FOUR_STAR
    TO BENEDICT_ARNOLD WITH GRANT OPTION;
```

Be extremely careful with statements like this one. ∎

Part II
Using SQL to Build Databases

"WHY A 4GL TOASTER? I DON'T THINK YOU'D ASK THAT QUESTION IF YOU THOUGHT A MINUTE ABOUT HOW TO BALANCE THE MAXIMIZATION OF TOAST DEVELOPMENT PRODUCTIVITY AGAINST TOASTER RESOURCE UTILIZATION IN A MULTI-DINER ENVIRONMENT."

In This Part...

There are four important stages in the life of a database:

- ✔ Creating the database
- ✔ Filling the database with data
- ✔ Manipulating and retrieving selected data
- ✔ Deleting the data

All these stages are covered in this book, but in Part II, I'll focus on database creation. SQL includes all the facilities necessary to create relational databases of any size or complexity. I'll explain what these facilities are and how to use them. I'll also describe some common problems that relational databases suffer from and tell you about provisions in SQL that can prevent such problems, or at least minimize their impact.

Chapter 5

Building and Maintaining a Simple Database Structure

● ●

● ●

*W*hen the world's first electronic computer (ENIAC) was activated right after the end of World War II, it operated on binary logic. It was essentially a large collection of interconnected switches, and each switch could be either on or off at any given time. The on and off states corresponded to the 1 and 0 of the binary number system. To use ENIAC, computer scientists had to feed it a sequence of ones and zeros, then have it perform a computation. The result was another sequence of ones and zeros. This arrangement was very easy for the computer, but very hard on the humans, who do not normally think in terms of ones and zeros. In those early days, there weren't more than a handful of computers on the planet. That was fortunate, because there weren't more than a handful of people who could program them.

As technology moved from vacuum tubes to transistors to integrated circuits, computers gained speed and power. They were able to take over more of the work, making it easier for the people. The first step was to move from binary machine language (first-generation language) programming to assembly language (second-generation language) programming. The next step was to go to high-level (third-generation) languages such as FORTRAN, COBOL, BASIC, Pascal, and C. Later, languages specifically designed for use with databases, such as dBASE, Paradox, and R:BASE (third-and-a-half-generation languages?) came into use. The latest step in this progression is the emergence of development environments that build applications with little or no procedural programming (fourth-generation languages or 4GLs). You can use these graphical object-oriented tools (also known as rapid application development or RAD tools) to assemble application components into production applications.

SQL, as I have noted before, is not a complete language. It does not fit tidily into one of the generational categories I just mentioned. It makes use of commands in the manner of a third-generation language, but is essentially non-procedural, like a fourth-generation language. The bottom line is it doesn't matter how you classify SQL. It is being used in conjunction with all the major third- and fourth-generation development tools. You can write the SQL code yourself, or you can move objects around on the screen and have the development environment generate equivalent SQL code for you. The commands that are sent to the remote database are pure SQL in either case.

In this chapter we'll step through the process of building, altering, and dropping a simple table using a RAD tool; and then we'll build, alter, and drop the same table using SQL.

Building a Simple Database with a RAD Tool

People use databases because they want to keep track of things that are important to them. Sometimes the things they want to track are simple and sometimes not. A good database management system will provide what you need in either case. Some DBMSs give you SQL. Others, called rapid application development (RAD) tools, give you an object-oriented graphical environment. Some DBMSs support both approaches. Let's build a simple single-table database with an object-oriented graphical database design tool, and see what is involved. I will use Borland's Delphi, but the procedure would be similar for other Windows-based development environments.

A likely scenario

The first step is to decide what facts you want to track. Let's consider a likely example. Imagine you have just won $101 million in the Arizona Powerball lottery. People you have not heard from in years, and friends that you had forgotten that you had, are coming out of the woodwork. Some have sure-fire, can't-miss business opportunities in which they would like you to invest. Others represent worthy causes that could benefit from your support. You are a responsible person, and you want to be a good steward of your new wealth. You realize that some of the business opportunities are probably not as good as others. Some of the causes are not as worthy as others. You had better put all the options into a database, so as not to lose any, and to help you make fair and equitable judgments.

You decide to track the following items:

- ✔ First Name
- ✔ Last Name
- ✔ Address 1
- ✔ City
- ✔ State
- ✔ Country
- ✔ Postal Code
- ✔ Phone
- ✔ How Known
- ✔ Proposal
- ✔ Business or Charity?

Since you don't want to get too elaborate, you decide to put all the listed items into a single database table. You fire up your development environment and stare at the screen shown in Figure 5-1.

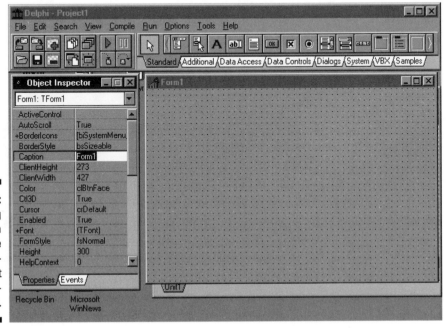

Figure 5-1:
Opening screen of a database development environment.

Too much is never enough

The screen contains a lot more information than previous-generation DBMS products used to display. In the old days (the 1980s) it was typical for a DBMS to present you with a blank screen, punctuated by a single-character operating system prompt. We have come a long way since then, but it is not necessarily any easier to determine what you should do first. Sometimes too much information is just as confusing as too little. Actually, once you become familiar with the RAD tools, you will be able to operate quite confidently and comfortably with them.

Borland's Delphi is a RAD tool. Its primary function is to develop applications of all types, including those that do not involve databases. In that sense it is similar to other RAD tools such as Microsoft's Visual Basic/Access combination, PowerBuilder, as well as Borland's dBASE for Windows and Paradox for Windows.

Delphi has a component named Database Desktop, which serves the same purpose as the SQL Data Definition Language. The Database Desktop provides graphical tools for creating, maintaining, and destroying tables. Other RAD environments will have similar tools, which operate in similar ways.

From the main Delphi screen, select Database Desktop from the Tools menu. The window shown in Figure 5-2 will appear.

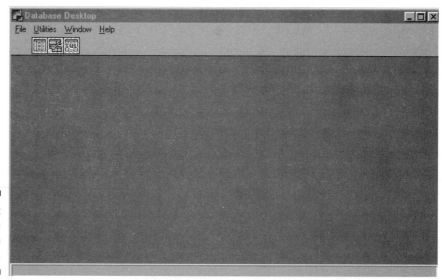

Figure 5-2:
Database
Desktop
window.

As you can see, the Database Desktop screen is marvelously free of clutter. In fact, it is marvelously free of just about everything. It does however, have a menu with a few choices on it. That's really all you need. From the File menu, select New I Table so you can define a new database table. This will cause Delphi to display the Table Type dialog box.

There are a number of database file formats in use on a variety of platforms. To be competitive, a development tool must be able to create and operate on at least most of the popular formats. Delphi gives you several to choose from. Select the INTRBASE file type from the list box in the center of the dialog box. Borland's Interbase is a mainframe class relational database which has a compatible version that runs on personal computers. It is accessible through SQL.

A really RAD way to create a table

After you select the INTRBASE file type, a table definition window like the one shown in Figure 5-3 will appear.

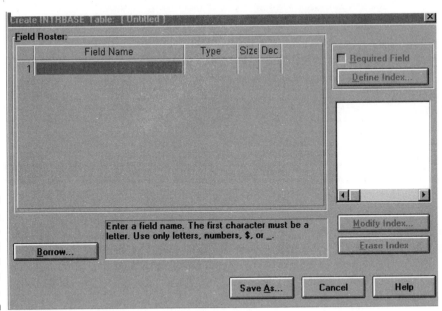

Figure 5-3:
Table definition window for the Interbase file type.

In the Field Roster you can enter the field name (which is the same as table column name), the field type, its size, and the number of decimal places (if applicable). Do this for all the fields that you have identified.

As a new multimillionaire, you will want to add one more field that hasn't been mentioned yet. So many people have offered you enticing business deals that a few of them have the same first and last names as other people in the group. To keep them straight, you decide to add a unique Proposal Number to each record in the database table. This way you will be able to tell one Jeff Stone from another.

Enter the field information into the Field Roster, including appropriate values for field type and size. When you are finished, the Field Roster will appear as shown in Figure 5-4.

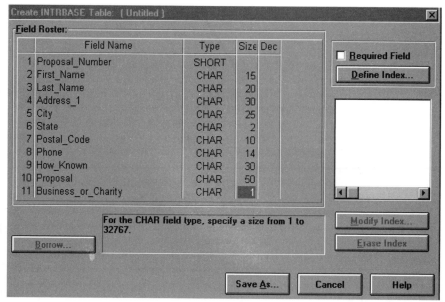

Figure 5-4: Completed field roster.

In the upper-right corner of the Create INTRBASE Table window is a check box named Required Field. Click this check box when the Field Roster cursor is in the Proposal_Number field and again when it is in the Last_Name field. This applies constraints that force the user to enter values in these fields. If you let the database user leave these fields blank, both could have a value of NULL. A null Proposal_Number would destroy the integrity of the table, since Proposal_Number is the unique key that differentiates one record from another. A null Last_Name would make it difficult to determine who is making the proposal. Avoid these problems by requiring the user to enter a value in these two fields. ■

Creating an index

Since the number of investment and charitable proposals could easily grow into the thousands, you will need a quick way to pull out records of interest. You may want to do this a variety of different ways. Say you want to look at all the proposals made by your brothers. You can isolate these effectively by basing your retrieval on the contents of the Last_Name field. For example:

```
SELECT * FROM POWERBALL
    WHERE LAST_NAME = 'Marx' ;
```

That strategy would not work for the proposals made by your brothers-in-law, but you could get them by looking at another field as in the following example:

```
SELECT * FROM POWERBALL
    WHERE HOW_KNOWN = 'brother-in-law' ;
```

These queries will work, but if POWERBALL is large (tens of thousands of records) they may not work very quickly. SQL will scan the entire table a row at a time, looking for entries that satisfy the WHERE clause. You can speed things up tremendously by applying indexes to the POWERBALL table.

An *index* is a table of pointers. Each row in the index points to a corresponding row in the data table. ■

You can define an index for each different way that you might want to access your data. When you add, change, or delete rows in the data table, there is no need to re-sort it. You only need to update the indexes. Updating an index can be done much faster than sorting an entire table. Once you have established an index with the desired ordering, you can use it to access rows in the data table almost instantaneously.

Since Proposal_Number is unique, as well as short, it will always be the quickest way to reach an individual record. To use it, however, you will have to know the proposal number of the record you want. You may want to create additional indexes, based on other fields, such as Last_Name, Postal_Code, or How_Known. For a table indexed on LAST_NAME, once a search has found the first row with a Last_Name of 'Marx', it has found them all, since the indexes for those rows are stored one right after another.

When you create an index, it adds overhead to your system, which tends to slow operations down a bit. You have to balance this against the speed you will gain by accessing records through the index. It pays to index fields that you will use frequently to access records in a large table. It doesn't pay to create indexes for fields that you will never use as retrieval keys. It also makes no sense to create indexes for fields that do not differentiate one record from another. For example the Business_Or_Charity field only divides the table records into two categories. It would not make a good index. ■

The effectiveness of a specific index will vary from one implementation to another. If you migrate a database from one platform to another, the indexes that gave the best performance on the first system may not be the best on the new platform. In fact, they may cause performance to be worse than if the database were not indexed at all. You must optimize your indexes for each specific DBMS and hardware configuration. Try various indexing schemes to see which gives the best overall performance, considering both retrieval and update speed. ■

To create indexes for our example table, click on the Define Index button in the Create INTRBASE Table dialog box. This will display the Define Index dialog box shown in Figure 5-5.

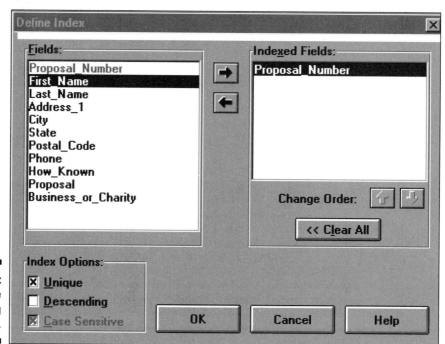

Figure 5-5:
Define
Index dialog
box.

From the fields listed on the left, select one or more that you want to serve as indexes. (Indexes made up of more than one field are called *composite indexes*.) The indexes will appear in the Indexed Fields panel on the right. Select the Proposal_Number field, and select the Unique property for it in the Index Options panel. An SQL table may have multiple indexes. When your selections are complete, click the OK button to create the index. You will be asked to name the index. Name it Proposal_Number. Of course you could name it Beauregard if you wanted to, but it will probably be easier to remember what it represents if you name it Proposal_Number.

You may now create additional indexes, using other fields. You can index Last_Name, Postal_Code, and How_Known in the same way that you indexed Proposal_Number, except that you do not specify the Unique option. These fields probably won't contain unique entries. In most cases it is good practice to have at least one index that uniquely identifies each row in its table. Since you already have one index that is guaranteed to be unique (Proposal_Number), other indexes need not be.

Once you have created all your indexes, you can save the new table structure. Press the Save As button on the Create INTRBASE Table dialog box. Another dialog box appears, asking for a file name. Enter the name (or alias) of the directory you want to add your new table to. An alias is just a shorthand substitute for a full directory path.

Of course, if you are using a RAD tool other than Borland Delphi, the specifics discussed in this section will not apply to you. However, you'll go through a roughly equivalent procedure to create a database table and its indexes. ■

Altering table structure

More often than not, the database tables you create will not be right the first time you build them. If you are working for someone else, it is a virtual certainty that your client will come to you after you have created your database and tell you that management wants to keep track of another data item, perhaps several more. If you are building a database for your own use, after you have created a structure deficiencies in it will become apparent that were totally invisible before you actually built it. Perhaps you start getting proposals from outside the USA and need to add a Country column. Or you decide that it would be helpful to include an e-mail address. In any case, you will have to go back in and restructure what you have created. All RAD tools have a restructure capability. To demonstrate a typical one, let's use Delphi to modify our POWERBALL proposal table.

Let us say we need to add another address field, since for some people one line of address is not enough. From the Database Desktop, choose File | Open | Table to display the Open Table dialog box. Specify the proper drive or alias, and directory, then specify the table name. This will put the table's structural skeleton on the screen, as shown in Figure 5-6.

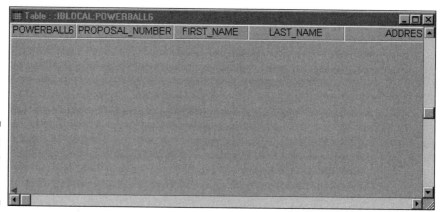

Figure 5-6:
POWERBALL6
table
structure.

You might think that you could add a column to the table by selecting
Table|Restructure Table from the menu. You would be wrong. The only
restructuring Delphi's Database Desktop allows to an SQL table is to add,
modify, or drop indexes. To add a second address field to your structure, you
will have to create a new table. Happily, you don't need to type in the entire
structure again. You can borrow the structure from the existing table, then
modify it.

From the Database Desktop menu, select File|New|Table. Specify INTRBASE
for table type to display the Create INTRBASE Table dialog box. Click on the
Borrow button to show the Borrow Table Structure dialog box. In the dialog
box, specify POWERBALL6 as the table from which to borrow. The structure
for POWERBALL6 will appear in the Create INTRBASE table dialog box.

You can now place the Field Roster cursor on line 5 (the line below
Address_1), and press the Insert key. This will open up a blank line on line 5,
pushing down the former contents of that line and everything below it. Enter
Address_2 as the field name, CHAR as the type, and 30 as the size. The result
is shown in Figure 5-7.

Note that the indexes you created for POWERBALL6 were not carried over to
this new table when you borrowed the structure of POWERBALL6. You will
have to create new indexes for the new table.

To create a table that is similar to an existing one, but with one or more
columns deleted, go through the same procedure outlined above, but with
the Field Roster cursor on the line to be deleted, press the Delete key instead
of the Insert key.

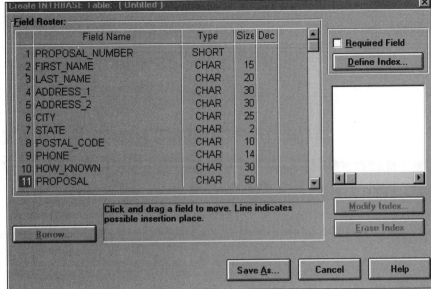

Figure 5-7: Create INTRBASE Table dialog box with borrowed structure and new line.

Dropping a table

In the course of creating a POWERBALL table with exactly the structure you want, you may have created a few intermediate forms that are not quite right. The presence of these bogus tables on your system may be confusing to people later, so it is best to get rid of them while you can still remember which is which. To do that, select Utilities | Delete from the Database Desktop main menu. The Delete dialog box shown in Figure 5-8 will appear on the screen.

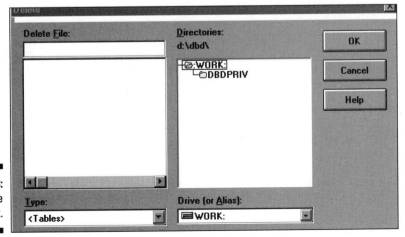

Figure 5-8: Delete dialog box.

By default Delphi assumes that the type of file you want to delete is a table. For our example, this is correct. However, the default drive and directory are incorrect. Specify the proper drive, directory, and table name, then click the OK button to delete the table. When the Database Desktop deletes a table, it deletes all related tables as well, including any indexes the table might have.

Building and Maintaining the Same Database with the SQL Data Definition Language (DDL)

All the database definition functions you can perform with a RAD tool such as Borland's Delphi can also be accomplished using SQL. Instead of clicking on menu choices with the mouse, you enter commands from the keyboard. Some people, who prefer to manipulate visual objects, find the RAD tools easy and natural to understand and use. Other people, more oriented toward stringing words together into logical statements, find SQL commands easier and more natural. Since some things are more easily represented with the object paradigm and others are more easily handled with SQL, it pays to be proficient at using both methods.

In the following sections, I will use SQL to perform the same table creation, alteration, and deletion operations that the RAD tool performed in the preceding section.

Creating a table

To create a database table with SQL, you must enter the same information that you would enter if you were creating it with a RAD tool. The difference is that the RAD tool will help you by providing a field roster or some similar data entry skeleton, and by preventing you from entering invalid field names, types, or sizes. SQL will not give you nearly as much help. You must know what you are doing before you start, rather than figuring it out along the way. You must enter the entire CREATE TABLE statement before SQL even looks at it, let alone gives you any indication as to whether there are any errors in it.

The statement that will create a proposal tracking table identical to the one created earlier will have the following syntax:

```
CREATE TABLE POWERBALL_SQL
   (PROPOSAL_NUMBER SMALLINT NOT NULL,
   FIRST_NAME CHAR (15),
   LAST_NAME CHAR (20) NOT NULL,
   ADDRESS_1 CHAR (30),
   ADDRESS_2 CHAR (30),
   CITY CHAR (25),
   STATE CHAR (2),
   POSTAL_CODE CHAR (10),
   PHONE CHAR (14),
   HOW_KNOWN CHAR (30),
   PROPOSAL CHAR (50),
   BUSIN_OR_CHARITY CHAR (1) );
```

As you can see, the information in the SQL statement is essentially the same as what you entered into the RAD tool. Notice that the NOT NULL constraint has been applied to the PROPOSAL_NUMBER and LAST_NAME fields. This is equivalent to marking the Required Field checkbox on the Create INTRBASE Table dialog box. In both cases, the user will be required to provide a value for any fields that have this constraint.

So which is the easier way to create a table, using SQL or a RAD tool? Probably the method you are used to will be the easier one for you. It's largely a matter of personal preference. The nice thing about SQL, however, is that it is universal. The same standard syntax will work, regardless of the database management system you are using.

SQL is a standard database language in the same way that COBOL is a standard programming language. If you had learned COBOL in the mid-1960s, that knowledge would still be very valuable today. On the other hand, if you had become an expert in Borland's ObjectVision RAD Tool in 1992, when it first appeared, you would have no market for that expertise now. ObjectVision is no longer on the market.

Any effort you put into learning SQL will have long-term payoffs, since SQL is going to be around for a long time, just as COBOL has been. Effort you put into becoming an expert in a particular development tool will probably yield a lesser return on investment. No matter how wonderful the latest RAD tool may be, you can be sure it will be superseded by newer technology within one to three years. If you can recover your investment in the tool in that time, great! Use it. If not, you may be wise to stick with the tried and true. Train your people in SQL and your training investment will pay dividends over a much longer period. ■

Creating an index

Indexes are a very important part of any relational database. They serve as pointers into the tables that contain the data of interest. With an index, you can go directly to a particular record, without having to scan the table sequentially, one record at a time, to find it. For large tables, indexes are a necessity. Without them, you may have to wait years rather than seconds for a result.

Well, I suppose you wouldn't wait years. Some retrievals might actually take that long if you let them run. Unless you have a computer that doesn't have anything better to do with its time, you would probably abort the retrieval and do without the result. Life goes on.

Amazingly, the SQL-92 specification does not provide a means to create an index! It is up to the DBMS vendors to provide their own implementations of the function. Since these implementations are not standardized, they may differ from one another. Most vendors provide the index creation function by adding a CREATE INDEX command to SQL. Even though two vendors might use the same words (CREATE INDEX), the way the command operates may not be the same. There will probably be a lot of implementation dependent clauses. You will have to carefully study your DBMS's documentation to determine how to create indexes with it.

Altering table structure

To change the structure of an existing table, you can use SQL's ALTER TABLE command. Interactive SQL at your client station is not as convenient as a RAD tool. The RAD tool will display your table's structure, which you can then modify. With SQL, you must know the table's structure, and how you wish to modify it, in advance. At the screen prompt, you must enter the appropriate command to perform the alteration. If, however, you want to embed the alteration instructions in an application program, SQL is usually the easiest way to do it.

To add a second address field to the POWERBALL6 table, use the following DDL command:

```
ALTER TABLE POWERBALL6
    ADD COLUMN ADDRESS_2 CHAR (30);
```

It doesn't take an SQL guru to decipher this code. In fact, even professed computer illiterates can probably figure it out. The command alters a table named POWERBALL6 by adding a column to it. The column is named ADDRESS_2, is of the CHAR data type, and is 30 characters long. This example demonstrates how easy it is to change the structure of database tables using SQL DDL commands.

Although SQL provides this statement for adding a column to a table, it doesn't have facilities for dropping a column, or for changing the name or data type of a column, so if you want to do any of those, then you have to create a new table and transfer the data. ■

Dropping a table

It is easy to get rid of database tables you no longer want that are cluttering up your hard disk. Just use the DROP TABLE command, like so:

```
DROP TABLE POWERBALL6 ;
```

What could be simpler? When you drop a table, all its data, as well as its meta-data, is erased. No vestige of the table remains.

Dropping an index

If you get rid of a table by issuing a DROP TABLE command, any indexes associated with that table are deleted at the same time. There are times, however, when you might want to keep a table, but remove an index from it. SQL-92 does not define a DROP INDEX command, but some implementations include it anyway. Such a command can come in handy when your system slows to a crawl and you discover that your tables are not optimally indexed. Correcting an index problem can bring about a dramatic performance improvement that will surprise and delight users who have become accustomed to response times reminiscent of pouring molasses on a cold day in Vermont.

Portability Considerations

Any SQL implementation that you are likely to use will have extensions that give it capabilities not covered in the SQL-92 specification. Some of these features are likely to be in the next release of the SQL specification, commonly referred to as SQL3. Others are unique to a particular implementation, and destined to stay that way.

Often these extensions make it easier to create an application that meets your needs, and you will be tempted to use them. Using them may be your best course, but if you do, be aware of the tradeoffs. If you ever want to migrate your application to another SQL implementation, you may have to rewrite those sections that used extensions that are not supported in your new environment. Think about the probability of such a migration at some time in the future, and also about whether the extension you are considering is unique to your implementation or fairly widespread. It may be better in the long run to forgo use of an extension, even if it will save you some time. On the other hand, there may be no reason not to use it. Consider each case carefully. The more you know about existing implementations and the trends in their development, the better decisions you will be able to make.

Chapter 6

Building a Multitable Database

*A*database is a representation or model of a physical or conceptual reality. The fidelity or resolution of that representation could be high (very detailed), low (only to a broad approximation), or somewhere in between.

It takes more time, money, and expertise to create a high-fidelity model of a system than a low-fidelity model — a lot more. Consequently, you should design your database structure so that it contains the level of detail that you need to serve your purpose, but no more than that.

Suppose you work for an automobile dealership. You want to create an inventory of all the vehicles you have in stock. You will probably want to track such facts as the year, model, color, engine, and options on each vehicle, so that you can know what you have available for sale. You probably do not want to maintain detailed records of every part in the engine, the transmission, the differential, or any other part of the car. Such data would be needed in the manufacturer's database, but not in the dealer's. On the other hand, you wouldn't want to leave out any fact that might be important to sales, such as a car's color.

Some items in the system you are modeling need to be major components of the database. Other items need to be present, but in a subsidiary capacity. Some aspects of the system don't need to be included in the model at all, because they don't affect the results that you want to get out of the database. In the auto dealer database model, clearly VEHICLE would be a major component. COLOR, on the other hand would be subsidiary to VEHICLE. ALTERNATOR_TYPE probably doesn't need to be included at all.

In this chapter I'll take you through an example of how to design a multitable database. The first step is to identify what to include and what not to include. The next step is to decide how the included items are related to each other, and set up tables accordingly. I'll discuss how to use keys, which provide a means of accessing individual records, and indexes, which allow you to access the records quickly.

It's not enough that a database hold your data. It must also protect the data from becoming corrupted. In the latter part of this chapter I'll discuss how to protect the integrity of your data. Normalization is one of the key methods for protecting the integrity of a database, so we'll discusses the various normal forms, and point out the kinds of problems that normalization solves.

Designing the Database

It's best to approach database design as a sequence of steps:

1. Decide what objects are relevant to the problem.

2. Determine which of these objects should be tables, and which should be columns in those tables.

3. Define tables according to your determination of how the objects should be organized.

4. Optionally, you may want to designate a table column or a combination of columns as a key. Keys provide a fast way of locating a particular row of interest in a table.

The following sections will discuss these steps in detail, as well as some other technical issues that come up during database design.

Defining objects

The first step in designing a database is to decide which aspects of the system are important enough to include in the model. Treat each of these aspects as an object and create a list containing the names of all the objects you can think of. At this stage, don't try to decide how these objects are related to each other. Just try to list them all.

It helps if you have a team of several people familiar with the system you are modeling. They can brainstorm and respond to each other's ideas. Working together, you will probably develop a more complete and more accurate set of objects. ▪

Once you feel you have a reasonably complete set of objects, you can move on to the next step: deciding how these objects relate to each other. Some of the objects will be major entities, crucial to giving you the results that you want. Others will be subsidiary to or components of those major entities. Some objects, you may decide, don't belong in the model at all.

Identifying tables and columns

Major entities translate into database tables. Each major entity will have a set of associated attributes, which translate into the columns of the table. For example, many business databases have a CUSTOMER table that keeps track of customers' names, addresses, and other permanent information. Each attribute of a customer, such as her name, street, city, state, zip code, phone number, and Internet address, would become columns in the CUSTOMER table.

There are no hard and fast rules about what to identify as tables, and which of the attributes in the system should belong to which table. There may be some reasons for assigning a particular attribute to one table, and other reasons for assigning the attribute to another table. You will have to make a judgment based on what information you want to get out of the database and how you want to use that information.

When deciding how to structure database tables, it is critical to involve the future users of the database, as well as the people who will be making decisions based on database information. If the "reasonable" structure you arrive at is not consistent with the way the information will be used, your system will be frustrating to use at best. It could even produce wrong information, which is much worse than being hard to use. Don't let this happen! Put careful effort into deciding how to structure your tables. ∎

Let's look at an example to demonstrate the thought process involved in creating a multitable database. Say you have just established VetLab, a clinical microbiology laboratory that tests biological specimens sent in by veterinarians. Clearly, there are several kinds of things that you will want to track:

- ✔ Clients
- ✔ Tests that you perform
- ✔ Employees
- ✔ Orders
- ✔ Results

Each of these entities has associated attributes. Each client has a name, address, and other contact information. Each test has a name and a standard charge. Employees have contact information, as well as a job classification and rate of pay. For each order you would need to know who ordered the test, when it was ordered, and what test was ordered. For each test result you would need to know the outcome of the test, whether it is preliminary or final, and the test order number.

Defining tables

Define a table for each entity, and a column for each attribute. Table 6-1 shows how you might define the VetLab tables.

Table 6-1: VetLab Tables

Table	Columns
CLIENT	Client Name
	Address 1
	Address 2
	City
	State
	Postal Code
	Phone
	Fax
	Contact Person
TESTS	Test Name
	Standard Charge
EMPLOYEE	Employee Name
	Address 1
	Address 2
	City
	State
	Postal Code
	Home Phone
	Office Extension
	Hire Date
	Job Classification
	Hourly/Salary/Commission
ORDERS	Order Number
	Client Name
	Test Ordered
	Responsible Salesperson
	Order Date
RESULTS	Result Number
	Order Number
	Result
	Date Reported
	Preliminary/Final

Create these tables, either with a rapid application development (RAD) tool, or with SQL's Data Definition Language (DDL) as follows:

```
CREATE TABLE CLIENT (
       CLIENT_NAME        CHARACTER (30)      NOT NULL,
       ADDRESS_1          CHARACTER (30),
       ADDRESS_2          CHARACTER (30),
       CITY               CHARACTER (25),
       STATE              CHARACTER (2),
       POSTAL_CODE        CHARACTER (10),
       PHONE              CHARACTER (13),
       FAX                CHARACTER (13),
       CONTACT_PERSON     CHARACTER (30) ) ;

CREATE TABLE TESTS (
       TEST_NAME          CHARACTER (30)      NOT NULL,
       STANDARD_CHARGE    CHARACTER (30) ) ;

CREATE TABLE EMPLOYEE (
       EMPLOYEE_NAME      CHARACTER (30)      NOT NULL,
       ADDRESS_1          CHARACTER (30),
       ADDRESS_2          CHARACTER (30),
       CITY               CHARACTER (25),
       STATE              CHARACTER (2),
       POSTAL_CODE        CHARACTER (10),
       HOME_PHONE         CHARACTER (13),
       OFFICE_EXTENSION   CHARACTER (4),
       HIRE_DATE          DATE,
       JOB_CLASSIFICATION CHARACTER (10),
       HOUR_SAL_COMM      CHARACTER (1) ) ;

CREATE TABLE ORDERS (
       ORDER_NUMBER       INTEGER             NOT NULL,
       CLIENT_NAME        CHARACTER (30),
       TEST_ORDERED       CHARACTER (30),
       SALESPERSON        CHARACTER (30),
       ORDER_DATE         DATE ) ;

CREATE TABLE RESULTS (
       RESULT_NUMBER      INTEGER             NOT NULL,
       ORDER_NUMBER       INTEGER,
       RESULT             CHARACTER(50),
       DATE_REPORTED      DATE,
       PRELIM_FINAL       CHARACTER (1) ) ;
```

These tables are related to each other by the attributes (columns) that they share.

- ✔ The CLIENT table is linked to the Orders table by the CLIENT_NAME column.
- ✔ The TESTS table is linked to the ORDERS table by the TEST_NAME (TEST_ORDERED) column.
- ✔ The EMPLOYEE table is linked to the ORDERS table by the EMPLOYEE_NAME (SALESPERSON) column.
- ✔ The RESULTS table is linked to the ORDERS table by the ORDER_NUMBER column.

For a table to be an integral part of a relational database, it is good practice to link it to at least one other table in the database by a common column. Figure 6-1 illustrates the relationships between the tables.

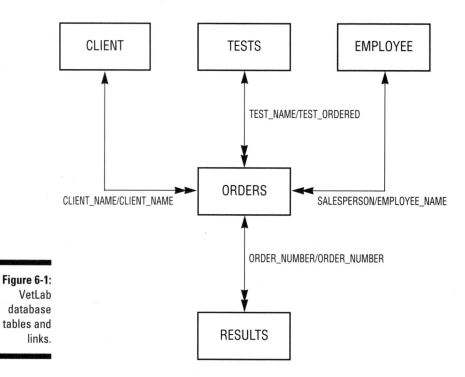

Figure 6-1:
VetLab
database
tables and
links.

The links in Figure 6-1 illustrate four different one-to-many relationships. The single arrowhead points to the "one" side of the relationship and the double arrowhead points to the "many" side. One client can make many orders, but each order is made by one and only one client. Each test can appear on many orders, but each order calls for one and only one test. Each order is taken by one and only one employee (salesperson), but each salesperson can (and hopefully will) take multiple orders. Each order can produce several preliminary test results and a final result, but each result is associated with one and only one order. As you can see in the figure, the attribute that links one table to another can have a different name in each table. Both attributes must, however, have matching data types.

Domains, character sets, collations, and translations

Although tables are the main components of a database, there are additional elements that play a part too. In Chapter 1 I defined the domain of a column in a table as the set of all values that the column may assume. Establishing clear-cut domains for the columns in a table, through the use of constraints, is an important part of designing a database.

Relational databases are not used only by people who communicate in standard American English. Other languages, some using other character sets, work equally well. Even if your data isn't in a foreign language, some applications may still require a specialized character set. SQL-92 allows you to specify the character set you want to use. In fact, you can have a different character set for each column in a table. This kind of flexibility is generally unavailable in languages other than SQL.

A *collation* is a set of rules that determine how strings in a character set compare with one another. Every character set has a default collation. In the default collation of the ASCII character set, 'A' comes before 'B' and 'B' comes before 'C'. In a comparison, 'A' is considered less than 'B' and 'C' is considered greater than 'B'. SQL-92 lets you apply different collations to a character set. Once again, this is a flexibility not generally available in other languages.

Sometimes data in a database is encoded in one character set, but you would like to deal with it in another character set. Perhaps you have data in the German character set, but your printer will not support German characters that are not included in the ASCII character set. A *translation* is a facility of SQL-92 that allows you to translate character strings from one character set to another. It may translate one character into two, such as a German 'ü' to an ASCII 'ue', or it may translate lowercase characters to uppercase. You could even translate one alphabet into another, such as Hebrew into ASCII.

Get into your database fast with keys

A good rule for database design is that every row in a database table should be distinguishable from every other row — that is, each row in the table should be unique. Sometimes you may want to extract data from your database for a specific purpose, such as a statistical analysis, and in so doing create tables where rows are not necessarily unique. For your limited purpose, this does not matter. However, tables that might be used in more than one way should not contain duplicate rows.

A key is an attribute or a combination of attributes that uniquely identifies a row in a table. To access a row in a database, you must have some way of distinguishing it from all the other rows. Keys, since they must be unique, provide such an access mechanism. Because a key must be unique, null values should not be allowed in keys. If null keys are allowed, two rows that have a null key field may not be distinguishable from each other.

In our veterinary lab example, designate appropriate columns as keys. In the CLIENT table, CLIENT_NAME would make a good key. It should distinguish each client from all others. Entry of a value in this column should be mandatory for every row in the table. TEST_NAME and EMPLOYEE_NAME make good keys for the TESTS and EMPLOYEE tables. ORDER_NUMBER and RESULT_NUMBER make good keys for the ORDERS and RESULTS tables. In each case, make sure that a unique value is entered for every row.

There are two kinds of keys, *primary keys* and *foreign keys*. The keys discussed in the previous paragraph are actually primary keys. They guarantee uniqueness. ■

To incorporate the idea of keys into our VetLab database, we can specify the primary key of a table when we create it. In this example, a single column is sufficient.

```
CREATE TABLE CLIENT (
    CLIENT_NAME       CHARACTER (30)     PRIMARY KEY,
    ADDRESS_1         CHARACTER (30),
    ADDRESS_2         CHARACTER (30),
    CITY              CHARACTER (25),
    STATE             CHARACTER (2),
    POSTAL_CODE       CHARACTER (10),
    PHONE             CHARACTER (13),
    FAX               CHARACTER (13),
    CONTACT_PERSON    CHARACTER (30)
    ) ;
```

In this example, the constraint NOT NULL given in the earlier definition of the CLIENT table has been replaced with the constraint PRIMARY KEY. The

PRIMARY KEY constraint implies the NOT NULL constraint, since a primary key cannot have a null value.

Sometimes no single column in a table can guarantee uniqueness. In such cases, you can use a *composite key*. A composite key is a combination of columns that together guarantee uniqueness. Imagine that some of VetLab's clients are chains that have offices in several cities. In that case, CLIENT_NAME would not be sufficient to distinguish two different branch offices of the same client. To handle this situation, you can define a composite key as follows:

```
CREATE TABLE CLIENT (
     CLIENT_NAME        CHARACTER (30)     NOT NULL,
     ADDRESS_1          CHARACTER (30),
     ADDRESS_2          CHARACTER (30),
     CITY               CHARACTER (25)     NOT NULL,
     STATE              CHARACTER (2),
     POSTAL_CODE        CHARACTER (10),
     PHONE              CHARACTER (13),
     FAX                CHARACTER (13),
     CONTACT_PERSON     CHARACTER (30),
     CONSTRAINT BRANCH PRIMARY KEY
          (CLIENT_NAME, CITY)
     ) ;
```

A *foreign key* is a column or group of columns in a table that corresponds to or *references* a primary key in another table in the database. A foreign key need not be unique, but it must uniquely identify the column (or columns) in the table that it references. If the CLIENT_NAME column is the primary key in the CLIENT table, every row in the CLIENT table must have a unique value in the CLIENT_NAME column. CLIENT_NAME is a foreign key in the ORDERS table. It corresponds to the primary key of the CLIENT table, but it need not be unique in the ORDERS table. In fact, you hope it is not unique. If each one of your clients gave you only one order, and then never ordered again, you would go out of business rather quickly. Hopefully, there are many rows in the ORDERS table that correspond with each row in the CLIENT table, indicating that all of your clients are repeat customers.

The following definition of the ORDERS table shows how the concept of foreign keys can be added to a CREATE statement.

```
CREATE TABLE ORDERS (
     ORDER_NUMBER       INTEGER             PRIMARY KEY,
     CLIENT_NAME        CHARACTER (30),
     TEST_ORDERED       CHARACTER (30),
     SALESPERSON        CHARACTER (30),
     ORDER_DATE         DATE
     CONSTRAINT NAME_FK FOREIGN KEY (CLIENT_NAME)
          REFERENCES CLIENT (CLIENT_NAME),
```

```
CONSTRAINT TEST_FK FOREIGN KEY (TEST_ORDERED)
    REFERENCES TESTS (TEST_NAME),
CONSTRAINT SALES_FK FOREIGN KEY (SALESPERSON)
    REFERENCES EMPLOYEE (EMPLOYEE_NAME)
 ) ;
```

Foreign keys in the ORDERS table link it to the primary keys of the CLIENT, TESTS, and EMPLOYEE tables.

Indexes

The SQL-92 specification does not address the topic of indexes, but that does not mean that they are rare, or even optional parts of a database system. Every implementation of SQL supports indexes; there is just no universal agreement on how they are supported. In Chapter 5 we showed how to create an index with Borland's Delphi, a rapid application development (RAD) tool. You will have to refer to the documentation for your particular DBMS to see how it implements indexes.

What's an index, anyway?

Data is generally positioned in a table in the order in which it was originally entered. That order may have nothing to do with the order in which you later want to process the data. Say, for instance, you want to process your CLIENT table in CLIENT_NAME order. The computer must first search the entire table to find the name that is closest to the front of the alphabet. After processing that row, you must search the entire table again to find the name that is the second closest to the front of the alphabet, and so on through the entire table. These searches take time. The larger the table, the longer the searches will take. What if you have a table with 100,000 rows? What if you have a table with a million rows? In some applications, such table sizes are not rare. To scan through the entire table a million times in order to sort a million rows becomes unreasonable. Even with a very fast computer, you may not live long enough to see the result.

Indexes can be a great time saver. An index is a subsidiary or support table that goes along with a data table. For every row in the data table, there is a corresponding row in the index table. In the index table, however, the order of the rows is different.

Table 6-2 shows a small example data table.

Table 6-2: CLIENT Table

CLIENT_NAME	ADDRESS_1	ADDRESS_2	CITY	STATE
Butternut Animal Clinic	5 Butternut Lane		Hudson	NH
Amber Veterinary, Inc.	470 Kolvir Circle		Amber	MI
Vets R Us	2300 Geoffrey Road	Suite 230	Anaheim	CA
Doggie Doctor	32 Terry Terrace		Nutley	NJ
The Equestrian Center	Veterinary Department	7890 Paddock Parkway	Gallup	NM
Dolphin Institute	1002 Marine Drive		Key West	FL
J. C. Campbell, Credit Vet	2500 Main Street		Los Angeles	CA
Wenger's Worm Farm	15 Bait Boulevard		Sedona	AZ

The rows are not in alphabetical order by CLIENT_NAME. In fact, they are not in any useful order at all. They are simply in the order in which somebody entered the data.

An index for this CLIENT table might look like Table 6-3.

Table 6-3: Client Name Index for the CLIENT Table

CLIENT_NAME	Pointer to data table
Amber Veterinary, Inc.	2
Butternut Animal Clinic	1
Doggie Doctor	4
Dolphin Institute	6
J. C. Campbell, Credit Vet	7
The Equestrian Center	5
Vets R Us	3
Wenger's Worm Farm	8

The index contains the field that forms the basis of the index (in this case CLIENT_NAME), and a pointer into the data table. The pointer in each index row gives the row number of the corresponding row in the data table.

Why would I want one?

If I want to process a table in CLIENT_NAME order, and I have an index that is arranged in CLIENT_NAME order, I can perform my operation almost as fast as I could if the data table itself was in CLIENT_NAME order. I can work through the index sequentially, moving immediately to each index row's corresponding data record by using the pointer in the index.

With an index the processing time of a table is proportional to N, where N is the number of records in the table. Without an index, the processing time for the same operation would be proportional to N^2. For small tables, the difference will be insignificant, but for large tables, it will be very great indeed. Some operations on large tables would not be practical at all without the help of indexes.

As an example, say you have a table with 100,000 records (N = 100,000) and it takes one millisecond (one thousandth of a second) to process each record. With an index, it would take 100 seconds to process the entire table. That is less than two minutes. Without an index, however, you would have to go through the table 100,000 times to achieve the same result. It would take 10,000,000 seconds. That is over 115 days. I think you will agree that there is a substantial difference between having to wait almost two minutes for a result, and having to wait almost 116 days. That is the difference that indexing can make.

If it takes way too long to process a large table that has no index, wouldn't it take just as long to create that index in the first place?

No. But it could still take a significant chunk of time.

If you have a large table (many thousands of records), and you want to create a new index for it, it will take a long time to create that index. How long depends on the size of your table and the speed of your system. However, you will save time overall, because subsequent references to the table will be made very rapidly.

Once an index has been created, it must be *maintained.* Your DBMS will maintain your indexes for you by updating them every time you update the corresponding data tables. This takes a little bit of extra time, but not too much. Once you have created an index, and it is being maintained, it will always be available to speed processing, no matter how many times you need to call on it.

Some DBMS products give you the ability to turn off index maintenance. You may want to do this in some real-time applications where updating indexes is taking a lot of time, and you have precious little to spare. You may elect to update the indexes as a separate operation during off-peak hours. ◼

Clearly, the best time to create an index is at the same time that you create its corresponding data table. If you create the index at the start, and begin maintaining it at the same time, you will not have to undergo the pain of building it later, with the entire operation taking place in a single, very long, session. Try to anticipate all the ways that you will want to access your data and create an index for each such possibility. ◼

Don't fall into the trap of creating an index for retrieval orders that you will probably never use. There is a performance penalty associated with maintaining an index, since it is an extra operation that the computer must perform every time it modifies the index field, or adds or deletes a data table row. For optimal performance, only create indexes that you will really use as retrieval keys, and only for tables with a large number of rows. Otherwise, indexes could actually degrade performance. ◼

You may have something like a monthly or quarterly report that requires the data in an odd order that you do not ordinarily need. Create an index just before running that periodic report, run the report, then drop the index, so that the DBMS won't be burdened with maintaining the index during the long period between reports. ◼

Integrity

A database is valuable only if you can be reasonably sure that the data in it is correct. In medical, aircraft, and spacecraft databases, incorrect data could lead to loss of life. Incorrect data in other applications may have less severe consequences, but it can still be damaging. The database designer must do everything possible to ensure that incorrect data never enters the database.

Some problems cannot be stopped at the database level. The application programmer must intercept these problems before they can damage the database. Everyone responsible for dealing with the database in any way must be conscious of the threats to data integrity and take appropriate action to nullify those threats.

There are several distinctly different kinds of integrity, and a number of kinds of problems that can affect integrity. In the following sections I'll discuss three types of integrity: entity, domain, and referential. I'll also look at some of the problems that can threaten database integrity.

Entity integrity

Every table in a database corresponds to an entity in the "real" world. That entity may be physical or conceptual, but in some sense its existence is independent of the database. A table has entity integrity if it is entirely consistent with the entity that it models. To have entity integrity, a table must have a primary key. The primary key uniquely identifies each row in a table. Without a primary key, it is not possible to uniquely retrieve a table row.

To maintain entity integrity, specify that the column or group of columns that comprise the primary key are NOT NULL. In addition, constrain the primary key to be UNIQUE. Some implementations of SQL will allow you to add such a constraint to the table definition. With others you will have to apply the constraint later, when you specify how data may be added to, changed, or deleted from the table. Perhaps the best way to ensure that your primary key is both NOT NULL and UNIQUE is to give it the PRIMARY KEY constraint when you create the table, as shown here:

```
CREATE TABLE CLIENT (
    CLIENT_NAME        CHARACTER (30)    PRIMARY KEY,
    ADDRESS_1          CHARACTER (30),
    ADDRESS_2          CHARACTER (30),
    CITY               CHARACTER (25),
    STATE              CHARACTER (2),
    POSTAL_CODE        CHARACTER (10),
    PHONE              CHARACTER (13),
    FAX                CHARACTER (13),
    CONTACT_PERSON     CHARACTER (30)
    ) ;
```

An alternative would be to use NOT NULL in combination with UNIQUE:

```
CREATE TABLE CLIENT (
    CLIENT_NAME        CHARACTER (30)    NOT NULL,
    ADDRESS_1          CHARACTER (30),
    ADDRESS_2          CHARACTER (30),
    CITY               CHARACTER (25),
    STATE              CHARACTER (2),
    POSTAL_CODE        CHARACTER (10),
    PHONE              CHARACTER (13),
    FAX                CHARACTER (13),
    CONTACT_PERSON     CHARACTER (30),
    UNIQUE (CLIENT_NAME) ) ;
```

Domain integrity

It is usually impossible to guarantee that a particular data item in a database is correct, but you can at least determine whether or not a data item is valid. Many data items have a limited number of possible values. If an entry is made that is not one of the possible values, it must be an error. For example, there are 50 states in the United States, plus the District of Columbia, Puerto Rico, and a few possessions. Each of these has a two-character code recognized by the U.S. Postal Service. If your database has a STATE column, you can enforce domain integrity by requiring that any entry into that column be one of the recognized two-character codes. If an operator enters a code that is not on the list of valid codes, domain integrity has been breached. If you test for domain integrity, you can refuse to accept any operation that will cause such a breach.

Domain integrity concerns arise when you are adding new data to a table with either the INSERT or the UPDATE statements. You can specify a domain for a column with a CREATE DOMAIN statement, before you use that column in a CREATE TABLE statement. For example:

```
CREATE DOMAIN LEAGUE_DOM CHAR (8)
    CHECK (LEAGUE IN ('American', 'National'));
CREATE TABLE TEAM (
    TEAM_NAME CHARACTER (20) NOT NULL,
    LEAGUE    CHARACTER (8)
    ) ;
```

The domain of the LEAGUE column includes only two valid values: American and National. Your DBMS will not allow an entry or update to the TEAM table to be committed, unless the LEAGUE column of the row being added has a value of either 'American' or 'National'.

Referential integrity

Even if every table in your system has entity integrity and domain integrity, you could still have a problem due to inconsistencies in the way one table relates to another. In most well-designed databases, every table contains at least one column that refers to a column in another table in the database. These references are important for maintaining the overall integrity of the database. However, they make update anomalies possible. *Update anomalies* are problems that can occur when you update the data in a row of a database table.

The relationships among tables are generally not bidirectional. One table is usually dependent on the other. For example, say you have a database with a

CLIENT table and an ORDERS table. It is possible that you might enter a client into the CLIENT table before she has made any orders. However, you would not enter an order into the ORDERS table unless there was already an entry in the CLIENT table for the client who made that order. The ORDERS table is dependent on the CLIENT table. This kind of arrangement is often called a parent-child relationship, where CLIENT is the parent table and ORDERS is the child table. The child is dependent on the parent. Generally the primary key of the parent table is the column (or group of columns) that appears in the child table. Within the child table it is called a foreign key. A foreign key may contain nulls and it need not be unique.

Update anomalies arise in several ways. For example, a client has moved away and you want to delete her from your database. If she had already made some orders, which were recorded in the ORDERS table, deleting her from the CLIENT table could present a problem. There would be records in the ORDERS (child) table for which there were no corresponding records in the CLIENT (parent) table. Similar problems arise if you add a record to a child table without making a corresponding addition to the parent table. Changes to the primary key of a row in a parent table will need to be reflected in the corresponding foreign keys in all child tables, or an update anomaly will result.

You can eliminate most referential integrity problems by carefully controlling the update process. In some cases you will need to cascade deletes from a parent table to its children. This means that if you delete a row from a parent table, you must perform the same action (delete) on all rows in its child tables whose foreign key matches the primary key of the deleted row in the parent table. For example:

```
CREATE TABLE CLIENT (
    CLIENT_NAME        CHARACTER (30)      PRIMARY KEY,
    ADDRESS_1          CHARACTER (30),
    ADDRESS_2          CHARACTER (30),
    CITY               CHARACTER (25)      NOT NULL,
    STATE              CHARACTER (2),
    POSTAL_CODE        CHARACTER (10),
    PHONE              CHARACTER (13),
    FAX                CHARACTER (13),
    CONTACT_PERSON     CHARACTER (30),
) ;

CREATE TABLE TESTS (
    TEST_NAME          CHARACTER (30)      PRIMARY KEY,
    STANDARD_CHARGE    CHARACTER (30)
    ) ;

CREATE TABLE EMPLOYEE (
    EMPLOYEE_NAME      CHARACTER (30)      PRIMARY KEY,
```

```
        ADDRESS_1           CHARACTER (30),
        ADDRESS_2           CHARACTER (30),
        CITY                CHARACTER (25),
        STATE               CHARACTER (2),
        POSTAL_CODE         CHARACTER (10),
        HOME_PHONE          CHARACTER (13),
        OFFICE_EXTENSION    CHARACTER (4),
        HIRE_DATE           DATE,
        JOB_CLASSIFICATION  CHARACTER (10),
        HOUR_SAL_COMM       CHARACTER (1)
        ) ;

CREATE TABLE ORDERS (
        ORDER_NUMBER        INTEGER             PRIMARY KEY,
        CLIENT_NAME         CHARACTER (30),
        TEST_ORDERED        CHARACTER (30),
        SALESPERSON         CHARACTER (30),
        ORDER_DATE          DATE
        CONSTRAINT NAME_FK FOREIGN KEY (CLIENT_NAME)
            REFERENCES CLIENT (CLIENT_NAME)
                ON DELETE CASCADE,
        CONSTRAINT TEST_FK FOREIGN KEY (TEST_ORDERED)
            REFERENCES TESTS (TEST_NAME),
                ON DELETE CASCADE,
        CONSTRAINT SALES_FK FOREIGN KEY (SALESPERSON)
            REFERENCES EMPLOYEE (EMPLOYEE_NAME)
                ON DELETE CASCADE
        ) ;
```

The constraint NAME_FK names CLIENT_NAME as a foreign key that references the CLIENT_NAME column in the CLIENT table. If a row in the CLIENT
table is deleted, all rows in the ORDERS table that have the same value in the
CLIENT_NAME column that was in the CLIENT_NAME column of the CLIENT
table will automatically be deleted also. The deletion has cascaded down
from the CLIENT table to the ORDERS table. The same is true for the foreign
keys in the ORDERS table that refer to the primary keys of the TESTS and
EMPLOYEE tables.

You might not want to cascade a deletion. Instead you may wish to change
the child table's foreign key to a NULL value. Consider the following example:

```
CREATE TABLE CLIENT (
        CLIENT_NAME         CHARACTER (30)      PRIMARY KEY,
        ADDRESS_1           CHARACTER (30),
        ADDRESS_2           CHARACTER (30),
        CITY                CHARACTER (25)      NOT NULL,
        STATE               CHARACTER (2),
```

```
            POSTAL_CODE      CHARACTER (10),
            PHONE            CHARACTER (13),
            FAX              CHARACTER (13),
            CONTACT_PERSON   CHARACTER (30),
            ) ;

    CREATE TABLE ORDERS (
            ORDER_NUMBER     INTEGER           PRIMARY KEY,
            CLIENT_NAME      CHARACTER (30),
            TEST_ORDERED     CHARACTER (30),
            SALESPERSON      CHARACTER (30),
            ORDER_DATE       DATE
            CONSTRAINT NAME_FK FOREIGN KEY (CLIENT_NAME)
                REFERENCES CLIENT (CLIENT_NAME),
            CONSTRAINT TEST_FK FOREIGN KEY (TEST_ORDERED)
                REFERENCES TESTS (TEST_NAME),
            CONSTRAINT SALES_FK FOREIGN KEY (SALESPERSON)
                REFERENCES EMPLOYEE (EMPLOYEE_NAME)
                    ON DELETE SET NULL
            ) ;
```

The constraint SALES_FK names the SALESPERSON column as a foreign key that references the EMPLOYEE_NAME column of the EMPLOYEE table. If a salesperson leaves the company, her row in the EMPLOYEE table will be deleted. New salespeople will eventually be assigned to her accounts, but for now deletion of her name from the EMPLOYEE table will cause all of her orders in the order table to be given a null value in the SALESPERSON column.

Another way to keep inconsistent data out of a database is to refuse to allow an addition to a child table until a corresponding row exists in its parent table. Yet another possibility is to refuse to allow changes to a table's primary key. If you refuse to allow rows in a child table that do not have a corresponding row in a parent table, you are preventing the occurrence of "orphan" rows in the child table. This helps maintain consistency across tables. If you disallow changes to a table's primary key, then you don't have to worry about updating foreign keys in other tables that depend on that primary key.

Potential problem areas

Data integrity is subject to assault from a variety of quarters. Some of these problems arise only in multitable databases, while others can happen even in databases that contain only a single table. You will want to recognize all of these potential threats, and minimize them.

Bad input data

The source documents or data files that you use to populate your database may contain bad data. It may not be the data you want at all, or it may be a corrupted version of the correct data. Range checks will tell you if the data has domain integrity. This will catch some, but clearly not all problems. Field values that are within the acceptable range, but are nonetheless incorrect, will not be identified as problems.

Operator error

Your source data may be correct, but incorrectly transcribed by the data entry operator. This can lead to the same kinds of problems as bad input data. Some of the solutions are the same too. Range checks help, but they are not a panacea. Another solution is to have all data independently validated by another operator. This is costly, since it takes twice the people and twice the time. In some cases, however, the extra effort and expense may be worth it, if data integrity is critical.

Mechanical failure

If you should experience a mechanical failure, such as a disk crash, while a database table is open, the data in the table could become corrupted. Good backups are your main defense against this problem.

Malice

Consider the possibility that someone may want to intentionally corrupt your data. Your first line of defense is to deny database access to anyone who might have a malicious intent, and restrict everyone else's access to what they need. Your second is to maintain data backups in a safe place. Periodically reevaluate the security features of your installation. It doesn't hurt to be a little paranoid.

Data redundancy

Data Redundancy is one of the big problems with the hierarchical database model, but it can plague relational databases too. Not only does it waste storage space and slow down processing, but it can lead to serious data corruption. If the same data item is stored in two different tables in a database, it may be possible for the item in one of those tables to be changed, while the corresponding item in the other table remains the same. This generates a discrepancy, and there may be no way of telling which version is correct. It is a good idea to hold data redundancy to a minimum. A certain amount of redundancy is necessary for the primary key of one table to serve as a foreign key in another. You should try to avoid any redundancy beyond that, however.

Once you have eliminated most redundancy from a database design, you may find that performance has become unacceptable. Redundancy is very often purposefully used to speed up processing. In the previous example, the ORDERS table has only the client's name to identify the source of each order. When you prepare an order, you have to join the ORDERS table with the CLIENT table to get the client's address. If this makes the program that prints orders run too slowly, you might decide to store the client's address redundantly in the ORDERS table. This would gain the advantage of printing the orders faster, at the expense of making it slower and more complicated to update the client's address.

It's very common for users to initially design a database with very little redundancy and with high degrees of normalization, and then when they find that important applications are running slowly, they selectively add redundancy and denormalize. The key word is *selectively.* The redundancy that you add back in is there for a purpose, and since you are acutely aware of both the redundancy and the hazard it represents, you take appropriate measures to assure that it doesn't cause more problems than it solves. ◾

Constraints

I talked earlier about constraints as mechanisms for assuring that data entered into a table column falls within the domain of that column. A constraint is an application rule that the DBMS enforces. When you define a database, you can include constraints (such as NOT NULL) in a table definition. The DBMS will make sure that no transaction is ever committed that would cause a constraint to be violated.

There are three different kinds of constraints: column constraints, table constraints, and assertions. A *column constraint* imposes a condition on a column in a table. A *table constraint* is a constraint on an entire table. An *assertion* is a constraint that affects more than one table. ◾

Column constraints

An example of a column constraint is shown in the following DDL (Data Definition Language) statement:

```
CREATE TABLE CLIENT (
    CLIENT_NAME      CHARACTER (30)      NOT NULL,
    ADDRESS_1        CHARACTER (30),
    ADDRESS_2        CHARACTER (30),
```

```
CITY                CHARACTER (25),
STATE               CHARACTER (2),
POSTAL_CODE         CHARACTER (10),
PHONE               CHARACTER (13),
FAX                 CHARACTER (13),
CONTACT_PERSON      CHARACTER (30)
) ;
```

The constraint NOT NULL has been applied to the CLIENT_NAME column. It specifies that CLIENT_NAME may not assume a null value. UNIQUE is another constraint that you can apply to a column. It specifies that every value in the column must be unique. The CHECK constraint is particularly useful in that it can take any valid expression as an argument. Consider this example:

```
CREATE TABLE TESTS (
    TEST_NAME           CHARACTER (30)     NOT NULL,
    STANDARD_CHARGE     CHARACTER (30) ) ;
        CHECK (STANDARD_CHARGE >= 0
            AND STANDARD_CHARGE <= 200)
    ) ;
```

VetLab's standard charge for a test should always be greater than or equal to zero. Also none of the standard tests costs more than $200. The CHECK clause will disallow any entries that fall outside of the range 0 <= STANDARD_CHARGE <= 200. Another way of stating the same constraint is:

```
CHECK (STANDARD_CHARGE BETWEEN 0 AND 200)
```

Table constraints

The PRIMARY KEY constraint specifies that the column it applies to is a primary key. It is a constraint on the entire table, and is equivalent to a combination of the NOT NULL and the UNIQUE column constraints. You can specify this constraint in a CREATE statement like this:

```
CREATE TABLE CLIENT (
    CLIENT_NAME         CHARACTER (30)     PRIMARY KEY,
    ADDRESS_1           CHARACTER (30),
    ADDRESS_2           CHARACTER (30),
    CITY                CHARACTER (25),
    STATE               CHARACTER (2),
    POSTAL_CODE         CHARACTER (10),
    PHONE               CHARACTER (13),
    FAX                 CHARACTER (13),
    CONTACT_PERSON      CHARACTER (30)
    ) ;
```

Assertions

An *assertion* specifies a restriction that applies to more than one table. In the following example, a search condition drawn from two tables is used to create an assertion.

```
CREATE TABLE ORDERS (
        ORDER_NUMBER        INTEGER             NOT NULL,
        CLIENT_NAME         CHARACTER (30),
        TEST_ORDERED        CHARACTER (30),
        SALESPERSON         CHARACTER (30),
        ORDER_DATE          DATE
        ) ;

CREATE TABLE RESULTS (
        RESULT_NUMBER       INTEGER             NOT NULL,
        ORDER_NUMBER        INTEGER,
        RESULT              CHARACTER(50),
        DATE_REPORTED       DATE,
        PRELIM_FINAL        CHARACTER (1)
        ) ;

CHECK (NOT EXISTS SELECT * FROM ORDERS, RESULTS
    WHERE ORDERS.ORDER_NUMBER = RESULTS.ORDER_NUMBER
    AND ORDERS.ORDER_DATE > RESULTS.DATE_REPORTED) ;
```

This assertion assures that no result is reported before its corresponding test is ordered.

Normalizing the Database

Some ways of organizing data are better than others. Some are more logical. Some are simpler. Some are better at preventing inconsistencies from arising after you start using the database.

There are a host of different problems (called modification anomalies) that can potentially plague a database, if it is not properly structured. To prevent these problems, normalize the database structure. *Normalization* generally entails splitting one database table into two, with each of the resulting tables being simpler than the original.

Modification anomalies are so named because they are generated when data is added to, changed, or deleted from a database table. ▪

To illustrate how modification anomalies can occur, consider the table shown in Figure 6-2.

SALES

Customer_ID	Product	Price
1001	Laundry detergent	12
1007	Toothpaste	3
1010	Chlorine bleach	4
1024	Toothpaste	3

Figure 6-2:
This SALES table leads to modification anomalies.

Your company sells household cleaning and personal care products, and you charge all customers the same price for each product. The SALES table keeps track of everything for you. Now assume that customer 1001 has moved out of the area and will no longer be a customer. You don't care what he has bought in the past, because he will not be buying again. You want to delete his row from the table. However, if you do so, you will lose not only the fact that customer 1001 has bought laundry detergent; you will also lose the fact that laundry detergent costs $12. This is called a *deletion anomaly*. In deleting one fact (that customer 1001 buys laundry detergent), you have inadvertently deleted another fact (that laundry detergent costs $12).

We can use the same table to illustrate an *insertion anomaly*. Say you want to add stick deodorant to your product line, at a price of $2. You cannot add this data to the SALES table until you have a customer who has bought stick deodorant.

The problem with the SALES table is that it deals with more than one thing. It deals with which products customers buy, and it also deals with what the products cost. The SALES table should be split into two tables, each one dealing with only a single theme or idea, as shown in Figure 6-3.

CUST_PURCH

Customer_ID	Product
1001	Laundry detergent
1007	Toothpaste
1010	Chlorine bleach
1024	Toothpaste

PROD_PRICE

Product	Price
Laundry detergent	12
Toothpaste	3
Chlorine bleach	4

Figure 6-3:
The SALES table has been split into two tables.

The figure shows that the SALES table has been divided into two tables, CUST_PURCH and PROD_PRICE. CUST_PURCH deals with the single idea of customer purchases. PROD_PRICE deals with the single idea of product pricing. You can now delete the row for customer 1001 from CUST_PURCH without losing the fact that laundry detergent costs $12. That fact is now stored in PROD_PRICE. Also, we can add stick deodorant to PROD_PRICE, whether anyone has bought it or not. Purchase information is stored elsewhere in the CUST_PURCH table.

The process of breaking up a table into multiple tables, each of which has a single theme is called *normalization*. ▪

A normalization operation that solves one problem may not affect others. It may be necessary to perform several successive normalization operations to reduce each of the resulting tables to a single theme. Each table in a database should deal with one and only one main theme. Sometimes it is hard to tell that a table is really dealing with two or even more themes.

Tables are classified according to the types of modification anomalies to which they are subject. In E. F. Codd's 1970 paper that first described the relational model, he identified three sources of modification anomalies and defined first, second, and third normal forms (1NF, 2NF, 3NF) as remedies to those types of anomalies. In the ensuing years, additional types of anomalies were discovered and new normal forms were specified to deal with them. Boyce-Codd normal form (BCNF), fourth normal form (4NF) and fifth normal form (5NF) each afforded a higher degree of protection against modification anomalies. It was not until 1981 however, when a paper by R. Fagin described domain/key normal form (DKNF), that it became possible to guarantee that a table was free of modification anomalies.

The normal forms are nested in the sense that a table that is in 2NF is automatically also in 1NF. Similarly a table in 3NF is automatically in 2NF, and so on. For most practical applications, putting a database in 3NF is sufficient to assure a high degree of integrity. However, to be absolutely sure, you will need to put the database into DKNF.

As I mentioned earlier, once you have normalized a database as much as possible, you may want to make selected denormalizations to improve performance. If you do, be fully aware of the types of anomalies that might now become possible.

First normal form

To be in first normal form (1NF), a table must have the following qualities:

✔ It is a two-dimensional table with rows and columns.

✔ Each row contains data that pertains to some thing or portion of a thing.

✔ Each column contains data for a single attribute of the thing being described.

✔ Each cell (intersection of a row and a column) of the table must be single valued.

✔ Entries in any column must all be of the same kind. For example, if the entry in one row of a column contains an employee name, all the other rows must contain employee names in that column too.

✔ Each column must have a unique name.

✔ No two rows may be identical (each row must be unique).

✔ The order of the columns and the order of the rows is not significant.

A table (relation) in first normal form will be immune to some kinds of modification anomalies but will still be subject to others. The SALES table shown in Figure 6-2 is in first normal form, and as has been shown, it is subject to deletion and insertion anomalies. It may be useful in some applications, but will be unreliable in others.

Second normal form

To appreciate second normal form, you must understand the idea of functional dependency.

A *functional dependency* is a relationship between or among attributes. One attribute is functionally dependent on another if the value of the second attribute determines the value of the first attribute. If we know the value of the second attribute, we can determine the value of the first attribute. ■

For example, if a table had attributes (columns) STANDARD_CHARGE, NUMBER_OF_TESTS, and TOTAL_CHARGE, which were related by the equation:

```
TOTAL_CHARGE = STANDARD_CHARGE * NUMBER_OF_TESTS
```

then TOTAL_CHARGE would be functionally dependent on both STANDARD_CHARGE and on NUMBER_OF_TESTS. If you know the values of STANDARD_CHARGE and NUMBER_OF_TESTS, you can determine the value of TOTAL_CHARGE.

Every table in first normal form must have a unique primary key. That key may be made up of one or more than one column. A key made up of more than one column is called a *composite key*. To be in second normal form

(2NF), all non-key attributes (columns) must be dependent on all of the key. Thus every relation that is in 1NF, with a single attribute key, is automatically in second normal form. If a relation has a composite key, all non-key attributes must be dependent on all components of the key. If you have a table where some non-key attributes are not dependent on all components of the key, break the table up into two or more tables such that in each of the new tables all non-key attributes are dependent on all of the primary key.

This all sounds pretty confusing. Let's look at an example to clarify matters. Consider a table similar to the SALES table in Figure 6-2. However, instead of recording only a single purchase for each customer, a row is added every time a customer buys an item they have never bought before. An additional difference is that "charter" customers, having CUSTOMER_IDs of 1001 to 1009, get a special discount from the normal price. Figure 6-4 shows some of its rows.

SALES_TRACK

Customer_ID	Product	Price
1001	Laundry detergent	11
1007	Toothpaste	2.70
1010	Chlorine bleach	4
1024	Toothpaste	3
1010	Laundry detergent	12
1001	Toothpaste	2.70

Figure 6-4: In the SALES_- TRACK table the CUSTOMER _ID and PRODUCT columns are a composite key.

Notice that in this table, CUSTOMER_ID does not uniquely identify a row. There are two rows where CUSTOMER_ID is 1001 and two where CUS-TOMER_ID is 1010. However, the combination of the CUSTOMER_ID column and the PRODUCT column does uniquely identify a row. These two columns taken together constitute a composite key.

If it weren't for the fact that some customers qualify for a discount and others don't, the table would not be in second normal form, because PRICE (a non-key attribute) would depend only on part of the key (PRODUCT). However, since some customers do qualify for a discount, PRICE depends on both CUSTOMER_ID and PRODUCT, and the table is in second normal form.

Third normal form

Tables in second normal form are still subject to some types of modification anomalies. These anomalies arise because transitive dependencies are possible.

A *transitive dependency* is one in which one attribute depends on a second attribute, which in turn depends on a third attribute. Deletions in a table with such a dependency can cause undesired loss of information. A relation in *third normal form* is a relation in second normal form with no transitive dependencies. ■

Let's look again at the SALES table in Figure 6-2, which you know to be in first normal form. As long as you constrain entries to allow only one row for each CUSTOMER_ID, you have a single attribute primary key, and the table is in second normal form. However, it is still subject to anomalies. For example, what if customer 1010 is unhappy with the chlorine bleach and returns it for a refund? We want to remove the third row from the table, which records the fact that customer 1010 has bought chlorine bleach. There is a problem: If we remove that row, we will also lose the fact that chlorine bleach has a price of $4. This is an example of a transitive dependency. PRICE depends on PRODUCT, which in turn depends on the primary key CUSTOMER_ID.

Breaking the SALES table into two tables solves the transitive dependency problem. The two tables shown in Figure 6-3, CUST_PURCH and PROD_PRICE, comprise a database that is in third normal form.

Domain key normal form

Once a database is in third normal form, most but not all chances of modification anomalies are eliminated. Normal forms beyond the third have been defined to squash those few remaining bugs. Boyce-Codd normal form (BCNF), fourth normal form (4NF), and fifth normal form (5NF) are examples of such. Each eliminates a possible modification anomaly but does not guarantee that all possible modification anomalies are prevented. Domain/key normal form (DKNF) does provide such a guarantee.

A relation is in *domain/key normal form* if every constraint on the relation is a logical consequence of the definition of keys and domains. A constraint in this definition is any rule that is precise enough that we can evaluate whether it is true or not. A key is a unique identifier of a row in a table. A domain is the set of allowed values of an attribute. ■

Let's look once again at the database in Figure 6-2, which is in 1NF, to see what it takes to put it in DKNF.

```
Table:  SALES (CUSTOMER_ID, PRODUCT, PRICE)

Key:  CUSTOMER_ID

Constraints:  1.  CUSTOMER_ID determines PRODUCT
              2.  PRODUCT determines PRICE
              3.  CUSTOMER_ID must be an integer > 1000
```

To enforce constraint 3, that CUSTOMER_ID must be an integer greater than 1000, we can simply define the domain for CUSTOMER_ID to incorporate this constraint. That will make the constraint a logical consequence of the domain of the CUSTOMER_ID column. Since PRODUCT depends on CUSTOMER_ID and CUSTOMER_ID is a key, there is no problem with constraint 1. It is a logical consequence of the definition of the key. Constraint 2 is a problem, however. PRICE depends on (is a logical consequence of) PRODUCT, and PRODUCT is not a key. The solution is to divide the SALES table into two tables, one of which has CUSTOMER_ID as a key and the other of which has PRODUCT as a key. This is, in fact, what we have in Figure 6-3. The database in Figure 6-3, besides being in 3NF, is also in DKNF.

Design your databases so that they are in domain/key normal form, if at all possible. When you do, enforcing key and domain restrictions will cause all constraints to be met. Modification anomalies will not be possible. If a database's structure is such that it cannot be put into domain/key normal form, the constraints must be built into the application program that uses the database, since the database does not guarantee that the constraints will be met. ▨

Abnormal form

Sometimes it pays to be abnormal. It is possible to get carried away with normalization, and go too far. You can break a database up into so many tables that it becomes unwieldy and inefficient. Performance can plummet. Often the optimal structure is somewhat denormalized. In fact, practical databases are almost never normalized all the way to DKNF. However, you should normalize the databases you design as much as possible to eliminate the possibility of data corruption due to modification anomalies.

When you have normalized the database as far as you can, make some retrievals. If performance is not satisfactory, examine your design to see if selective denormalization would improve performance without sacrificing integrity. You will probably find that by carefully adding redundancy in strategic locations, and denormalizing, you can arrive at a database that is both efficient and safe from anomalies.

Part III
Retrieving Information

The 5th Wave   By Rich Tennant

"CALL ME CRAZY, BUT I'VE GOT A HUNCH THIS VIRUS WAS GENERATED INTERNALLY."

In This Part ...

SQL provides a rich set of tools for manipulating data in a relational database. As you might expect, SQL has mechanisms for adding new data, updating existing data, retrieving data, and deleting obsolete data. There is nothing extraordinary about these capabilities. Where SQL shines is in its ability to isolate the exact data you want from all the rest and present it to you in an understandable form. SQL's comprehensive Data Manipulation Language (DML) provides this critically important capability.

In this part, we delve deep into the riches of the DML. You'll learn how to use SQL tools to massage raw data into a form suitable for your present purposes, whatever they may be, and then retrieve the result as useful information.

Chapter 7

Manipulating Database Data

. . . .

. . . .

As I explained in Chapters 4 and 5, creating a sound database structure is critical. However, the stuff that we are *really* interested in is the data itself, not its structure. There are four things you will want to do with data — add it to tables, retrieve and display it, change it, and delete it from tables.

The SQL Data Manipulation Language (DML)

In principle, database manipulation is quite simple. It's not difficult to understand how to add data to a table. You can do it either one row at a time, or in a batch. It's also easy to change, delete, or retrieve table rows in practice. The main challenge is selecting the rows you want to change, delete, or retrieve. Sometimes retrieving data is like trying to put together a jigsaw puzzle whose pieces are mixed in with the pieces of a hundred other puzzles. The data you want may be stored in the same database with a much larger volume of data you don't want. Happily, if you can specify what you want precisely enough with an SQL SELECT statement, the computer will do all the searching for you.

SQL in proprietary tools

Actually, you may not need to use an SQL SELECT statement. If you are interacting with your database through a DBMS, it probably has proprietary tools for manipulating data. You can use these tools, many of which are quite intuitive, to add to, delete from, change, or query your database.

In a client-server system, the relational database on the server generally understands only SQL. When you develop a database application with a DBMS or RAD tool, you can create data entry screens that contain fields corresponding to database table fields. You can group the fields logically on the screen and explain them using supplemental text. The user, sitting at a client machine, can easily examine or change the data in the fields.

Let's say the user changes the value of some fields. The DBMS "front end" on the client takes the user input typed into the screen form, translates it into an SQL UPDATE state-

ment, then sends the UPDATE statement to the server. The DBMS "back end" on the server executes the statement. This means that people manipulating data on a major system relational database are using SQL whether they realize it or not. They may be using it directly, or indirectly through a translation process.

Many DBMS front ends give you the choice of using either their proprietary tools or SQL. In some cases, the proprietary tools can't express everything that can be expressed with SQL. If you need to perform an operation that the proprietary tool can't handle, you may be forced to use SQL. So it's a good idea to become very familiar with SQL, even if most of the time you'll be using a proprietary tool. To successfully perform an operation that is too complex for your proprietary tool, you will need a clear understanding of what SQL is capable of, and how it works.

Retrieving Data

The most frequently performed data manipulation task is retrieving selected information from a database. You may want to retrieve the contents of one specific row out of thousands in a table. You may want to retrieve all the rows that satisfy a condition or a combination of conditions. You may even want to retrieve all the rows in the table. One SQL statement, the SELECT statement, does all of these things for you.

The simplest use of the SELECT statement is to retrieve all the data in all the rows of a specified table. Here's how:

```
SELECT * FROM CUSTOMER ;
```

The asterisk (*) is a *wildcard* character that means "everything." In this context it is a shorthand substitute for listing all the column names of the CUSTOMER table. As a result of this statement all the data in all the rows and columns of the CUSTOMER table will be displayed.

SELECT statements can be much more complicated than this. In fact, they can be so complicated that they are virtually indecipherable. This is due to the fact that multiple modifying clauses can be tacked onto the basic statement. In Chapter 10 I'll analyze these modifying clauses in detail. Here I'll briefly discuss the WHERE clause, which is the most commonly used method of restricting the rows returned by a SELECT statement.

A SELECT statement with a WHERE clause has the general form:

```
SELECT column_list FROM table_name
    WHERE condition ;
```

The column list specifies which of the columns in the table you want to display. The statement displays only the columns you list. The FROM clause specifies which table you want to display columns from. The WHERE clause excludes rows that do not satisfy a specified condition. The condition may be simple (for example WHERE CUSTOMER_STATE = 'NH') or it may be compound (for example, WHERE CUSTOMER_STATE='NH' AND STATUS='Active').

Here's what a compound condition looks like inside a SELECT statement:

```
SELECT CUSTOMER_NAME, CUSTOMER_PHONE FROM CUSTOMER
    WHERE CUSTOMER_STATE = "NH"
    AND STATUS = "Active" ;
```

This statement returns the names and phone numbers of all active customers living in New Hampshire. The AND keyword means that both conditions, CUSTOMER_STATE = 'NH' and STATUS = 'ACTIVE', must be met in order for a row to qualify for retrieval.

Creating Views

A database that has been designed according to sound principles is structured to maximize the integrity of the data. This is often not the best structure when it comes to looking at the data. Several different applications may all make use of the same data, but each application might have a different emphasis. One of the most powerful features of SQL is its ability to display *views* of the data, structured differently from the way the data is actually stored in the database tables.

The tables that are the sources for the columns and rows in a view are called *base tables*. ▪

I talked about views as part of the data definition language (DDL) in Chapter 4. Let's take another look at them here in the context of retrieving and manipulating data.

A SELECT statement always returns a result in the form of a virtual table. A view is a special kind of virtual table. It is distinguished from other virtual tables by the fact that its definition is recorded in the database's meta-data. This gives a view a degree of persistence not possessed by other virtual tables. You can manipulate a view just like you can manipulate a real table. The difference is that a view's data does not have an independent existence. It is derived from the table or tables from which the view's columns are drawn. Each application can have its own unique views of the same data.

Consider the VetLab database created in Chapter 6. It has five tables, named CLIENT, TESTS, EMPLOYEE, ORDERS, and RESULTS. The national marketing manager would like to see which states the company's orders are coming from. Part of this information is in the CLIENT table and part is in the ORDERS table. The quality control officer would like to compare the date a test was ordered to the date the final result was reported. This requires some data from the ORDERS table and some from the RESULTS table. To satisfy these needs, and others that are sure to arise, you can create views that, in each specific case, give you exactly the data you want.

For the marketing manager you could create a view, as shown in Figure 7-1 with the following statement:

```
CREATE VIEW ORDERS_BY_STATE
    (CLIENT_NAME, STATE, ORDER_NUMBER)
  AS SELECT CLIENT_NAME, STATE, ORDER_NUMBER
  FROM CLIENT, ORDERS
  WHERE CLIENT.CLIENT_NAME = ORDERS.CLIENT_NAME ;
```

The new view has three columns, CLIENT_NAME, STATE, and ORDER_NUMBER. CLIENT_NAME appears in both the CLIENT and the ORDERS table, and serves as the link between them. STATE information is drawn from the CLIENT table, and the ORDER_NUMBER of each order is taken from the ORDERS table. In the preceding example the names of the columns in the new view are explicitly declared. This is not strictly necessary, however, when the names are the same as the names of the corresponding columns in the source tables. The next example shows a similar CREATE VIEW statement, but with the view column names implied rather than explicitly stated.

The quality control officer requires a different view (Figure 7-2) from the one used by the marketing manager:

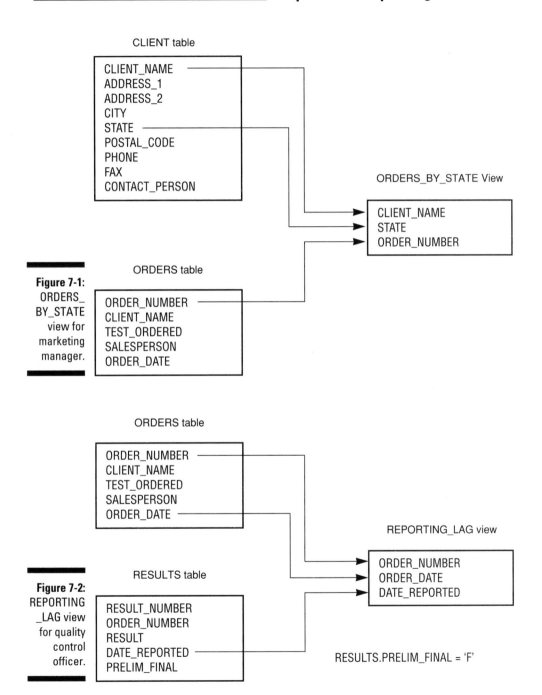

CLIENT table

ORDERS_BY_STATE View

Figure 7-1: ORDERS_ BY_STATE view for marketing manager.

ORDERS table

ORDERS table

REPORTING_LAG view

Figure 7-2: REPORTING _LAG view for quality control officer.

RESULTS table

RESULTS.PRELIM_FINAL = 'F'

```
CREATE VIEW REPORTING_LAG
   AS SELECT ORDER_NUMBER, ORDER_DATE, DATE_REPORTED
   FROM ORDERS, RESULTS
   WHERE ORDERS.ORDER_NUMBER = RESULTS.ORDER_NUMBER
   AND RESULTS.PRELIM_FINAL = 'F' ;
```

This view will contain order date information from the ORDERS table and final report date information from the RESULTS table. Only rows that have an 'F' in the PRELIM_FINAL column of the RESULTS table will appear in the REPORTING_LAG view.

The SELECT clauses in the two previous examples contain only column names. However, it is also possible to include expressions in the SELECT clause. Suppose the owner of VetLab is having a birthday, and he wants to give all his customers a 10-percent discount to celebrate. He can create a view based on the ORDERS table and the TESTS table. It might be constructed as follows:

```
CREATE VIEW BIRTHDAY
   (CLIENT_NAME, TEST_ORDERED, ORDER_DATE, STANDARD_CHARGE)
   AS SELECT CLIENT_NAME, TEST, ORDER_DATE,
      "STANDARD_CHARGE * .9"
   FROM ORDERS, TESTS
   WHERE TEST_ORDERED = TEST_NAME ;
```

Note that the second column in the BIRTHDAY view, TEST, corresponds to the column named TEST_ORDERED in the ORDERS table, which also corresponds to the column named TEST_NAME in the TESTS table. Figure 7-3 shows how this view is created.

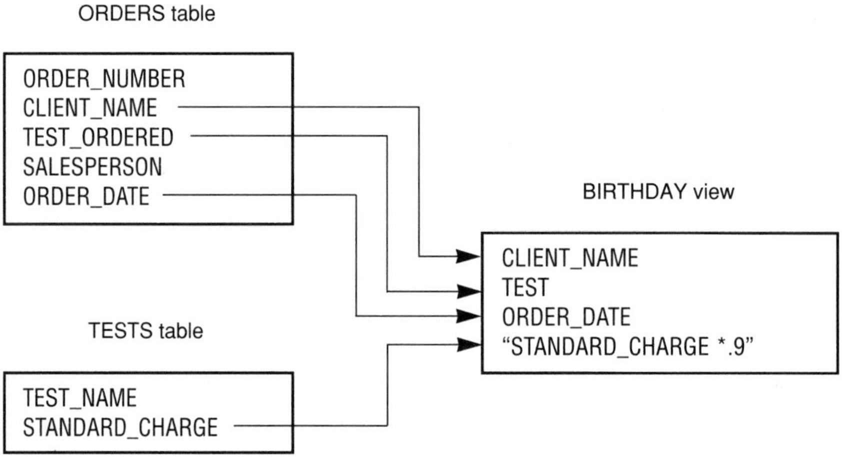

ORDERS table

Figure 7-3:
View created to show birthday discounts.

You can build a view based on multiple tables, as in the preceding examples, or you can build a view based on only one table. If you don't need some of the columns or rows in a table, create a view to remove them from sight, then deal with the view rather than the original table. This protects the user from confusion or distraction caused by looking at parts of the table that are not relevant to the task at hand.

Another reason for creating a view is to provide security for its underlying tables. You may want to make some of the columns in your tables available for inspection, while hiding others. You can create a view that includes only the columns that you want to make available and grant broad access to the view, while restricting access to the tables that the view is drawn from. Chapter 13 talks about database security, and describes how to grant and revoke data access privileges. ▪

Updating Views

When you create a table, it is automatically capable of accommodating insertions, updates, and deletions. This is not necessarily true of views, however. When you update a view, you are actually updating its underlying table. Some views, however, may draw components from two or more tables. Which table gets updated? Another problem has to do with the SELECT list. A view may have an expression for a SELECT list. How do you update an expression? Suppose you had a view created by the followng statement:

```
CREATE VIEW COMP AS SELECT NAME, SALARY+COMM AS PAY
    FROM EMPLOYEE ;
```

Could you then update PAY as follows?

```
UPDATE COMP SET PAY = PAY + 100 ;
```

No. That wouldn't make any sense. The underlying table has no column named PAY. Keep these two rules in mind when you consider updating views:

- ✔ Views whose FROM clause references more than one table cannot be updated.
- ✔ Views whose SELECT clause contains one or more expressions cannot be updated.

Adding New Data

Every database table starts out empty. After you create a table, either with SQL's DDL or a RAD tool, it will be nothing but a structured shell, containing no data. To make the table useful, you will have to put some data into it. That data may already be stored in digital form, or it may not.

Data that is not already in digital form will probably have to be entered, one record at a time, by a person using a keyboard and monitor. Data entered through optical scanners and voice recognition systems are exceptions to this, but their use is still relatively rare. Data that is already in digital form, but perhaps not in the format of the database tables you are using, first needs to be translated into the appropriate format, then inserted into the database. You may also want data that already exists in the proper format to be transferred to a new database. Depending on the current form of the data, you may be able to transfer it into your database in one operation, or you may have to enter it one record at a time. Each data record you enter would correspond to a single row in a database table.

Adding data one row at a time

Most DBMSs support *form-based data entry*. This feature lets you create a screen form that has a field for every column in a database table. Text on the form makes it easy to determine what data should go into each field. The data entry operator enters all the data for a single row into the form. After the DBMS accepts the new row, it clears the form to accept another one. In this way, you can easily add data to a table one row at a time.

Form-based data entry is easy to use, and less susceptible to data entry errors than a list of comma-delimited values. The main problem with form-based data entry is that it is nonstandard. Each different DBMS has its own method of creating forms. This is no problem for the data entry operator. You can make the form look much the same from one DBMS to another. It is the application developer who must return to the bottom of the learning curve every time she changes development tools. Another possible problem with form-based data entry is that some implementations may not allow a full range of validity checks on the data being entered.

The best way to maintain a high level of data integrity in a database is to keep bad data out of it in the first place. You can prevent some bad data from being entered by applying constraints to the fields on a data entry form. This lets you be sure that only data values of the proper type, and that fall within a predefined range, will be accepted. Of course this won't prevent all possible errors, but it will catch some of them.

If the form design tool in your DBMS does not allow you to apply all the validity checks that you need to assure data integrity, you may want to build your own screen, accept data entries into variables, and check the entries using application program code. When you are sure that all the values that have been entered for a table row are valid, you can then have your code add that row using the SQL INSERT command. ■

When you are entering the data for a single row into a database table, the INSERT command has the following syntax:

```
INSERT INTO table_1 [(column_1, column_2, ..., column_n)]
    VALUES (value_1, value_2, ..., value_n)
```

As indicated by the square brackets ([ ]), the listing of the column names is optional. The default column list order is the order of the columns in the table. If you put the VALUES in the same order as the columns in the table, they will be placed in the proper columns, whether those columns are specified explicitly or not. If you want to specify the VALUES in some order other than the order of the columns in the table, then you must list the column names, putting them in an order that corresponds to the order of the VALUES.

For example, to enter a record into the CUSTOMER table:

```
INSERT INTO CUSTOMER (CUSTOMER_ID, FIRST_NAME, LAST_NAME,
    STREET, CITY, STATE, ZIPCODE, PHONE)
    VALUES (vcustid, 'David', 'Taylor', '235 Nutley Ave.',
    'Nutley', 'NJ', '07110', '(201) 555-1963')
```

The first VALUE, *vcustid*, is a variable that you would increment with your program code after each new row of the table is entered. This guarantees that there is no duplication of the CUSTOMER_ID. CUSTOMER_ID is the primary key for this table, and therefore must be unique. The rest of the values are data items, rather than variables that contain data items. Of course, you could hold the data for these columns in variables also. The INSERT statement works equally well with variables or with an explicit copy of the data itself as arguments of the VALUES keyword.

Adding data only to selected columns

Sometimes you want to note the existence of an object, even though you do not have all the facts on it yet. If there is a database table for such objects, you can insert a row for the new object without filling in the data in all the columns. If you want the table to be in at least first normal form, you must insert enough data to distinguish the new row from all the other rows in the table. (For a discussion of first normal form, see Chapter 6.) If you insert the new row's primary key, that will be sufficient. In addition to the primary key, insert any other data about the object that you have. Columns that you do not enter data into will contain nulls.

An example of such a partial row entry is

```
INSERT INTO CUSTOMER (CUSTOMER_ID, FIRST_NAME, LAST_NAME)
    VALUES (vcustid, 'Tyson', 'Taylor')
```

Only the customer's unique identification number and name are inserted into the database table. The other columns in this row contain null values.

Adding a block of rows to a table

Loading a database table one row at a time using INSERT statements can get awfully tedious, particularly if that is all you do all day. Even entering the data into a carefully human-engineered ergonomic screen form gets tiring after a while. Clearly, if there is a reliable way to enter the data automatically, there are going to be occasions when automatic entry is better than having a human sit at a keyboard and type.

Automatic data entry is feasible if the data already exists in electronic form, because sometime in the past, somebody somewhere manually entered the data into a computer. If this is true, then there is no point in repeating history. The transfer of data from one data file to another is something a computer can do with a minimum of human involvement. Once the characteristics of the source data and the desired form of the destination table are known, the computer can (in principle) perform the transfer automatically.

Copying from a foreign data file

Suppose you are building a database for a new application. Some of the data you need already exists in a computer file. The file may be a flat file or a table in a database that operates in a DBMS different from the one you are using. The data may be in ASCII or EBCDIC code, or in some arcane proprietary format. What should you do?

The first thing you should do is hope and pray that the data you want is in a format that has seen widespread use. If it is in a popular format, there is a good chance that a format conversion utility exists that will translate it into one or more other popular formats. Your development environment will probably be able to import at least one of these formats. If you are really lucky, your development environment will be able to handle the data's current format directly. On personal computers, the dBASE and Paradox formats are probably the most widely used. If the data you want is in one of those formats, conversion should be easy. If the format of the data is something less common, you may have to do a two-step conversion.

As a last resort, you can always turn to one of the professional data translation services. These businesses specialize in translating computer data from one format to another. They have the capability of dealing with hundreds of different formats, most of which nobody has ever heard of. Give them a tape or disk with the data in its original format and they will return to you the same data translated into whatever format you specify.

Transferring rows from one table to another

A much less severe problem than dealing with foreign data is taking data that already exists in one table in your database and combining it with the data in another table. This works great if the structure of the second table is identical to the structure of the first table. Every column in the first table has a corresponding column in the second table, and the data types of the corresponding columns match. You can combine the contents of the two tables using the UNION relational operator. The result will be a virtual table containing data from both source tables. I'll discuss the relational operators, including UNION, in Chapter 11.

Transferring only selected columns and rows from one table to another

More often than not the data in the source table will *not* exactly match the structure of the table into which you want to insert the data. Perhaps only some of the columns match — and these are the columns you want to transfer. By combining SELECT statements with a UNION, you can specify which columns from the source tables to include in the virtual result table. By including WHERE clauses in the SELECT statements, you can restrict the rows placed into the result table to those that satisfy specific conditions. WHERE clauses are covered extensively in Chapter 10.

Suppose you had two tables, named PROSPECT and CUSTOMER, and you wanted to list everyone living in the state of Maine who appears in either table. You could create a virtual result table with the desired information with the following command:

```
SELECT FIRST_NAME, LAST_NAME
    FROM PROSPECT
      WHERE STATE = 'ME'
UNION
SELECT FIRST_NAME, LAST_NAME
    FROM CUSTOMER
      WHERE STATE = 'ME' ;
```

The SELECT statements specify that the columns included in the result table are FIRST_NAME and LAST_NAME. The WHERE clauses restrict the rows included to those that have the value 'ME' in the STATE column. The STATE column is not included in the result table, but is present in both the PROSPECT and CUSTOMER tables. The UNION operator combines the results from the SELECT on PROSPECT with the results of the SELECT on CUSTOMER, deletes any duplicate rows, then displays the result.

Another way to copy data from one table in a database to another is to nest a SELECT statement within an INSERT statement. This method (a subselect) does not create a virtual table; it actually duplicates the selected data. For example, you could take all the rows from the CUSTOMER table and insert them into the PROSPECT table. If you later wanted to isolate those customers that live in Maine, a simple SELECT with one condition in the WHERE clause would do it.

```
INSERT INTO PROSPECT
    SELECT * FROM CUSTOMER
    WHERE STATE = 'ME' ;
```

 Even though this operation creates redundant data (customer data is now stored in both the PROSPECT table and the CUSTOMER table), you may want to do it anyway, to improve the performance of retrievals. Be aware of the redundancy, and make sure that you do not insert, update, or delete rows in one place without inserting, updating, or deleting the corresponding rows in the other place. ▪

Updating Existing Data

In our world the one thing you can count on is change. If you don't like the current state of affairs, just wait a while. Before long things will be different. Since the world is constantly changing, the databases we use to model aspects of that world need to change too. A customer may change his address. The quantity of a product in stock may change (hopefully someone buys one now and then). A basketball player's season performance statistics will change each time she plays in another game. These are the kinds of typical events that require a database to be updated.

SQL provides the UPDATE statement for changing data in a table. With a single UPDATE, you can change one, some, or all the rows in a table. The UPDATE statement has this syntax:

```
UPDATE table_name
    SET column_1 = expression_1, column_2 = expression_2,
```

```
..., column_n = expression_n
[WHERE predicates] ;
```

The WHERE clause is optional. It specifies the rows that will be updated. If there is no WHERE clause, all the rows in the table will be updated. The SET clause specifies the new values for the columns that you are changing.

Consider the CUSTOMER table shown in Table 7-1.

Table 7-1: CUSTOMER Table

Name	City	Area_Code	Telephone
Abe Abelson	Springfield	(714)	555-1111
Bill Bailey	Decatur	(714)	555-2222
Chuck Wood	Philo	(714)	555-3333
Don Stetson	Philo	(714)	555-4444
Dolph Stetson	Philo	(714)	555-5555

Customer lists change occasionally, as people move, change their phone number, and so on. Let's say that Abe Abelson moves from Springfield to Kankakee. You can update his record in the table with this UPDATE statement:

```
UPDATE CUSTOMER
   SET CITY = 'Kankakee', TELEPHONE = '666-6666'
   WHERE NAME = 'Abe Abelson' ;
```

This will cause the change shown in Table 7-2.

Table 7-2: CUSTOMER Table after UPDATE to One Row

Name	City	Area_Code	Telephone
Abe Abelson	Kankakee	(714)	666-6666
Bill Bailey	Decatur	(714)	555-2222
Chuck Wood	Philo	(714)	555-3333
Don Stetson	Philo	(714)	555-4444
Dolph Stetson	Philo	(714)	555-5555

You can use a similar statement to update multiple rows. Assume that Philo has experienced explosive population growth and now requires its own area code. You can change all rows for customers who live in Philo with a single UPDATE statement.

```
UPDATE CUSTOMER
   SET AREA_CODE = '(619)'
   WHERE CITY = 'Philo' ;
```

The table will now look like Table 7-3.

Table 7-3: CUSTOMER Table after UPDATE to Several Rows

Name	City	Area_Code	Telephone
Abe Abelson	Kankakee	(714)	666-6666
Bill Bailey	Decatur	(714)	555-2222
Chuck Wood	Philo	(619)	555-3333
Don Stetson	Philo	(619)	555-4444
Dolph Stetson	Philo	(619)	555-5555

It's even easier to update all the rows of a table than it is to update only some of them. No WHERE clause is needed. Let's imagine that the city of Rantoul has acquired major political clout and has annexed not only Kankakee, Decatur, and Philo, but all the cities and towns in the database. We can update all the rows with a single statement.

```
UPDATE CUSTOMER
   SET CITY = 'Rantoul' ;
```

Table 7-4 shows the result.

Table 7-4: CUSTOMER Table after UPDATE to All Rows

Name	City	Area_Code	Telephone
Abe Abelson	Rantoul	(714)	666-6666
Bill Bailey	Rantoul	(714)	555-2222
Chuck Wood	Rantoul	(619)	555-3333
Don Stetson	Rantoul	(619)	555-4444
Dolph Stetson	Rantoul	(619)	555-5555

The WHERE clause used to restrict the rows to which an UPDATE statement applies could contain a subselect. This would allow you to update rows in one table based on the contents of another table.

As an example of a subselect within an UPDATE, let's say you are a wholesaler, and your database has a VENDOR table containing the names of all the manufacturers you buy products from. You also have a PRODUCT table containing the names of all the products you sell and the prices you charge for them. The VENDOR table has columns VENDOR_ID, VENDOR_NAME, STREET, CITY, STATE, and ZIP. The PRODUCT table has PRODUCT_ID, PRODUCT_NAME, VENDOR_ID, and SALE_PRICE.

Your vendor, Cumulonimbus Corporation, decides to raise the prices of all its products by 10 percent. To maintain your own profit margin, you'll have to raise your prices on products you obtain from Cumulonimbus by 10 percent. You can do this with the following UPDATE statement:

```
UPDATE PRODUCT
   SET SALE_PRICE = (SALE_PRICE * 1.1)
   WHERE VENDOR_ID IN
      (SELECT VENDOR_ID FROM VENDOR
      WHERE VENDOR_NAME = 'Cumulonimbus Corporation') ;
```

The subselect finds the VENDOR_ID that corresponds to Cumulonimbus. The VENDOR_ID field in the PRODUCT table is then used to find the rows that need to be updated. The prices on all Cumulonimbus products will increase by 10 percent, while the prices on all other products will not be affected. I'll discuss subselects more extensively in Chapter 12.

Deleting Obsolete Data

As time passes, some data gets old and loses its usefulness. You may want to remove it from its table. Unneeded data in a table slows performance, consumes memory, and can confuse users. You may want to transfer older data to an archive table, then take the archive off line. That way, in the unlikely event that you will ever need to look at that data again, you can recover it. In the meantime it won't be slowing down your everyday processing. Whether you decide that obsolete data is worth archiving or not, you will eventually come to the point where you want to delete it. SQL provides for the removal of rows from database tables with the DELETE statement.

You can delete all the rows in a table with a single DELETE statement, or you can restrict the deletion to only selected rows by adding a WHERE clause. The syntax is similar to the syntax of a SELECT statement, except there is no specification of columns. If you delete a table row, all the data in all that row's columns is removed.

As an example, say that your customer David Taylor has just moved to Tahiti and will not buy from you any more. You can remove him from your CUS-TOMER table with the following statement:

```
DELETE FROM CUSTOMER
    WHERE FIRST_NAME = 'David' AND LAST_NAME = 'Taylor' ;
```

Assuming you have only one customer named David Taylor, this will make the intended deletion. If there is any chance that two of your customers might be named David Taylor, you can add more conditions to the WHERE clause (such as STREET or PHONE or CUSTOMER_ID) to make sure you delete only the one you intend to delete.

Chapter 8
Specifying Values

● ●

In This Chapter

▶ Using variables to eliminate redundant coding

▶ Maintaining a system activity log

▶ Retrieving information on multiple table rows with a single command

▶ Extracting frequently required information from a database table field

▶ Combining simple values into complex expressions

● ●

*I*n the preceding chapters, I emphasized the importance of database struc-ture for maintaining database integrity. Database structure *is* very impor-tant, and it is often not given its due. However, we mustn't forget that the most important thing is the data itself. After all, the values held in the fields that form the intersections of the rows and columns of a database table are the raw materials from which we can derive meaningful relationships and trends.

Values can be represented several ways. They can be represented directly, or they can be derived. This chapter describes the various kinds of values, as well as functions and expressions.

Functions look at data and calculate a value based on the data. *Expressions* are combinations of data items that SQL can evaluate to produce a single value. ■

Values

SQL recognizes several different kinds of values: row values, literal values, variables, special variables, and column references.

Atoms aren't indivisible either

In the nineteenth century, scientists believed that an atom was the irreducible smallest possible piece of matter. That is why they named it atom, which comes from the Greek word *atomos*, which means indivisible. Now we know that atoms are not indivisible: they are made up of protons, neutrons, and electrons. Protons and neutrons in turn are made up of quarks, gluons, and virtual quarks. Even these things may not be indivisible. Who knows?

The value of a field in a database table is called atomic, even though many fields aren't indivisible either. A DATE value has components of month, year, and day. A TIMESTAMP value has components of hour, minute, seconds, and so on. A REAL or FLOAT value has components of exponent and mantissa. A CHAR value has components that can be accessed by SUBSTRING. So calling database field values atomic is true to the analogy of atoms of matter. Both modern applications of the term "atomic," however, are not true to the word's original meaning.

Row values

The most visible values in a database are the table *row values*. These are the values contained in each row of a database table. A row value is typically made up of multiple components, since each column in a row will contain a value. A *field* is the intersection of a single column with a single row. It contains a *scalar* or *atomic* value. A value that is scalar or atomic has only a single component.

Literal values

In SQL a value may be represented as either a variable or a constant. Sensibly enough, the value of a variable may change from time to time. The value of a constant never changes, which is why it is called a *constant*. An important kind of constant is the *literal* value. You might consider a literal to be a WYSIWYG value, because What You See Is What You Get. The representation is itself the value. ∎

Just as SQL has many different data types, there are many different types of literals. Table 8-1 shows some examples of literals of the various data types.

Notice that the literals of the nonnumeric types are enclosed in single quotes. This helps to prevent confusion: however, it can also cause problems.

Table 8-1: Example Literals of Various Data Types

Data type	Example literal
INTEGER	186282
SMALLINT	186
NUMERIC	186282.42
DECIMAL	186282.42
REAL	6.02257E-23
DOUBLE PRECISION	3.1415926535897E00
FLOAT	6.02257E-23
CHARACTER(15)	'GREECE '
VARCHAR (CHARACTER VARYING)	'lepton'
NATIONAL CHARACTER(15)	'ΕΛΛΑΣ '[1]
NATIONAL CHARACTER VARYING	'λεπτον'[2]
BIT(12)	B'100111001110'[3]
BIT(12)	X'9CE'[4]
BIT VARYING(16)	B'1001111000111'
BIT VARYING(16)	X'F7'
DATE	DATE '07-20-1969'
TIME(2)	TIME '13:41:32.50'
TIMESTAMP(0)	TIMESTAMP '04-17-1995 14:18:00'
TIME WITH TIMEZONE(4)	TIME '13:41:32.5000-08:00'
TIMESTAMP WITH TIMEZONE(0)	TIMESTAMP '04-17-1995 14:18:00+02:00'
INTERVAL DAY	INTERVAL '7' DAY

NOTES:

[1]This is the word Greeks use when naming their own country in their own language. The English equivalent is 'Hellas.'

[2]This is the word 'lepton' in Greek national characters.

[3]BIT and BIT VARYING values that start with a 'B' are interpreted as binary numbers.

[4]BIT and BIT VARYING values that start with an 'X' are interpreted as hexadecimal numbers.

> What if a literal is a character string that contains a single quote? In that case, type two single quotes to show that the quote mark you are typing is a part of the character string and not an indicator of the end of the string. For example, you would type 'Earth''s atmosphere' to represent the character literal 'Earth's atmosphere'. ■

Variables

It's great to be able to manipulate literals and other kinds of constants when you are dealing with a database. However, in many cases you would have to do a lot more work if you didn't have variables. A *variable* is a quantity whose value can change. Let's look at an example to see why variables are valuable.

Let's say you are a retailer who has several classes of customers. You give your high-volume customers the best price, your medium-volume customers the next best price, and your low-volume customers the highest price. You want all prices to be indexed to your cost of goods. For your F-117A product, you decide to charge your best customers (Class C) 1.4 times your cost of goods. You charge your next best customers (Class B) 1.5 times your cost of goods, and your worst (Class A) customers 1.6 times your cost.

You store your cost of goods and the prices you charge in a table named PRICING. To implement your new pricing structure, you issue the following SQL commands:

```
UPDATE PRICING
   SET PRICE = COST * 1.4
   WHERE PRODUCT = 'F-117A'
      AND CLASS = 'C' ;
UPDATE PRICING
   SET PRICE = COST * 1.5
   WHERE PRODUCT = 'F-117A'
      AND CLASS = 'B' ;
UPDATE PRICING
   SET PRICE = COST * 1.6
   WHERE PRODUCT = 'F-117A'
      AND CLASS = 'A' ;
```

This code is fine, and will do what you want it to do, for now. But what if aggressive competition begins to eat into your market share? You may have to reduce your margins to remain competitive. You will have to enter something like the following commands:

```
UPDATE PRICING
   SET PRICE = COST * 1.25
```

```
         WHERE PRODUCT = 'F-117A'
            AND CLASS = 'C' ;
UPDATE PRICING
   SET PRICE = COST * 1.35
   WHERE PRODUCT = 'F-117A'
      AND CLASS = 'B' ;
UPDATE PRICING
   SET PRICE = COST * 1.45
   WHERE PRODUCT = 'F-117A'
      AND CLASS = 'A' ;
```

If you are in a volatile market, you may have to rewrite your SQL code repeatedly. This can be very tedious, particularly if you have a large number of products, and the price multiplier can vary from one product to the next. You can minimize this problem if you replace literals (such as 1.45) with variables (such as :multiplierA). Then you could perform your updates like this:

```
UPDATE PRICING
   SET PRICE = COST * :multiplierC
   WHERE PRODUCT = 'F-117A'
      AND CLASS = 'C' ;
UPDATE PRICING
   SET PRICE = COST * :multiplierB
   WHERE PRODUCT = 'F-117A'
      AND CLASS = 'B' ;
UPDATE PRICING
   SET PRICE = COST * :multiplierA
   WHERE PRODUCT = 'F-117A'
      AND CLASS = 'A' ;
```

Now whenever market conditions cause you to change your pricing, you need only change the values of the variables :multiplierC, :multiplierB, and :multiplierA. These variables are *parameters* that are passed to the SQL code, which uses them to compute new prices.

Sometimes you will see variables used in this way called *parameters*, and at other times *host variables*. They are called parameters within applications written in SQL module language, and host variables when you are using embedded SQL. ∎

Embedded SQL means that SQL statements are embedded into the code of an application written in a host language. Alternatively you can use *SQL module language* to create an entire module of SQL code. The module would then be called by the host language application. Either method could give you the capabilities you want. The approach you use will depend on your particular implementation of SQL. ∎

Special variables

When a user on a client machine connects to a database on a server, this establishes a *session*. If the user has connected to several databases, the session associated with the most recent connection is considered the current session, and previous sessions are considered dormant. SQL-92 defines several special variables that are valuable on multiuser systems. They keep track of who the users are. The special variable SESSION_USER holds a value that is equal to the user authorization identifier of the current SQL session. If you write a program that performs a monitoring function, you can interrogate SESSION_USER to find out who is executing SQL statements.

An SQL module may have a user-specified authorization identifier associated with it. This value is stored in the CURRENT_USER variable. If a module has no such identifier, then CURRENT_USER has the same value as SESSION_USER.

The SYSTEM_USER variable contains the operating system's identifier of a user. This may differ from that user's identifier in an SQL module. For example, a user may log onto the system as LARRY, but identify himself to a module as PLANT_MGR. The value in SESSION_USER will be PLANT_MGR. If no explicit specification of the module identifier was made, then CURRENT_USER will also contain PLANT_MGR. SYSTEM_USER would hold the value LARRY.

One use of the SYSTEM_USER, SESSION_USER, and CURRENT_USER special variables is to track who is using the system. You can maintain a log table, and periodically insert into it the values contained in SYSTEM_USER, SESSION_USER, and CURRENT_USER. Here is an example:

```
INSERT INTO USAGELOG (SNAPSHOT)
    VALUES ('User ' || SYSTEM_USER ||
        ' with ID ' || SESSION_USER ||
        ' active at ' || CURRENT_TIMESTAMP) ;
```

This statement would produce log entries similar to the following:

```
User LARRY with ID PLANT_MGR active at 04-17-1995 14:18:00
```

Column references

Columns contain values, one in each row of a table. SQL statements often make reference to such values. A fully qualified column reference consists of the table name, a period, then the column name (for example, PRICING.PRODUCT). Consider this statement:

```
SELECT PRICING.COST
   FROM PRICING
   WHERE PRICING.PRODUCT = 'F-117A' ;
```

PRICING.PRODUCT is a column reference. It contains the value 'F-117A'. PRIC-ING.COST is also a column reference, but we won't know its value until after the preceding SELECT statement has been executed.

Since it only makes sense to reference columns in the current table, it is generally not necessary to use fully qualified column references. The following statement is completely equivalent to the previous one.

```
SELECT COST
   FROM PRICING
   WHERE PRODUCT = 'F-117A' ;
```

However, there are times when you may be dealing with more than one table. Two tables in a database might well both contain one or more columns that have the same name. If this happens, you will have to fully qualify column references for those columns to guarantee that the column you get is indeed the one you want.

For example, say your company has facilities at Hollis and at Jefferson, and you maintain separate employee records for each site. The employee table at Hollis is named EMP_HOLLIS and the employee table at Jefferson is named EMP_JEFFERSON. You would like a list of all employees who work at both sites, so you need to find all employees who are in both tables. The following SELECT will give you what you want:

```
SELECT F_NAME, L_NAME
   FROM EMP_HOLLIS, EMP_JEFFERSON
   WHERE EMP_HOLLIS.EMP_ID = EMP_JEFFERSON.EMP_ID ;
```

Since the employee's ID number is unique and will be the same regardless of work site, it can be used as a link between the two tables. This retrieval will return only the names of employees who appear in both tables.

Functions

A function is a simple to moderately complex operation that is not performed by one of the SQL commands, but comes up fairly often in practice. The functions provided by SQL perform tasks that would otherwise have to be performed by application code in the host language within which your SQL statements are embedded. SQL has two main categories of functions: set (or aggregate) functions, and value functions.

Summarizing with set functions

The set functions apply to sets of rows in a table rather than to a single row. They summarize some characteristic of the current set of rows. That set may include all the rows in the table, or a subset specified by a WHERE clause. I'll discuss WHERE clauses extensively in Chapter 10. Set functions are sometimes called aggregate functions because they take information from multiple rows, process it in some way, and deliver a single-row answer. That answer is an aggregation of the information in the rows making up the set.

To illustrate the use of the set functions, consider the following table, a list of nutrition facts for 100 grams of certain selected foods.

Food	Calories	Protein (grams)	Fat (grams)	Carbohydrate (grams)
Almonds, roasted	627	18.6	57.7	19.6
Asparagus	20	2.2	0.2	3.6
Bananas, raw	85	1.1	0.2	22.2
Beef, lean hamburger	219	27.4	11.3	
Chicken, light meat	166	31.6	3.4	
Opossum, roasted	221	30.2	10.2	
Pork, ham	394	21.9	33.3	
Beans, lima	111	7.6	0.5	19.8
Cola	39			10.0
Bread, white	269	8.7	3.2	50.4
Bread, whole wheat	243	10.5	3.0	47.7
Broccoli	26	3.1	0.3	4.5
Butter	716	0.6	81	0.4
Jelly beans	367		0.5	93.1
Peanut brittle	421	5.7	10.4	81.0

The information in the table above is stored in a database table named FOODS. Blank fields contain the value NULL. The set functions COUNT, AVG, MAX, MIN, and SUM can tell us important facts about the data in this table.

COUNT

The COUNT function tells us how many rows are in the table, or how many rows in the table meet certain conditions. The simplest usage would be

```
SELECT COUNT (*)
    FROM FOODS ;
```

This yields a result of 15, since it counts all rows in the FOODS table. The following statement would produce the same result:

```
SELECT COUNT (CALORIES)
    FROM FOODS ;
```

Since there is an entry in the CALORIES column in every row of the table, the count is the same. However, if a column contains nulls, the rows corresponding to those nulls are not counted.

```
SELECT COUNT (CARBOHYDRATE)
    FROM FOODS ;
```

This statement returns a value of 11, since four of the fifteen rows in the table contain nulls in the carbohydrate column.

 A field in a database table may have a null value for a variety of reasons. One common reason is that the actual value is not known, or not known yet. Or the value may be known, but not entered yet. Sometimes, if a value is known to be zero, the data entry operator will not bother to enter anything in a field, leaving it a null. This is not a good practice. Zero is a definite value, and can be included in computations. Null is not a definite value, and SQL does not include null values in computations ■

You can also use the COUNT function, in combination with DISTINCT, to determine how many distinct values exist in a column. Consider the following statement:

```
SELECT COUNT (DISTINCT FAT)
    FROM FOODS ;
```

The answer returned is 13. 100 grams of asparagus has exactly the same fat content as 100 grams of bananas (0.2 grams). 100 grams of lima beans has exactly the same fat content as 100 grams of jelly beans (0.5 grams). Thus there are only 13 distinct fat values in the table.

AVG

The AVG function calculates and returns the average of the values in the specified column. Of course, the AVG function can only be used on columns that contain numeric data.

```
SELECT AVG (FAT)
    FROM FOODS ;
```

The result is 14.3. This number is as high as it is primarily due to the presence of butter in the database. You might wonder what the average fat content would be if butter were not included. To find out, add a WHERE clause to your statement.

```
SELECT AVG (FAT)
    FROM FOODS
    WHERE FOOD <> 'Butter' ;
```

The average fat value drops all the way down to 9.6 grams per 100 grams of food.

MAX

The MAX function returns the maximum value found in the specified column. The statement

```
SELECT MAX (FAT)
    FROM FOODS ;
```

returns a value of 81 (the fat content in 100 grams of butter).

MIN

The MIN function returns the minimum value found in the specified column. The statement

```
SELECT MIN (CARBOHYDRATE)
    FROM FOODS ;
```

returns a value of 0.4, since the nulls are not treated as zeros.

SUM

The SUM function returns the sum of all the values found in the specified column. The statement

```
SELECT SUM (CALORIES)
    FROM FOODS ;
```

returns 3924, which is the total calorie content of all fifteen foods.

Value functions

There are a number of operations that are applied in a wide variety of contexts. Since they are needed so often, it makes sense to incorporate them into SQL as value functions. SQL has relatively few value functions compared to PC database management systems such as Paradox or dBASE, but the few that it does have are probably the ones that you will want to use most often. There are three different types of value functions:

- String value functions
- Numeric value functions
- Datetime value functions

String value functions

String value functions take one character string (or bit string) as an input and produce another character string (or bit string) as an output. There are six such functions:

- SUBSTRING
- UPPER
- LOWER
- TRIM
- TRANSLATE
- CONVERT

SUBSTRING

Use the SUBSTRING function to extract a substring from a source string. The source string may be either a character string or a bit string. The extracted substring will be of the same type as the source string. For example, if the source string is a character string, the substring will also be a character string. Here's the syntax of the SUBSTRING function:

```
SUBSTRING (string_value FROM start [FOR length])
```

The clause in square brackets ([]) is optional. The substring extracted from *string_value* begins with the character (or bit) represented by *start* and continues for *length* characters (or bits). If the FOR clause is absent, the substring extracted extends from the *start* character to the end of the string. Consider the following example:

```
SUBSTRING ('Bread, whole wheat' FROM 8 FOR 7)
```

The substring extracted is 'whole w'. It starts with the eighth character of the source string and has a length of seven characters. On the surface this doesn't seem like a very valuable function. If I have a literal such as 'Bread, whole wheat' I don't need a function to figure out what the eighth through the fourteenth characters are. SUBSTRING really is a valuable function however, because the string value doesn't have to be a literal. It can be any expression that evaluates to a character string. Thus, I could have a variable named *fooditem* that takes on different values at different times. The expression

```
SUBSTRING (fooditem FROM 8 FOR 7)
```

would extract the desired substring regardless of what character string was currently represented by the *fooditem* variable. All the value functions are similar in that they can operate on expressions that evaluate to values as well as on the literal values themselves.

There are a couple of things to watch out for when using the SUBSTRING function. Make sure that the substring you specify actually falls within the source string. If you ask for a substring starting at character eight when the source string is only four characters long, you will get a null result. This means you must have some idea of the form of your data before you specify a substring function. You also don't want to specify a negative substring length, because the end of a string cannot precede the beginning. ∎

If a column is of the VARCHAR type, you may not know, for a particular row, how far the field extends. This does not present a problem for the SUBSTRING function. If the length you specify goes beyond the right edge of the field, SUBSTRING will return whatever it has found. It will not return an error.

Say you had the following statement:

```
SELECT * FROM FOODS
    WHERE SUBSTRING (FOOD FROM 8 FOR 7) = 'white' ;
```

This will return the row for white bread from the FOODS table, even though the value in the FOOD column ('Bread, white') is less than 14 characters long.

If any operand in the substring function has a null value, SUBSTRING will return a null result. ∎

To extract a substring from a bit string, incorporate a 'B' in the string value argument, such as in the following example:

```
SUBSTRING (B'0111000110101' FROM 4 FOR 6)
```

This returns a value of B'100011'. The substring starts with the fourth bit of the source string and proceeds for six bits.

UPPER

The UPPER value function converts a character string to all uppercase characters. For example:

This statement	Returns
UPPER ('e. e. cummings')	'E. E. CUMMINGS'
UPPER ('Isaac Newton, PhD)	'ISAAC NEWTON, PHD'

A string that is already all in uppercase is unaffected by the UPPER function.

LOWER

The LOWER value function converts a character string to all lowercase characters. For example:

This statement	Returns
LOWER ('TAXES')	'taxes'
LOWER ('E. E. Cummings')	'e. e. cummings'

A string that is already all in lowercase is unaffected by the LOWER function.

TRIM

Use the TRIM function to trim off leading or trailing blanks (or other characters for that matter) from a character string. The following examples show how to use TRIM:

This statement	Returns
TRIM (LEADING ' ' FROM ' treat ')	'treat '
TRIM (TRAILING ' ' FROM ' treat ')	' treat'
TRIM (BOTH ' ' FROM ' treat ')	'treat'
TRIM (BOTH 't' from 'treat')	'rea'

The default trim character is the blank, so the following syntax would also be legal:

```
TRIM (BOTH FROM ' treat ')
```

It would give the same result as the third example above — 'treat'.

TRANSLATE and CONVERT

The TRANSLATE and CONVERT functions take a source string expressed in one character set and transform it into a string in another character set. Examples might be English to Kanji, or Hebrew to French. These transformations are specified by conversion functions that are implementation specific. Consult the documentation of your implementation for details.

It would be great if translating from one language to another was as easy as invoking an SQL TRANSLATE function. Unfortunately it is not that easy. All TRANSLATE does is translate a character in the first character set to the corresponding character in the second character set. It could, for example translate 'Ελλασ' to 'Ellas'. It would not translate 'Ελλασ' to 'Greece'. ■

Numeric value functions

Numeric value functions may take data of a variety of types as input, but the output is always a numeric value. There are five numeric value functions:

- ✔ POSITION
- ✔ CHARACTER_LENGTH
- ✔ OCTET_LENGTH
- ✔ BIT_LENGTH
- ✔ EXTRACT

POSITION

POSITION searches for a specified target string within a specified source string. It returns the character position where the target string begins. The syntax is

```
POSITION (target IN source)
```

Here are a few examples:

This statement	*Returns*
POSITION ('B' IN 'Bread, whole wheat')	1
POSITION ('Bre' IN 'Bread, whole wheat')	1
POSITION ('wh' IN 'Bread, whole wheat')	7
POSITION ('whi' IN 'Bread, whole wheat')	0
POSITION (" IN 'Bread, whole wheat')	1

If the target string is not found, the POSITION function returns a zero value. If the target string has zero length (as in the last example), the POSITION function always returns a value of one. If any operand in the function has a null value, the result will be a null value.

CHARACTER_LENGTH

The CHARACTER_LENGTH function returns the number of characters in a character string. For example the statement:

```
CHARACTER_LENGTH ('Opossum, roasted')
```

returns 17.

As I noted before in regard to the SUBSTRING function, this function is not particularly useful if its argument is a literal such as 'Opossum, roasted'. It is just as easy for me to write 17 as it is to write CHARACTER_LENGTH ('Opossum, roasted'). In fact it is easier to write 17. This function becomes useful when its argument is an expression rather than a literal value. ■

OCTET_LENGTH

In music, a vocal ensemble made up of eight singers is called an octet. Typically the parts represented are first and second soprano, first and second alto, first and second tenor, and first and second bass. In computer terminology, an ensemble of eight data bits is called a byte. The word "byte" is clever in that it is clearly related to "bit" but implies something larger than a bit. This is nice, but there is nothing in the word 'byte' to convey the concept of "eightness." By borrowing the musical term, a more apt description of a collection of eight bits is possible.

In practically all modern computers, eight bits are used to represent a single alphanumeric character. More complex character sets (such as Chinese) require sixteen bits to represent a single character. The OCTET_LENGTH function counts and returns the number of octets (bytes) in a string. If the string is a bit string, OCTET_LENGTH returns the number of octets needed to hold that number of bits. If the string is an English language character string (with one octet per character) it will return the number of characters in the string. If the string is a Chinese character string, the number returned will be twice the number of Chinese characters. Here are some examples:

```
OCTET_LENGTH ('Beans, lima')  11
OCTET_LENGTH (B'10111010011')   returns 2
```

The second string is 11 bits long, so it would take two octets to hold it.

Some character sets use a variable number of octets for different characters. In particular, some character sets for supporting mixtures of Kanji and Latin characters use "escape" characters to switch between the two character sets. A string that contains both Latin and Kanji may have, say 30 characters, and require 30 octets if all of the characters are Latin, and 62 characters if all of the characters are Kanji (60 characters plus a leading and trailing shift character), and 150 characters if the characters alternate between Latin and Kanji (since each Kanji character would need two octets for the character, and one octet each for the leading and trailing shift characters). The OCTET_LENGTH function returns the number of octets required for the current value of the string. ■

BIT_LENGTH

If you understand CHARACTER_LENGTH and OCTET_LENGTH, the BIT_LENGTH ought to be easy. It returns the length of a bit string. If the string is 6 bits long, it will return a 6. If the string is 15 bits long it will return a 15. For example the statement

```
BIT_LENGTH (B'01100111')
```

returns 8.

EXTRACT

The EXTRACT function extracts a single field from a datetime or an interval. For example the statement

```
EXTRACT (MONTH FROM DATE '1995-04-22')
```

returns 4.

Datetime value functions

SQL has three functions that return information about the current date, current time, or both. CURRENT_DATE returns the current date; CURRENT_TIME returns the current time, and CURRENT_TIMESTAMP returns (surprise) both the current date and the current time. CURRENT_DATE does not take an argument, but CURRENT_TIME and CURRENT_TIMESTAMP both take a single argument. The argument specifies the precision for the seconds part of the time value returned. The Datetime data types are described in Chapter 3, and the concept of precision is explained there as well.

Here are some examples.

This statement	Returns
CURRENT_DATE	1995-07-22
CURRENT_TIME (1)	08:36:57.3
CURRENT_TIMESTAMP (2)	1995-07-22 08:36:57.38

The date returned by CURRENT_DATE is DATE type data, not CHARACTER. The time returned by CURRENT_TIME (*p*) is TIME type data, and the timestamp returned by CURRENT_TIMESTAMP (*p*) is TIMESTAMP type data. Since SQL retrieves date and time information from your computer's system clock, it is correct for the time zone in which the computer is located.

In some applications, you may want to deal with dates, times, or timestamps as character strings to take advantage of the functions that operate on character data. You can do a type conversion with the CAST expression, which is described in Chapter 9. ■

Value Expressions

An expression may be simple or very complex. It can contain literal values, column names, parameters, host variables, subqueries, logical connectives, and arithmetic operators. Regardless of its complexity, an expression must reduce to a single value.

For this reason SQL expressions are commonly called *value expressions*. It is possible to combine multiple value expressions into a single expression, as long as the component value expressions reduce to values that are of compatible data types. ■

There are five different kinds of value expression in SQL-92. They are

✔ String value expressions

✔ Numeric value expressions

✔ Datetime value expressions

✔ Interval value expressions

✔ Conditional value expressions

String value expressions

The simplest string value expression would be a single string value specification. Other possibilities are a column reference, a set function, a scalar subquery, a CASE expression, a CAST expression, or a complex string value expression. I'll discuss CASE and CAST value expressions in Chapter 9. Only one operator is allowed in a string value expression — the concatenation operator. Any of the expressions just mentioned may be concatenated with another expression to create a more complex string value expression. The concatenation operator is represented by a pair of vertical lines (| |). Here are some examples of string value expressions:

Expression	*Produces*
'Peanut ' || 'brittle'	'Peanut brittle'
'Jelly' || ' ' || 'beans'	'Jelly beans'
FIRST_NAME || ' ' || LAST_NAME	'Joe Smith'
B'1100111' || B'01010011'	B'110011101010011'
'' || 'Asparagus'	'Asparagus'
'Asparagus' || ''	'Asparagus'
'As' || '' || 'par' || '' || 'agus'	'Asparagus'

As the preceding table shows, when you concatenate a string to a zero-length string, the result is the same as the original string.

Numeric value expressions

In numeric value expressions you can apply the addition, subtraction, multiplication, and division operators to numeric type data. The expression must reduce to a numeric value. The components of a numeric value expression may be of different data types, as long as they are all numeric. The data type of the result will depend on the data types of the components from which it is derived. The SQL-92 standard does not rigidly specify the type that will result from any specific combination of source expression components because of differences among hardware platforms.

Here are some examples of numeric value expressions:

–27

49+83

5*(12-3)

PROTEIN+FAT+CARBOHYDRATE

FEET/5280

COST * :multiplierA

Datetime value expressions

Datetime value expressions perform operations on data that deal with dates and times. They can contain components that are of the types DATE, TIME, TIMESTAMP, or INTERVAL. The result of a datetime value expression is always of a datetime type (either DATE, TIME, or TIMESTAMP). For example,

```
CURRENT_DATE + INTERVAL '7' DAY
```

gives the date of one week from today. Times are maintained in Universal Coordinated Time (UCT), but you can specify an offset to make the time correct for any particular time zone. For your system's local time zone, you can use the simple syntax given in the following example:

```
TIME '22:55:00' AT LOCAL
```

Alternatively you could specify it the long way:

```
TIME '22:55:00' AT TIME ZONE INTERVAL '-08:00' HOUR TO MINUTE
```

This shows that the time is referenced to Portland, Oregon's time zone, which is eight hours earlier than Greenwich, England.

Interval value expressions

When you subtract one datetime from another, you get an interval. It makes no sense to *add* one datetime to another, so SQL does not permit you to do so. If you add two intervals together or subtract one interval from another interval, the result is an interval. An interval can also be either multiplied or divided by a numeric constant.

Recall that there are two types of interval, year-month and day-time. To avoid ambiguities, you must specify which to use in an interval expression. For example:

```
(BIRTHDAY_65 - CURRENT_DATE) YEAR TO MONTH
```

gives the interval in years and months until you reach retirement age.

```
INTERVAL '17' DAY + INTERVAL '23' DAY
```

gives an interval of 40 days.

```
INTERVAL '9' MONTH * 5
```

approximates the total number of months that a mother of five has been pregnant (assuming she's not expecting number six!). ▪

Intervals can be negative as well as positive, and may be made up of any value expression or combination of value expressions that evaluates to an interval.

Conditional value expressions

The value of a conditional value expression depends on a condition. The conditional value expressions CASE, NULLIF, and COALESCE are significantly more complex than the other kinds of value expressions. In fact, they are so complex that there is not enough room here to talk about them. I will give them extensive coverage in Chapter 9.

Chapter 9

Advanced SQL-92 Value Expressions

● ●

In This Chapter

▶ Updating one column in a table row based on the value of another column

▶ Using the CASE expression to avoid computations that are sure to lead to errors

▶ Replacing special characters in a database table with nulls

▶ Converting a data item from one data type to another

▶ Saving data entry time with row value expressions

● ●

*I*n Chapter 3 I described SQL as a data sublanguage. Its sole function is to operate on data in a database. As such, it lacks many of the features of a conventional procedural language. As a result, developers using SQL have been forced to switch back and forth between SQL and the host language they are using to control the flow of execution. This repeated switching complicates matters at development time and negatively impacts performance at run time.

New features have been added to SQL-92 that reduce an application's reliance on its host language. Tasks that in older implementations required a switch back to the host language can now be performed within SQL. One of these new features (the CASE expression) provides a long-sought conditional structure. A second new feature (CAST) gives the facility of converting data in a table from one type to another. A third new feature (the row value expression) lets you operate on a list of values where previously only a single value was possible. If for example, your list of values is a list of columns in a table, you can perform an operation on all those columns using a very simple syntax.

CASE Conditional Expressions

Every complete computer language has some kind of conditional statement or command. Most have several. Probably the most common is the IF..THEN..ELSE..ENDIF structure. If the condition following the IF keyword evaluates to True, then the block of commands following the THEN keyword is executed. If the condition is not True, then the block of commands following the ELSE keyword is executed. The ENDIF keyword signals the end of the structure. This structure is great for any decision that can go one of two ways. It is less applicable to decisions that can have more than two outcomes.

The CASE statement handles situations where you may want to do more than two different things based on more than two conditions. ■

SQL's CASE expression is different from the CASE statements found in other languages in that it is an expression rather than a statement. In SQL, you can place a CASE expression almost anyplace where a value is legal. At run time a CASE expression evaluates to a value. The CASE statements found in other languages do not evaluate to a value, but rather execute a block of statements.

The key point to remember is that CASE in SQL is an expression, and thus only a part of a statement; not a statement in its own right. ■

The CASE expression can be used two different ways. The first is to use it with search conditions. It searches for rows in a table where specified conditions are True. If a search condition is found to be True for a table row, the statement containing the CASE expression makes a specified change to that row.

The second way you can use a CASE expression is to compare a table field to a value specified in the CASE expression. The outcome of the statement containing the CASE expression, for each table row, depends on which of several specified values the table field is equal to.

Let's look at examples in the following sections to make these concepts clearer. First I'll give two examples of using CASE with search conditions. One example searches a table and makes different changes to table values, based on a condition. This is called *translation oriented* use of CASE. The second checks the values in the table during the search for conditions that will cause errors. This is called an *exception avoidance* use of CASE. ■

The last section on CASE will look at an example of the *value form* of CASE.

Using CASE with search conditions

One powerful way to use the CASE expression is to search a table for rows in which a specified search condition is True. When used in this way the CASE expression has the following syntax:

```
CASE
    WHEN condition₁ THEN result₁
    WHEN condition₂ THEN result₂
    ...
    WHEN condition_n THEN result_n
    ELSE result_x
END
```

The first qualifying row (the first row that meets the conditions of the WHERE clause, if any) is examined to see if $condition_1$ is True. If it is, the CASE expression is given a value of $result_1$. If $condition_1$ is not True, then the row is evaluated for $condition_2$. If $condition_2$ is True, then the CASE expression is given the value of $result_2$, and so on. If none of the stated conditions are True, then the CASE expression is given the value of $result_x$. The ELSE clause is optional. If there is no ELSE clause and none of the specified conditions is True, the expression is given a null value. After the CASE expression is applied to the first qualifying row in a table, and the appropriate action is taken, the next row is processed. This continues until the entire table has been processed.

Updating values based on a condition

Since a CASE expression can be embedded within an SQL statement, in almost any place where a value is possible, it gives you tremendous flexibility. You can use it within an UPDATE statement to make different changes to table values, based on a condition. Consider the following example:

```
UPDATE FOODS
    SET RATING = CASE
                    WHEN FAT < 1
                        THEN 'very low fat'
                    WHEN FAT < 5
                        THEN 'low fat'
                    WHEN FAT < 20
                        THEN 'moderate fat'
                    WHEN FAT < 50
                        THEN 'high fat'
                    ELSE 'heart attack city'
                END
```

The WHEN conditions are evaluated in order until the first True, after which the rest are ignored. For this reason you don't have to code the preceding example as

```
WHEN FAT < 1
      THEN 'very low fat'
WHEN FAT >= 1 AND FAT < 5
      THEN 'low fat'
WHEN FAT >= 5 AND FAT < 20
      THEN 'moderate fat'
WHEN FAT >= 20 AND < 50
      THEN 'high fat'
ELSE 'heart attack city'
```

A table in Chapter 8 showed the fat content of 100 grams of certain selected foods. A database table holding that information has a column named 'RAT-ING' that gives a quick assessment of the meaning of the fat content. If you were to run the above update on the FOODS table, asparagus would be assigned a value of 'very low fat,' chicken would be assigned a value of 'low fat,' and roasted almonds would fall into the 'heart attack city' category.

Avoiding conditions that cause errors

Another valuable use of CASE is exception avoidance: checking for conditions that cause errors.

Consider a case that determines compensation for salespeople. Companies that compensate their salespeople by straight commission often start out a new person by giving them a "draw" against commission to get them started. In the following example, new salespeople are given a draw against commission that is withdrawn gradually as their commissions rise.

```
UPDATE SALES_COMP
   SET COMP = COMMISSION + CASE
                             WHEN COMMISSION <> 0
                                 THEN DRAW/COMMISSION
                             WHEN COMMISSION = 0
                                 THEN DRAW
                        END
```

If the salesperson's commission is zero, the structure in this example avoids a division by zero operation, which would surely cause an error. If the salesperson has a non-zero commission, total compensation is the commission plus a draw that is reduced proportionately to the size of the commission.

The THEN expressions in a CASE expression must all be of the same type: all numeric, all character, or all date. The result of the CASE expression will be of the same type. ∎

Using CASE with values

You can use a more compact form of the CASE expression when you are comparing a test value for equality with a series of other values. This is useful within a SELECT or UPDATE statement, when a table has a limited number of values in a column, and you want to associate a corresponding result value to each of those column values. When used in this way, the CASE expression has the following syntax:

```
CASE value_t
    WHEN value_1 THEN result_1
    WHEN value_2 THEN result_2
    ...
    WHEN value_n THEN result_n
    ELSE result_x
END
```

If the test value ($value_t$) is equal to $value_1$, then the expression takes on the value $result_1$. If $value_t$ is not equal to $value_1$, but is equal to $value_2$, then the expression takes on the value $result_2$. Each comparison value is tried in turn all the way down to $value_n$, until a match is achieved. If none of the comparison values equals the test value, the expression takes on the value $result_x$. Once again, if the optional ELSE clause is not present, and none of the comparison values match the test value, the expression is given a null value.

For an actual example of how the value form works, consider a case where you have a table containing the names and ranks of various military officers. You want to list the names preceded by the correct abbreviation for each rank. The following statement would do it:

```
SELECT CASE RANK
           WHEN 'general'            THEN 'Gen.'
           WHEN 'colonel'            THEN 'Col.'
           WHEN 'lieutenant colonel' THEN 'Lt. Col.'
           WHEN 'major'              THEN 'Maj.'
           WHEN 'captain'            THEN 'Capt.'
           WHEN 'first lieutenant'   THEN '1st. Lt.'
           WHEN 'second lieutenant'  THEN '2nd. Lt.'
           ELSE 'Mr.'
       END,
          LAST_NAME
       FROM OFFICERS ;
```

The result will be a list similar to the following:

```
Capt.  Midnight
Col.   Sanders
Gen.   Schwartzkopf
Maj.   Disaster
Mr.    Nimitz
```

Chester Nimitz was an admiral in the United States Navy during World War II. Since his rank is not one of those listed in the CASE expression, his title is determined by the ELSE clause.

As another example, say that Captain Midnight has just been promoted to major, and we want to update the OFFICERS database accordingly. Assume the variable *officer_last_name* contains the value 'Midnight' and the variable *new_rank* contains an integer (4) that corresponds to Midnight's new rank according to the following table:

new_rank	Rank
1	general
2	colonel
3	lieutenant colonel
4	major
5	captain
6	first lieutenant
7	second lieutenant
8	Mr.

We can record the promotion with the following SQL code:

```
UPDATE OFFICERS
   SET RANK = CASE :new_rank
                   WHEN 1 THEN 'general'
                   WHEN 2 THEN 'colonel'
                   WHEN 3 THEN 'lieutenant colonel'
                   WHEN 4 THEN 'major'
                   WHEN 5 THEN 'captain'
                   WHEN 6 THEN 'first lieutenant'
                   WHEN 7 THEN 'second lieutenant'
                   WHEN 8 THEN 'Mr.'
              END
   WHERE LAST_NAME = :officer_last_name
```

An alternative syntax for the CASE with values is

```
CASE
    WHEN value_t = value_1 THEN result_1
    WHEN value_t = value_2 THEN result_2
    ...
    WHEN value_t = value_n THEN result_n
    ELSE result_x
END ■
```

A special CASE — NULLIF

If there is one thing we can be sure of in this world, it is change. Sometimes things change from one known state to another. Other times we thought we knew something, but later found out that we didn't know it after all. Classical thermodynamics as well as modern chaos theory tell us that it is natural for systems to migrate from a well-known, ordered state into a disordered state that cannot be predicted. Anyone who has monitored the status of a teenager's room for a period of a week after it was cleaned will vouch for the accuracy of these theories.

Database tables contain definite values in fields whose contents are known. Usually, if the value of a field is unknown, the field contains the null value. With SQL you can use a CASE expression to change the contents of a table field from a definite value to a null. The null indicates that we no longer know the value of the field. Let's consider an example.

Imagine you own a small airline that offers flights between Southern California and Washington State. Until recently, some of your flights have stopped at San Jose International Airport to refuel before continuing on. However, you have just lost your right to fly into San Jose. From now on you will have to make your refueling stop at either San Francisco International or Oakland International. At this point, you do not yet know which flights will stop at which airport, but you definitely do know that none of them will be stopping at San Jose any more. You have a FLIGHT database that contains important information about each of your routes, and now you want to update it to remove all references to San Jose. One way to do it is:

```
UPDATE FLIGHT
    SET REFUEL_STOP = CASE
                        WHEN REFUEL_STOP = 'San Jose'
                            THEN NULL
                        ELSE REFUEL_STOP
                    END ;
```

Since occasions frequently arise where you would want to replace a known value with a null, SQL-92 has a shorthand notation to accomplish it. The previous example expressed in the shorthand form is as follows:

```
UPDATE FLIGHT
   SET REFUEL_STOP = NULLIF(REFUEL_STOP, 'San Jose') ;
```

One can read this as, "Update the FLIGHT database by setting column REFUEL_STOP to null if the existing value of REFUEL_STOP is 'San Jose'. Otherwise, make no change."

NULLIF comes in even handier when you are converting data that was originally accumulated for use with a program written in a standard programming language such as COBOL or FORTRAN. Standard programming languages don't have nulls, so it's common to represent the "not known" or "not applicable" concept with special values. For example, a numeric -1 might represent a "not known" value for SALARY, and a character string "***" might represent a "not known" or "not applicable" value for JOBCODE. If you want to represent those "not known" and "not applicable" states in an SQL-compatible database with nulls, you need to convert the special values to nulls. The following example makes this conversion for an employee table, where some salary values are unknown.

```
UPDATE EMP
   SET SALARY = CASE SALARY
                     WHEN -1 THEN NULL
                     ELSE SALARY
                END ;
```

You can perform this conversion more conveniently with NULLIF:

```
UPDATE EMP
   SET SALARY = NULLIF(SALARY, -1) ;
```

Another special CASE — COALESCE

COALESCE, like NULLIF, is a shorthand form of a particular CASE expression. It deals with a list of values that may or may not be null. If one of the values in the list is non-null, the COALESCE expression takes on that value. If more than one value in the list is non-null, the expression takes on the value of the first non-null item in the list. If all the values in the list are null, the expression takes on the null value.

A CASE expression that had this function would have the form:

```
CASE
   WHEN value₁ IS NOT NULL
```

```
        THEN value₁
    WHEN value₂ IS NOT NULL
        THEN value₂
    ...
    WHEN valueₙ IS NOT NULL
        THEN valueₙ
    ELSE NULL
END
```

The corresponding COALESCE shorthand is:

```
COALESCE(value₁, value₂, ..., valueₙ)
```

The COALESCE expression takes on the value of the first non-null item in the list. If all items are null, the expression takes on the null value. You may want to use a COALESCE expression after you have performed an OUTER JOIN operation (discussed in Chapter 11). In such cases COALESCE can save you a lot of typing.

CAST Data Type Conversions

In Chapter 3 we discussed the different data types that SQL recognizes and supports. Ideally, there is a perfect choice of data type for each column in a database table. However, in this non-ideal world it is not always clear what that perfect choice should be. When defining a database table, you may assign a data type to a column that works perfectly for your current application. Later, you may want to expand the scope of your application, or write an entirely new application that makes a different use of the data. This new use may require a data type different from the one you originally chose.

You may want to compare a column of one type in one table with a column of a different type in a different table. For example you may have dates stored as character data in one table and as date data in another. Even if both columns contain the same things (dates, for example) the fact that the types are different may prevent you from doing the comparison. In SQL-86 and SQL-89, type incompatibility could be a big problem. SQL-92, however, offers an easy-to-use solution in the CAST expression.

The CAST expression converts table data or host variables of one type to another type. Once the conversion has been made, you can proceed with the operation or analysis that you originally envisioned.

Naturally, there are restrictions. You can't just indiscriminately convert data of any type into any other. The data being converted must be compatible with the new data type. For example, you can use CAST to convert the CHAR(10) character string '1995-04-26' to the DATE type. You could not, however, use CAST to convert the CHAR(10) character string 'rhinoceros' to the DATE type. You cannot convert an INTEGER to the SMALLINT type, if it exceeds the maximum size of a SMALLINT. ■

An item of any of the character types can be converted to any other type (such as numeric or date), providing the value of the item has the form of a literal of the new type. Conversely, an item of any type can be converted to any of the character types, providing the value of the item has the form of a literal of the original type.

Here are some additional possible conversions:

- ✔ Any bit string to a character string. The bits are treated as if they are the bits that make up characters.

- ✔ Any numeric type to any other numeric type. If converting to a type of less fractional precision, the system will round or truncate the result.

- ✔ Any exact numeric to a single component interval, such as INTERVAL DAY or INTERVAL SECOND.

- ✔ Any DATE to a TIMESTAMP. The time part of the TIMESTAMP will be filled in with zeros.

- ✔ Any TIME to a TIME with a different fractional seconds precision or a TIMESTAMP. The date part of the TIMESTAMP will be filled in with the current date.

- ✔ Any TIMESTAMP to either a DATE, a TIME, or a TIMESTAMP with a different fractional seconds precision.

- ✔ Any year-month INTERVAL to an exact numeric or another year-month INTERVAL with different leading field precision.

- ✔ Any day-time INTERVAL to an exact numeric or another day-time INTERVAL with different leading field precision.

Using CAST within SQL

Let's say that you work for a sales company that keeps track of prospective customers as well as of customers who have actually bought something. The prospective customers are in a table named PROSPECT, and each one is distinguished by a unique Prospect ID number, which is stored as a CHAR(5) type. The paying customers are in a table named CUSTOMER, and they are distinguished by a unique Customer ID number which is of SMALLINT type.

You would like to generate a list of all customers who appear in both tables. Use CAST to do it as follows:

```
SELECT * FROM CUSTOMER
   WHERE CUSTOMER.CUSTOMER_ID =
      CAST(PROSPECT.PROSPECT_ID AS SMALLINT)
```

Using CAST between SQL and the host language

The key use of CAST is to deal with data types that are in SQL but not in the host language you are using. For example,

✔ SQL has DECIMAL and NUMERIC, but FORTRAN and Pascal don't.

✔ SQL has FLOAT and REAL, but standard COBOL doesn't.

✔ SQL has DATETIME, and no language does.

Suppose that you want to use FORTRAN or Pascal to access tables that have DECIMAL(5,3) columns, and you don't want the inaccuracies that would result from converting those values to the REAL data type of FORTRAN and Pascal. You can do this by CASTing the data to and from character-string host variables. You would retrieve a numeric salary of 198.37 as a CHAR(10) value of '0000198.37'. Then, if you wanted to update that salary to 203.74, you could place that value in a CHAR(10) as '0000203.74'. First use CAST to change the SQL DECIMAL (5,3) data type to the CHAR (10) type for the specific employee whose ID number is stored in the host variable *:emp_id_var*:

```
SELECT CAST(SALARY AS CHAR(10)) INTO :salary_var
      FROM EMP
      WHERE EMPID = :emp_id_var ;
```

Then the application examines the resulting character string value in *:salary_var*, and possibly sets it to a new value of '000203.74', and then updates the database with the following SQL code:

```
UPDATE EMP
   SET SALARY = CAST(:salary_var AS DECIMAL(5,3))
      WHERE EMPID=:emp_id_var;
```

It's awkward to deal with character-string values such as '000198.37' in FORTRAN or Pascal, but you can write a set of subroutines to do the necessary manipulations. You can then retrieve and update any SQL data from any host language, and be able to get and set exact values.

The general idea is that CAST is most valuable for converting between host types and the database, rather than for converting within the database. ▪

Row Value Expressions

In SQL-86 and SQL-89, most operations deal with a single value or single column in a table row. To operate on multiple values you must build complex expressions using logical connectives (which we will discuss in Chapter 10).

SQL-92 introduces row value expressions, which operate on a list of values or columns rather than a single value or column. A *row value expression* is a list of value expressions enclosed in parentheses and separated by commas. You can operate on an entire row at once, or on a selected subset of the row. ▪

In Chapter 7 we saw how to use the INSERT statement to add a new row to an existing table. It uses a row value expression. Consider the example

```
INSERT INTO FOODS
    (FOODNAME, CALORIES, PROTEIN, FAT, CARBOHYDRATE)
    VALUES
    ('Cheese, cheddar', 398, 25, 32.2, 2.1)
```

('Cheese, cheddar', 398, 25, 32.2, 2.1) is a row value expression. When used in an INSERT statement in this way, a row value expression can contain null and default values. A default value is the value that a table column assumes if no other value is specified. For example,

```
('Cheese, cheddar', 398, NULL, 32.2, DEFAULT)
```

is a legal row value expression.

You can add multiple rows to a table by putting multiple row value expressions in the VALUES clause, as follows:

```
INSERT INTO FOODS
    (FOODNAME, CALORIES, PROTEIN, FAT, CARBOHYDRATE)
    VALUES
    ('Lettuce', 14, 1.2, 0.2, 2.5),
    ('Margarine', 720, 0.6, 81.0, 0.4),
    ('Mustard', 75, 4.7, 4.4, 6.4),
    ('Spaghetti', 148, 5.0, 0.5, 30.1)
```

Row value expressions can be used to save typing in comparisons. Say you have two tables of nutritional values, one compiled in English and the other in Spanish. You want to find those rows in the English language table that correspond exactly to rows in the Spanish language table. Without a row value expression, you might formulate something like the following:

```
SELECT * FROM FOODS
    WHERE FOODS.CALORIES = COMIDA.CALORIA
        AND FOODS.PROTEIN = COMIDA.PROTEINA
        AND FOODS.FAT = COMIDA.GORDO
        AND FOODS.CARBOHYDRATE = COMIDA.CARBOHIDRATO
```

Row value expressions allow you to code the same logic as follows:

```
SELECT * FROM FOODS
    WHERE (FOODS.CALORIES, FOODS.PROTEIN, FOODS.FAT,
        FOODS.CARBOHYDRATE)
    =
        (COMIDA.CALORIA, COMIDA.PROTEINA, COMIDA.GORDO,
        COMIDA.CARBOHIDRATO)
```

In this example, not much typing is saved. The benefit would be greater if more columns were being compared, but not much greater. In cases of marginal benefit like this, it may be better to stick with the older syntax because its meaning is clearer.

There is one benefit to using a row value expression rather than its coded equivalent; the row-value expression is *a lot* faster. In principle, a very clever implementation could analyze the coded version and implement it the same as the row-value version, but in practice this is a difficult optimization that is not done by any DBMS currently on the market (as far as I know). ▪

Chapter 10

Zeroing In on the Data You Want

● ●

In This Chapter

▶ Specifying the tables you want to work with

▶ Separating rows of interest from all the rest

▶ Building effective WHERE clauses

▶ Handling null values

▶ Building compound expressions with logical connectives

▶ Grouping query output by column

▶ Putting query output in order

● ●

A database management system has two main functions: storing data and providing easy access to it. There is nothing special about storing data. A file cabinet can do that. The hard part is providing easy access. In order for data to be useful, you must be able to separate the (usually) small amount you do want from the huge amount you don't want.

SQL lets you use some characteristic of the data itself to determine whether a particular table row is of interest or not. In particular the SELECT, DELETE, and UPDATE statements need to convey to the database engine (that part of the DBMS that actually interacts with the data) which rows to select, delete, or update, and which rows to leave alone. You can accomplish this discrimination by adding *modifying clauses* to your SELECT, DELETE, and UPDATE statements.

Modifying Clauses

The modifying clauses available in SQL are FROM, WHERE, HAVING, GROUP BY, and ORDER BY. The FROM clause tells which table or tables to operate on. The WHERE and HAVING clauses specify a characteristic of the data that determines whether a particular row should be included in the current operation or not. The GROUP BY and ORDER BY clauses specify how the retrieved rows should be displayed. Table 10-1 provides a summary.

Table 10-1: Modifying Clauses and Functions

Modifying Clause	Function
FROM	Specifies which tables to take data from
WHERE	Filters out rows that do not satisfy the search condition
GROUP BY	Separates rows into groups, based on the values in the grouping columns
HAVING	Filters out groups that do not satisfy the search condition
ORDER BY	Sorts the results of prior clauses to produce final output

If you have more than one of these clauses, they must appear in the following order:

```
SELECT column_list
    FROM table_list
    [WHERE search_condition]
    [GROUP BY grouping_column]
    [HAVING search_condition]
    [ORDER BY ordering_condition]
```

The WHERE clause is a filter that passes rows that meet the search condition and rejects those that don't. The GROUP BY clause rearranges the rows passed by the WHERE clause according to the value of the grouping column. The HAVING clause is another filter that takes each group formed by the GROUP BY clause and passes those groups that meet the search condition, rejecting the rest. The ORDER BY clause sorts whatever is left after all the preceding clauses have been processed. As indicated by the square brackets ([ ]), the WHERE, GROUP BY, HAVING, and ORDER BY clauses are optional.

The clauses are evaluated in the order FROM, WHERE, GROUP BY, HAVING, and finally SELECT, with the clauses operating in a "pipeline" manner, in which each clause takes as input the result of the prior clause, and produces an output for the next clause. Or, in functional notation:

SELECT(HAVING(GROUP BY(WHERE(FROM...))))

ORDER BY operates after SELECT, which explains why ORDER BY can only reference columns that are in the SELECT list. ORDER BY cannot reference other columns in the FROM table(s). ■

FROM Clauses

The FROM clause is easy to understand if only one table is specified. For example,

```
SELECT * FROM SALES ;
```

returns all the data in all the rows of every column in the SALES table. It is possible, however, to specify more than one table in a FROM clause. Consider this example:

```
SELECT *
    FROM CUSTOMER, SALES ;
```

This statement will form a virtual table that combines the data from the CUS-TOMER table with the data from the SALES table. Each row in the CUSTOMER table will be combined with every row in the SALES table to form the new table. This means that the new virtual table formed will contain the number of rows in the CUSTOMER table multiplied by the number of rows in the SALES table. If the CUSTOMER table has ten rows and the SALES table has a hundred, the new virtual table will have a thousand rows.

This operation is called the *Cartesian product* of the two source tables. The Cartesian product is actually a type of join. Joins are covered in detail in Chapter 11. ▆

In most applications, the majority of the rows formed by taking the Cartesian product of two tables will be garbage. In the case of the virtual table formed from the CUSTOMER and SALES tables, only the rows where the CUSTOMER_ID from the CUSTOMER table matches the CUSTOMER_ID from the SALES table will be of interest. You can filter out the rest with a WHERE clause.

WHERE Clauses

We have already encountered the WHERE clause several times in previous chapters. We were able to use it in those places without really explaining it because its meaning and use are so intuitively obvious. An operation (such as a SELECT, DELETE, or UPDATE) is performed only on table rows WHERE a stated condition is True. The syntax of the WHERE clause is:

```
SELECT column_list
    FROM table_name
    WHERE condition
```

```
DELETE FROM table_name
    WHERE condition

UPDATE table_name
    SET column₁=value₁, column₂=value₂, ..., columnₙ=valueₙ
    WHERE condition
```

In all cases the condition in the WHERE clause may be simple or arbitrarily complex. Multiple conditions may be joined together by the logical connectives AND, OR, and NOT (discussed later in this chapter) to create a single condition.

The following statements are examples of typical WHERE clauses:

```
WHERE CUSTOMER.CUSTOMER_ID = SALES.CUSTOMER_ID
WHERE FOODS.CALORIES = COMIDA.CALORIA
WHERE FOODS.CALORIES < 219
WHERE FOODS.CALORIES > 3 * base_value
WHERE FOODS.CALORIES < 219 AND FOODS.PROTEIN > 27.4
```

The conditions expressed in these WHERE clauses are called predicates. A *predicate* is an expression that asserts a fact about values. ■

For example, the predicate FOODS.CALORIES < 219 is True if the value for the current row of the column FOODS.CALORIES is less than 219. If the assertion is True, the condition is satisfied. An assertion may either be True, False, or unknown. The unknown case arises when one or more elements in the assertion are null. The *comparison predicates* (=, <, >, <>, <=, and >=) are the most common, but SQL has a number of others that greatly increase your ability to distinguish or "filter out" a desired data item from others in the same column. Here's a list of the predicates that give you that filtering ability:

- Comparison predicates
- BETWEEN
- IN [NOT IN]
- LIKE [NOT LIKE]
- NULL
- ALL, SOME, ANY
- EXISTS
- UNIQUE
- OVERLAPS
- MATCH

I'll discuss all of these in the following sections.

Comparison predicates

The preceding examples show typical uses of comparison predicates, in which one value is compared to another. For every row in which the comparison evaluates to a True value, the WHERE clause is satisfied and the operation (SELECT, UPDATE, DELETE, or whatever) is performed. For example, consider the following SQL statement:

```
SELECT * FROM FOODS
    WHERE CALORIES < 219 ;
```

This statement will display all rows from the FOODS table that have a value less than 219 in the CALORIES column.

There are six comparison predicates, listed in Table 10-2.

Table 10-2: SQL's Comparison Predicates

Comparison	*Symbol*
Equal	=
Not equal	<>
Less than	<
Less than or equal	<=
Greater than	>
Greater than or equal	>=

BETWEEN

Sometimes you want to select a row if the value in a column falls within a specified range. One way to do this is with comparison predicates. For example you could formulate a WHERE clause to select all the rows in the FOODS table that have a value in the CALORIES column greater than 100 and less than 300:

```
WHERE FOODS.CALORIES > 100 AND FOODS.CALORIES < 300
```

This comparison does not include foods that have a calorie count of exactly 100 or 300, only those values that fall in between. To include the end points you could write:

```
WHERE FOODS.CALORIES >= 100 AND FOODS.CALORIES <= 300
```

Another way of specifying a range that includes the end points is to use a BETWEEN predicate in the following manner:

```
WHERE FOODS.CALORIES BETWEEN 100 AND 300
```

This clause is functionally identical to the one preceding it, which used comparison predicates. As you can see, this formulation saves some typing and is also perhaps a little more intuitive than the one using two comparison predicates joined by the logical connective AND.

The BETWEEN keyword may be somewhat confusing because it does not tell you explicitly whether the end points are included or not. In fact they are included. It also does not explicitly tell you that the first term in the comparison must be equal to or less than the second. If, for example, FOODS.CALORIES contained a value of 200, the following clause would return a true value:

```
WHERE FOODS.CALORIES BETWEEN 100 AND 300
```

However, a clause that would seem to be equivalent would return the opposite result, False:

```
WHERE FOODS.CALORIES BETWEEN 300 AND 100 ■
```

If you use BETWEEN, you must be able to guarantee that the first term in your comparison is always equal to or less than the second term. ■

The BETWEEN predicate can be used with character, bit, and datetime data types as well as with the numeric types. You might see something like the following:

```
SELECT FIRST_NAME, LAST_NAME
   FROM CUSTOMER
   WHERE CUSTOMER.LAST_NAME BETWEEN 'A' AND 'Mzzz'
```

This will return all customers whose last name is in the first half of the alphabet.

IN and NOT IN

The IN and NOT IN predicates deal with whether (or not) their arguments are included in a set. For example, you might have a table listing suppliers of a commodity that your company purchases on a regular basis. You want to know the phone numbers of those suppliers located in the Pacific Northwest. You could find them by using comparison predicates, like this:

```
SELECT company, phone
   FROM SUPPLIER
   WHERE state = 'OR' OR state = 'WA' OR state = 'ID' ;
```

However, you could also use the IN predicate to do the same thing:

```
SELECT company, phone
   FROM SUPPLIER
   WHERE state IN ('OR', 'WA', 'ID') ;
```

This formulation is a little more compact than the one using comparison predicates and logical OR.

The NOT IN version works the same way. Say you have locations in California, Arizona, and New Mexico and, to save sales tax, you want to consider suppliers located anywhere *except* in those states. Use the following construction:

```
SELECT company, phone
   FROM SUPPLIER
   WHERE state NOT IN ('CA', 'AZ', 'NM')
```

When you use the IN keyword like this, it saves you a little typing. The more elements there are in the set, the more typing you save. However, saving a little typing is not that great an advantage. You could still do the same job with comparison predicates.

There may be another good reason to use the IN predicate rather than comparison predicates, even if it does not save much typing. Your DBMS will probably implement the two methods differently, and one of the methods may be significantly faster than the other. You may want to run a performance comparison on the two ways of expressing inclusion in (or exclusion from) a group, then use the technique that produces the quickest results. ■

There is another area in which the IN keyword is valuable. When it is part of a subquery, it allows you to pull information from two tables to obtain results that could not be derived from a single table. I'll cover subqueries in Chapter 12, but here is an example that shows how a subquery uses the IN keyword.

Suppose you want to display the names of all customers who have bought the F-117A product in the last 30 days. Customer names are in the CUSTOMER table and sales transaction data is in the TRANSACT table. You could use this query:

```
SELECT FIRST_NAME, LAST_NAME
   FROM CUSTOMER
   WHERE CUSTOMER_ID IN
      (SELECT CUSTOMER_ID
          FROM TRANSACT
          WHERE PRODUCT_ID = F-117A
          AND TRANS_DATE >= (CURRENT_DATE - 30)) ;
```

The sub-SELECT of the TRANSACT table is nested within the outer SELECT of the CUSTOMER table. The inner SELECT finds the CUSTOMER_ID numbers of all customers who have bought the F-117A product in the last 30 days. The outer SELECT displays the first and last names of all customers whose CUSTOMER_ID was retrieved by the inner SELECT.

LIKE and NOT LIKE

Use the LIKE predicate to compare two character strings for a partial match. Partial matches can be valuable when you have some idea of the string you are searching for, but do not know its exact form. You can also use partial matches to retrieve multiple rows that contain similar strings in one of the table's columns.

To identify partial matches, SQL makes use of two *wildcard characters*. The percent sign (%) can stand for any string of characters, zero or more characters in length. The underscore (_) stands for any single character. Table 10-3 provides some examples showing how to use LIKE.

Table 10-3: SQL's LIKE Predicate

Statement	*Values Returned*
WHERE WORD LIKE 'intern%'	intern internal international internet interns
WHERE WORD LIKE '%Peace%'	Justice of the Peace Peaceful Warrior
WHERE WORD LIKE 't_p_'	tape taps tipi tips tops type

The NOT LIKE predicate retrieves all rows that do *not* satisfy a partial match including one or more wildcard characters. For example,

```
WHERE PHONE NOT LIKE '503%'
```

returns all the rows in the table for which the phone number does not start with '503'.

You may want to search for a string that includes a percent sign or an underscore. In this case, you want SQL to interpret the percent sign as a percent sign, not as a wildcard character. You can do this by typing an *escape character* just prior to the character you want to be taken literally. You can choose any character to be the escape character, as long as it does not appear in the string being tested. For example:

```
SELECT QUOTE
    FROM BARTLETTS
    WHERE LIKE '20#%%'
        ESCAPE '#' ;
```

The first % is escaped by the preceding # sign, so it is interpreted as a percent sign. The second % is not escaped, so it is interpreted as a wildcard. This query would find, for instance:

```
20% of the salespeople produce 80% of the results
```

It would also find:

```
20% ▓
```

NULL

The NULL predicate finds all rows where the value in the selected column is null. For the FOODS table given in Chapter 8, several rows have null values in the CARBOHYDRATE column. You can retrieve their names with a statement such as:

```
SELECT (FOOD)
    FROM FOODS
    WHERE CARBOHYDRATE IS NULL ;
```

This query returns the following values:

```
Beef, lean hamburger
Chicken, light meat
```

```
Opossum, roasted
Pork, ham
```

As you would expect, including the NOT keyword reverses the result.

```
SELECT (FOOD)
   FROM FOODS
   WHERE CARBOHYDRATE IS NOT NULL ;
```

This returns all the rows in the table *except* the four listed above.

The statement CARBOHYDRATE IS NULL is not the same as CARBOHYDRATE = NULL. To illustrate this point, assume that in the current row of the FOODS table, both CARBOHYDRATE and PROTEIN are null. From this you can draw the following conclusions:

"CARBOHYDRATE IS NULL" is True

"PROTEIN IS NULL" is True

"CARBOHYDRATE IS NULL AND PROTEIN IS NULL" is True

"CARBOHYDRATE = PROTEIN" is unknown

"CARBOHYDRATE = NULL" is an illegal expression

It would be meaningless to use the keyword NULL in a comparison, because the answer would always be "unknown". ■

Why is CARBOHYDRATE = PROTEIN defined as unknown, even though CARBOHYDRATE and PROTEIN have the same (null) value? Because NULL means "I don't know." You don't know what CARBOHYDRATE is, and you don't know what PROTEIN is, therefore you don't know if those (unknown) values are the same. Maybe CARBOHYDRATE is 37 and PROTEIN is 14, or maybe CARBOHYDRATE is 93 and PROTEIN is 93. If you don't know either the carbohydrate value or the protein value, then you can't say whether they are the same.

ALL, SOME, ANY

Thousands of years ago, the Greek philosopher Aristotle formulated a system of logic that became the basis for much of Western thought. Its essence is to start with a set of premises that are known to be true, apply valid operations to them, and thereby arrive at new truths. An example of this procedure would be:

Premise 1: All Greeks are human.

Premise 2: All humans are mortal.

Conclusion: All Greeks are mortal.

Another example:

> Premise 1: Some Greeks are women.
>
> Premise 2: All women are human.
>
> Conclusion: Some Greeks are human.

Another way of stating the same logical idea is:

> If any Greeks are women and all women are human, then some Greeks are human.

The first example uses the *universal quantifier* ALL in both premises, allowing a sound deduction to be made about all Greeks in the conclusion. The second example uses the *existential quantifier* SOME in one premise, allowing a deduction to be made about some Greeks in the conclusion. The third example uses the existential quantifier ANY, which is a synonym for SOME, to come to the same conclusion reached in the second example.

ANY can be ambiguous

The original SQL used the word ANY for existential quantification. This turned out to be confusing and error prone, since the English language connotations of "any" are sometimes universal and sometimes existential:

✔ "Do any of you people know where Baker Street is?"

✔ "I can eat more eggs than any of you people".

The first sentence is probably asking if *some* people know where Baker Street is. "Any" is being used as an existential quantifier. The second sentence, however, is a boast that is stating that I can eat more eggs than *all* of you people. In this case "any" is being used as a universal quantifier.

Thus, for the standard, the word "ANY" was retained for compatibility with early products, but the word SOME was added as a less confusing synonym.

Let's look at how SOME and ALL apply in SQL.

Consider an example in baseball statistics. Baseball is a physically demanding sport, especially for pitchers. A pitcher must throw the baseball from the pitcher's mound to home plate from 90 to 150 times in the course of a game. This can be very tiring, and many times the pitcher becomes ineffective and must be replaced by a relief pitcher. It is an outstanding achievement for the pitcher who started a game to pitch the entire game without relief.

Suppose you are keeping track of the number of complete games pitched by all major league pitchers. In one table you list all the American League pitchers and in another table you list all National League pitchers. Both tables contain the players' first name, last name, and number of complete games pitched.

The American League allows a designated hitter (DH), who need not play a defensive position, to hit in the place of any of the nine players who do play defense. Usually the DH bats for the pitcher, since pitchers are notoriously poor hitters. Say you have a theory that, on the average, American League starting pitchers should throw more complete games than National League starting pitchers, because designated hitters allow hard-throwing but weak-hitting American League pitchers to stay in close games, while comparable National League pitchers, who must bat for themselves, would be removed for a pinch hitter in a close game. To test your theory, you formulate the following query:

```
SELECT FIRST_NAME, LAST_NAME
   FROM AMERICAN_LEAGUER
   WHERE COMPLETE_GAMES > ALL
      (SELECT COMPLETE_GAMES
         FROM NATIONAL_LEAGUER) ;
```

The subquery (the inner SELECT) returns a list of the number of complete games pitched by all National Leaguers. The outer query returns the first and last names of all American Leaguers who have pitched more complete games than ALL of the National Leaguers. This is somewhat confusing. The query will *not* return the names of American League pitchers who have pitched more complete games than all National League pitchers combined. It will return the names of those American League pitchers who have pitched more complete games than the pitcher who has thrown the most complete games in the National League.

Consider this similar statement:

```
SELECT FIRST_NAME, LAST_NAME
   FROM AMERICAN_LEAGUER
   WHERE COMPLETE_GAMES > ANY
      (SELECT COMPLETE_GAMES
         FROM NATIONAL_LEAGUER) ;
```

In this case the existential quantifier ANY is used instead of the universal quantifier ALL. The subquery (the inner, nested query) is identical to the subquery in the previous example. It retrieves a complete list of the complete game statistics for all the National League pitchers. The outer query returns the first and last names of all American League pitchers who have pitched more complete games than ANY National League pitcher. Since it is a virtual certainty that there is at least one National League pitcher who has not pitched a complete game, all American League pitchers who have pitched at least one complete game will probably be included in the result.

If you replace the keyword ANY with the equivalent keyword SOME, the result will be the same. If it is true that at least one National League pitcher has not pitched a complete game, then we can say that SOME National League pitcher has not pitched a complete game.

EXISTS

Use the EXISTS predicate in conjunction with a subquery, to find out whether the subquery returns any rows at all. If the subquery returns at least one row, then the EXISTS condition is satisfied, and the outer query is performed. Consider the example:

```
SELECT FIRST_NAME, LAST_NAME
  FROM CUSTOMER
  WHERE EXISTS
    (SELECT *
      FROM SALES
      WHERE SALES.CUSTOMER_ID = CUSTOMER.CUSTOMER_ID);
```

The SALES table contains a record of all a company's sales. It includes the CUSTOMER_ID of the customer who made each purchase, as well as other pertinent information. The CUSTOMER table contains each customer's first and last names, but no information about specific transactions.

The subquery in the preceding example will return a row for every sale to a customer who is listed in the CUSTOMER table. The outer query will return the first and last names of the customers who made the purchases recorded in the SALES table.

EXISTS is equivalent to a comparison of COUNT with zero, as the following query shows:

```
SELECT FIRST_NAME, LAST_NAME
  FROM CUSTOMER
  WHERE 0 <>
    (SELECT COUNT(*)
      FROM SALES
      WHERE SALES.CUSTOMER_ID = CUSTOMER.CUSTOMER_ID);
```

For every row in the SALES table whose CUSTOMER_ID is equal to a CUSTOMER_ID in the CUSTOMER table, this statement displays the FIRST_NAME and LAST_NAME columns in the CUSTOMER table. This means that, for every sale in the SALES table, the name of the customer who made the purchase is displayed.

UNIQUE

Like the EXISTS predicate, the UNIQUE predicate is used with a subquery. While the EXISTS predicate evaluates to True only if the subquery returns at least one row, the UNIQUE predicate evaluates to True only if no two of the rows returned by the subquery are identical. In other words, the UNIQUE predicate evaluates to True only if all rows returned by its subquery are unique. For example:

```
SELECT FIRST_NAME, LAST_NAME
  FROM CUSTOMER
  WHERE UNIQUE
    (SELECT CUSTOMER_ID FROM SALES
        WHERE SALES.CUSTOMER_ID = CUSTOMER.CUSTOMER_ID);
```

This will retrieve the names of all new customers who have only one sale recorded in the SALES table.

OVERLAPS

Use the OVERLAPS predicate to find out if two intervals of time overlap each other. This is useful in avoiding scheduling conflicts. If the two intervals overlap, the predicate returns a True value. If they do not, it returns a False value.

You can specify an interval in two ways, either as a start time and an end time, or as a start time and a duration. Here are a few examples:

```
(TIME '2:55:00', INTERVAL '1' HOUR)
OVERLAPS
(TIME '3:30:00', INTERVAL '2' HOUR)
```

returns a True because 3:30 is less than one hour after 2:55.

```
(TIME '9:00:00', TIME '9:30:00')
OVERLAPS
(TIME '9:29:00', TIME '9:31:00')
```

returns a True because there is one minute of overlap between the two intervals.

```
(TIME '9:00:00', TIME '10:00:00')
OVERLAPS
(TIME '10:15:00', INTERVAL '3' HOUR)
```

returns a False because the two intervals do not overlap.

```
(TIME '9:00:00', TIME '9:30:00)
OVERLAPS
(TIME '9:30:00', TIME '9:35:00)
```

returns a False because even though the two intervals are contiguous, they do not overlap.

MATCH

In Chapter 6 I discussed referential integrity, which has to do with maintaining consistency in a multitable database. You can lose integrity by adding a row to a child table that does not have a corresponding row in the child's parent table. You could cause similar problems by deleting a row from a parent table when rows corresponding to that row exist in a child table.

Let's say your business has a CUSTOMER table that keeps track of all your customers, and a SALES table that records all sales transactions. You would not want to add a row to SALES until the customer making the purchase exists in the CUSTOMER table. You would not want to delete a customer from the CUSTOMER table, if that customer had made purchases that existed in the SALES table. Before performing an insertion or deletion, you may want to check the candidate row to make sure inserting or deleting it will not cause integrity problems. The MATCH predicate is designed to perform such a check.

Let's examine the use of the MATCH predicate through an example that employs the CUSTOMER and SALES tables. CUSTOMER_ID is the primary key of the CUSTOMER table and acts as a foreign key in the SALES table. Every row in the CUSTOMER table must have a unique, non-null CUSTOMER_ID. CUSTOMER_ID will not be unique in the SALES table, because repeat customers will buy more than once. This is fine and does not threaten integrity, because CUSTOMER_ID is a foreign key rather than a primary key in that table.

It would seem that CUSTOMER_ID could be null in the SALES table because someone could walk in off the street, buy something, and walk out again without allowing you to enter his name and address into the CUSTOMER table. This would create a row in the child table with no corresponding row in the parent table. To overcome this problem, you could create a generic customer in the CUSTOMER table and assign all such anonymous sales to that customer. ∎

Say a customer steps up to the cash register and claims that she bought an F-117A Stealth fighter on May 1, 1996. She now wants to return it because it shows up like an aircraft carrier on opponent radar screens. You can verify her claim by searching your SALES database for a match. First retrieve her CUSTOMER_ID into the variable *vcustid*, then

```
... WHERE (vcustid, F-117A, 05/01/96)
        MATCH
        (SELECT CUSTOMER_ID, PRODUCT_ID, SALE_DATE
            FROM SALES)
```

If a sale was recorded for that customer ID for that product on that date, the MATCH predicate returns a True value. Give the customer her money back. Note that if any of the values in the first argument of the MATCH predicate are null, a True value is always returned.

The MATCH predicate and UNIQUE predicate were added to SQL for the same reason — they provide a way to explicitly perform the tests that are defined for the implicit referential integrity (RI) and UNIQUE constraints. ∎

The general form of the MATCH predicate is

```
Row_value MATCH  {UNIQUE | PARTIAL | FULL } Subquery
```

The UNIQUE, PARTIAL, and FULL options relate to rules that come into play when the *Row_value* has one or more columns that are null. The rules for the MATCH predicate are a copy of corresponding referential integrity rules.

Referential integrity rules

Referential integrity rules require that the values of a column or columns in one table match the values of a column or columns in another table. The columns in the first table are referred to as the "foreign key," and the columns in the second table are referred to as the "primary key" or "unique key." For example, you might declare a column called EMP_DEPTNO in an EMPLOYEE table to be a foreign key referencing the DEPTNO column of a DEPT table. This ensures that if an employee is recorded in the EMPLOYEE table as being in department 123, that there will be a row in the DEPT table where DEPTNO is 123.

This is fairly straightforward when the foreign key and primary key consist of a single column. They can, however, consist of multiple columns. For example, the DEPTNO value may only be unique within a LOCATION, so that to uniquely identify a DEPT row you must specify both a LOCATION and a DEPTNO. For example, if both the Boston and Tampa offices have a department 123, then you'd have to identify the departments as ('Boston', '123') and

('Tampa', '123'). In this case, the EMPLOYEE table will need to have two columns to identify a DEPT. Let's call those columns EMP_LOC and EMP_DEPTNO. If an employee works in department 123 in Boston, then the EMP_LOC and EMP_DEPTNO values will be 'Boston' and '123'. And, the foreign key declaration in EMPLOYEE will be

```
FOREIGN KEY (EMP_LOC, EMP_DEPTNO)
    REFERENCES DEPT (LOCATION, DEPTNO)
```

When the values of EMP_LOC and EMP_DEPTNO are both non-null or both null, the referential integrity rules are the same as for single-column keys whose values are null or non-null. But when EMP_LOC is null and EMP_DEPTNO is non-null, or EMP_DEPTNO is non-null and EMP_DEPTNO is null, new rules are needed. What should the rules be when you insert or update the EMPLOYEE table with EMP_LOC and EMP_DEPTNO values of (NULL, '123') or ('Boston', NULL). There are three main alternatives, referred to as FULL, PARTIAL, and UNIQUE. I'll summarize these alternatives:

- ✔ FULL. Prohibit partial nulls. For example, ('Boston', '123') and (NULL, NULL) are okay, but ('Boston', NULL) and (NULL, '123') would both be illegal.

- ✔ PARTIAL. Allow partial nulls, and validate the non-null values. For example, allow ('Boston', NULL) if and only if there is at least one DEPT with LOCATION 'Boston'; and allow (NULL, '123') if and only if there is at least one DEPT with DEPTNO '123'.

- ✔ UNIQUE. Allow partial nulls, and specify that if *any* column is null, the foreign key is regarded as completely null. For example, treat ('Boston', NULL) and (NULL, '123') the same as (NULL, NULL).

The UNIQUE rule initially sounds peculiar. It says that you allow an EMPLOYEE row ('Boston', NULL) even though there is no DEPT row with LOCATION 'Boston'. The reason you might want to do this is to deal with the following case.

Suppose you want to insert an employee that you know will work in Boston, even though you don't yet know which department in Boston he'll work in. Moreover, the department he'll work in may not yet exist. In fact, there may not yet be *any* departments for Boston. You would follow these steps:

1. You insert one or more rows into DEPT that have a LOCATION 'Boston' and also have some DEPTNO.

2. You update the EMPLOYEE row and change ('Boston', NULL) to ('Boston', '123'). At this point, the referential integrity validation of the UPDATE will require that there be a DEPT row for ('Boston', '123').

Rule by committee

The UNIQUE rule was specified in the SQL-89 version of the standard as the default, before the other alternatives had been proposed or debated. Then, during development of the SQL-92 version of the standard, the other alternatives were proposed. Some people strongly preferred the PARTIAL rules, and argued that they should be the only rules. They felt that the SQL-89 (UNIQUE) rules were so undesirable that they should be considered a bug, and the PARTIAL rules should be specified as a correction. Other people preferred the UNIQUE rules, and felt that the PARTIAL rules were obscure, error-prone, and inefficient. Still other people preferred

the additional discipline of the FULL rules. The issue was finally settled by providing the three keywords, so that the user could choose whichever approach she preferred.

Because the UNIQUE rules were specified in SQL-89, before the additional alternatives were provided, the UNIQUE alternative is the default, for compatibility. This explains why if any of the values in the first argument of the MATCH predicate are null, a True value is always returned. This is because UNIQUE is the default, and for UNIQUE, any null value means "don't perform the check."

Logical Connectives

Often, as you have seen in a number of previous examples, applying one condition in a query is not enough to return the rows that you want from a table. In some cases, the rows must satisfy two or more conditions. In other cases, if a row satisfies any of two or more conditions, it qualifies for retrieval. There are also occasions when we want to retrieve only rows that do *not* satisfy a specified condition. To meet these needs, SQL has the logical connectives AND, OR, and NOT.

AND

If multiple conditions must all be True before a row is retrieved, use the AND logical connective. Consider this example:

```
SELECT INVOICE_NO, SALE_DATE, SALESPERSON, TOTAL_SALE
   FROM SALES
   WHERE SALE_DATE >= 05/01/96
      AND SALE_DATE <= 05/07/96 ;
```

In the WHERE clause two conditions must be met:

■ ✔ SALE_DATE must be greater than or equal to May 1, 1996.

■ ✔ SALE_DATE must be less than or equal to May 7, 1996.

Only rows that record sales occurring during the week of May 1 meet both conditions. The query returns only these rows.

Note that the AND connective is strictly logical. This can sometimes be confusing, since the word "and" is commonly used with a looser meaning. For example, suppose your boss says to you "I'd like to see the sales for Ferguson and Ford." He said "Ferguson and Ford," so you might write this SQL query:

```
SELECT *
   FROM SALES
   WHERE SALESPERSON = 'Ferguson'
      AND SALESPERSON = 'Ford';
```

Well, don't take that answer back to your boss. This is more what he had in mind:

```
SELECT *
   FROM SALES
   WHERE SALESPERSON IN ('Ferguson', 'Ford') ; ■
```

OR

If any one of two or more conditions must be True to qualify a row for retrieval, use the OR logical connective. Here is an example:

```
SELECT INVOICE_NO, SALE_DATE, SALESPERSON, TOTAL_SALE
   FROM SALES
      WHERE SALESPERSON = 'Ford'
         OR TOTAL_SALE > 200 ;
```

This query will retrieve all of Ford's sales, regardless of how large they are, as well as all sales of over $200, regardless of who made them.

NOT

The NOT connective negates a condition. If the condition would normally return a True value, adding NOT will cause it to return a False value. If it would normally return a False value, adding NOT will cause it to return a True value. For example:

```
SELECT INVOICE_NO, SALE_DATE, SALESPERSON, TOTAL_SALE
   FROM SALES
      WHERE NOT (SALESPERSON = 'Ford') ;
```

This query returns rows for all sales transactions completed by salespeople other than Ford.

When using AND, OR, or NOT, sometimes it is not clear what the scope of the connective is. To be safe, use parentheses to make sure that the connective is applied to the predicate you want. In the preceding example, the NOT connective applies to the entire predicate (SALESPERSON = 'Ford'). ■

GROUP BY Clauses

When you retrieve rows from a table with a SELECT statement, they will be returned in the order in which they appear in their source table. Usually, this order is not the most meaningful. Often you will want to group related rows together so that you can get a sense of the overall content of each group. The GROUP BY clause allows you to specify a column (or several columns) as a *grouping column*. In the output table, all rows with an identical value in the grouping column will be grouped together.

Suppose you are a sales manager, and you want to look at sales performance for a particular week, with the information grouped by salesperson. The following example shows one way to do it:

```
SELECT INVOICE_NO, SALE_DATE, SALESPERSON, TOTAL_SALE
   FROM SALES
   WHERE SALE_DATE >= 05/01/96
      AND SALE_DATE <= 05/07/96
   GROUP BY SALESPERSON ;
```

The result is:

INVOICE_NO	SALE_DATE	SALESPERSON	TOTAL_SALE
1	05/01/96	Ferguson	1.98
3	05/02/96	Ferguson	249.00
5	05/03/96	Ferguson	4.95
7	05/04/96	Ferguson	12.95
4	05/02/96	Ford	7.50
9	05/07/96	Ford	2.50
10	05/07/96	Ford	2.49
2	05/01/96	Podolocek	3.50
6	05/04/96	Podolocek	3.50
8	05/05/96	Podolocek	5.00

The physical order of the SALES table is by INVOICE_NO, but the GROUP BY clause in the SELECT statement has reordered the rows in the virtual table. Rows are now grouped by salesperson sorted in ascending alphabetical order. Some implementations give you the option of sorting the groups in descending alphabetical order. There is no reordering within a group.

HAVING Clauses

A HAVING clause is a filter that places a further restriction on the virtual table created by a GROUP BY clause. Just as a WHERE clause weeds out unwanted individual rows in a query, a HAVING clause weeds out unwanted groups.

Taking our example from the previous section, say the sales manager wants to focus on the performance of Ford and Podolocek, disregarding the performance of all the other salespeople. She can do so by adding a HAVING clause to the previous query.

```
SELECT INVOICE_NO, SALE_DATE, SALESPERSON, TOTAL_SALE
   FROM SALES
   WHERE SALE_DATE >= 05/01/96
      AND SALE_DATE <= 05/07/96
   GROUP BY SALESPERSON
   HAVING SALESPERSON = 'Ford'
      OR SALESPERSON = 'Podolocek' ;
```

The result is:

INVOICE_NO	SALE_DATE	SALESPERSON	TOTAL_SALE
4	05/02/96	Ford	7.50
9	05/07/96	Ford	2.50
10	05/07/96	Ford	2.49
2	05/01/96	Podolocek	3.50
6	05/04/96	Podolocek	3.50
8	05/05/96	Podolocek	5.00

The argument of the HAVING clause must contain a condition that compares the value of a grouping column to a constant value.

ORDER BY Clauses

Use the ORDER BY clause to display the output table of a query in either ascending or descending alphabetical order. While the GROUP BY clause gathers rows into groups and sorts the groups into alphabetical order, ORDER BY sorts individual rows. The ORDER BY clause must be the last clause specified in a query. If the query also contains a GROUP BY clause, the output rows are first arranged into groups. The ORDER BY clause then sorts the rows within each group. If there is no GROUP BY clause, the entire table is considered to be a group and the ORDER BY clause sorts all its rows according to the column (or columns) specified in the ORDER BY clause.

To illustrate, let's consider the data in the SALES table. Recall that the SALES table has columns for INVOICE_NO, SALE_DATE, SALESPERSON, and TOTAL_SALE. If you simply

```
SELECT * FROM SALES ;
```

you will see all of the SALES data, but in an arbitrary order. On one implementation this may be the order that the rows were inserted, and on another implementation it may be the order of the most recent updates. The order can also change unexpectedly when the database is physically reorganized. So most of the time you'll want to specify the order in which you want to put the rows. For example, you might want to see the rows ordered by the SALE_DATE:

```
SELECT * FROM SALES ORDER BY SALE_DATE ;
```

This will return all of the rows in the SALES table, ordered by SALE_DATE.

For rows that have the same SALE_DATE, the default order depends on the implementation. However, you can specify how to sort the rows that share the same SALE_DATE. For example, you may want to see the SALES for each SALE_DATE ordered by INVOICE_NO:

```
SELECT * FROM SALES ORDER BY SALE_DATE, INVOICE_NO ;
```

This will first order the SALES by SALE_DATE, then for each SALE_DATE it will order the SALES by INVOICE_NO. Don't confuse this with the following query:

```
SELECT * FROM SALES ORDER BY INVOICE_NO, SALE_DATE ;
```

This will first order the SALES by INVOICE_NO, then for each different INVOICE_NO it will order the SALES by SALE_DATE.

Here's another example:

```
SELECT * FROM SALES ORDER BY SALESPERSON, SALE_DATE ;
```

This will first order by SALESPERSON, then by SALE_DATE. After you look at the data in that order, you may want to invert it:

```
SELECT * FROM SALES ORDER BY SALE_DATE, SALESPERSON ;
```

This orders the rows first by SALE_DATE and then by SALESPERSON.

All of these orderings are ascending (ASC), which is the default sort order. The last SELECT shows earlier SALES first, and will show SALES for 'Adams' before 'Baker'. If you prefer descending (DESC) order, you can specify it for one or more of the order columns:

```
SELECT * FROM SALES
ORDER BY SALE_DATE DESC, SALESPERSON ASC ;
```

This specifies a descending order for sales date, showing the more recent sales first, but an ascending order for salespeople, putting them in normal alphabetical order.

Chapter 11

Relational Operators

. . . .

In This Chapter

▶ Combining tables with similar structures

▶ Combining tables with different structures

▶ Deriving meaningful data from multiple tables

. . . .

*S*QL was designed as a query language for relational databases. Up until now I've presented simple databases, and in most cases my examples have dealt with only one table. It's now time to grow up and put the relational in relational database. After all, relational databases are so named because they consist of multiple *related* tables.

Because the data in a relational database is distributed across multiple tables, there are times when a query has to draw data from more than one table. In fact, this is usually the case. SQL-92 has operators that combine data from multiple sources into a single result table. These are the UNION, INTERSECTION, and EXCEPT operators, as well as a family of JOIN operators. Each combines data from multiple tables in a different way.

UNION

The UNION operator is the SQL implementation of relational algebra's union operator. It is useful when you want to draw information from two or more tables that all have the same structure.

By "the same structure" I mean that the tables must all have the same number of columns, and that corresponding columns all have identical data types and lengths. When these criteria are met, the tables are *union-compatible*. The union of two tables returns all the rows that appear in either table, eliminating duplicates. ■

Recal our baseball statistics database, introduced in Chapter 10. Say it contains two union-compatible tables named AMERICAN and NATIONAL. Both tables have three columns, and corresponding columns are all of the same type. In fact, corresponding columns have identical column names (this is not required for union-compatibility).

NATIONAL tells us the names and number of complete games pitched by National League pitchers. AMERICAN gives us the same information about pitchers in the American League. The UNION of the two tables will give us a virtual result table containing all the rows in the first table plus all the rows in the second table. For this example, lets put just a few rows in each table to illustrate the operation.

```
SELECT * FROM NATIONAL

FIRST_NAME   LAST_NAME   COMPLETE_GAMES
----------   ---------   --------------
Sal          Maglie                  11
Don          Newcombe                 9
Sandy        Koufax                  13
Don          Drysdale                12


SELECT * FROM AMERICAN

FIRST_NAME   LAST_NAME   COMPLETE_GAMES
----------   ---------   --------------
Whitey       Ford                    12
Don          Larson                  10
Bob          Turley                   8
Allie        Reynolds                14


SELECT * FROM NATIONAL
UNION
SELECT * FROM AMERICAN

FIRST_NAME   LAST_NAME   COMPLETE_GAMES
----------   ---------   --------------
Allie        Reynolds                14
Bob          Turley                   8
Don          Drysdale                12
Don          Larson                  10
Don          Newcombe                 9
Sal          Maglie                  11
Sandy        Koufax                  13
Whitey       Ford                    12
```

I've been using the asterisk (*) as shorthand for all the columns in a table. This is fine most of the time, but it can get you into trouble when you are using relational operators in embedded or module language SQL. What if one or more new columns are added to one table and not to another, or different columns are added to the two tables? Then the two tables will no longer be union-compatible, and your program will be invalid the next time it is recompiled. Even if the same new columns are added to both tables, so that they are still union-compatible, your program is probably not prepared to deal with this additional data. So it is generally a good idea to explicitly list the columns that you want, rather than to rely on the "*" shorthand. When you are entering ad hoc SQL from the console, the asterisk is probably all right, since you can quickly display table structure to verify union-compatibility if your query is not successful. ■

The UNION operation normally eliminates any duplicate rows that result from its operation. Most of the time this is the desired behavior. However, sometimes you may want to preserve duplicate rows. On those occasions use UNION ALL.

Referring to our example, suppose "Bullet" Bob Turley had been traded in midseason from the New York Yankees in the American League to the Brooklyn Dodgers in the National League. Suppose further that during the season he pitched eight complete games for each team. The ordinary UNION displayed above would throw away one of the two lines containing Turley's data. It would seem that he had pitched only eight complete games in the season when in fact he had hurled a remarkable 16 complete games. The following query would give us the true facts:

```
SELECT * FROM NATIONAL
UNION ALL
SELECT * FROM AMERICAN
```

It is sometimes possible to form the UNION of two tables even if they are not union-compatible. If the columns you want in your result table are present and compatible in both tables, you can perform a UNION CORRESPONDING operation. Only the specified columns will be considered, and they will be the only columns displayed in the result table.

Baseball statisticians keep entirely different statistics on pitchers from the ones they keep on outfielders. However, some information is common. In both cases first name, last name, putouts, errors, and fielding percentage are recorded. Outfielders, of course, do not have a won/lost record, a saves record, or a number of other things that pertain only to pitching. We can still perform a UNION that takes data from the OUTFIELDER table and from the PITCHER table to give us some overall information about defensive skill.

```
SELECT *
    FROM OUTFIELDER
UNION CORRESPONDING
    (FIRST_NAME, LAST_NAME, PUTOUTS, ERRORS, FIELD_PCT)
SELECT *
    FROM PITCHER ;
```

The result table will hold the first and last names of all the outfielders and pitchers, along with the number of putouts, errors, and the fielding percentage of each player. As with the simple UNION, duplicates are eliminated. Thus if a player spent some time in the outfield as well as being a pitcher, the UNION CORRESPONDING operation would lose some of his statistics.

Each name in the list following the CORRESPONDING keyword must be a name that exists in both of the unioned tables. If you omit this list of names, there will be an implicit list of all names that appear in both tables. However, this implicit list of names may change when new columns are added to one or both of the tables, so it is better to explicitly list the column names. ∎

INTERSECT

The UNION operation produces a result table containing all rows that appear in *any* of the source tables. If you want only rows that appear in *all* the source tables, you can use the INTERSECT operation, which is the SQL implementation of relational algebra's intersect operation. I'll illustrate INTERSECT by returning to the fantasy world in which Bob Turley was traded to the Dodgers in midseason.

```
SELECT * FROM NATIONAL

FIRST_NAME    LAST_NAME    COMPLETE_GAMES
----------    ---------    --------------

Sal           Maglie                   11
Don           Newcombe                  9
Sandy         Koufax                   13
Don           Drysdale                 12
Bob           Turley                    8


SELECT * FROM AMERICAN

FIRST_NAME    LAST_NAME    COMPLETE_GAMES
----------    ---------    --------------

Whitey        Ford                     12
Don           Larson                   10
Bob           Turley                    8
Allie         Reynolds                 14
```

Only rows that appear on all source tables will show up in the INTERSECT operation's result table.

```
SELECT *
   FROM NATIONAL
INTERSECT
SELECT *
   FROM AMERICAN

FIRST_NAME  LAST_NAME  COMPLETE_GAMES
----------  ---------  --------------
Bob         Turley                  8
```

The result table tells us that Bob Turley was the only pitcher to throw the same number of complete games in both leagues. A rather obscure distinction for old Bullet Bob.

The ALL and CORRESPONDING keywords function in an INTERSECT operation the same way they do in a UNION operation. If you use ALL, duplicates are retained in the result table. If you use CORRESPONDING, the intersected tables need not be union-compatible, although the corresponding columns need to have matching types and lengths.

Consider another example. A municipality keeps track of the pagers carried by police officers, fire fighters, street sweepers, and other city employees. A database table called PAGERS contains data on all pagers in active use. Another table named OUT, with an identical structure, contains data on all pagers that for one reason or another have been taken out of service. There should never be a situation where a pager exists in both tables. You can test to see if such an unwanted duplication has occurred with an INTERSECT operation:

```
SELECT *
   FROM PAGERS
INTERSECT CORRESPONDING (PAGER_ID)
SELECT *
   FROM OUT
```

If the result table contains any rows at all, you know there is a problem. Any PAGER_ID entries that appear in the result table should be investigated. The corresponding pager is either active or out of service. It cannot be both. After the problem is detected, you can perform a DELETE operation on one of the two tables to restore database integrity.

EXCEPT

The UNION operation acts on two source tables and returns all rows that appear in *either* table. The INTERSECT operation returns all rows that appear in *both* the first and the second table. In contrast, the EXCEPT operation returns all rows that appear in the first table that *do not* also appear in the second table.

Let's return to our municipal pager database example. Say that a group of pagers that had been declared out of service and returned to the vendor for repairs have now been fixed and placed back into service. The PAGERS table was updated to reflect the returned pagers, but for some reason the returned pagers were not removed from the OUT table as they should have been. You can display the Pager ID numbers of the pagers in the OUT table, with the reactivated ones eliminated, using an EXCEPT operation.

```
SELECT *
    FROM OUT
EXCEPT CORRESPONDING (PAGER_ID)
SELECT *
    FROM PAGERS
```

This returns all the rows in the OUT table whose PAGER_ID is not also present in the PAGERS table.

Joins

The UNION, INTERSECT, and EXCEPT operators are valuable in multitable databases where the tables are union-compatible. There are many cases, however, when you will want to draw data from multiple tables that have very little in common. Joins are powerful relational operators that combine data from multiple tables into a single result table. The source tables may have little (or even nothing) in common with each other.

SQL-92 supports a number of different types of joins. The best one to choose in a given situation will depend on what result you are trying to achieve.

Basic join

Any multitable query is a type of join. The source tables are joined in the sense that the result table includes information taken from all of the source tables. The simplest join is a two-table SELECT in which there are no WHERE clause qualifiers. Every row of the first table is joined to every row of the second table. The result table is the Cartesian product of the two source tables. (I discussed the notion of Cartesian product in Chapter 10, in connection with the FROM clause.) The number of rows in the result table is equal to the number of rows in the first source table multiplied by the number of rows in the second source table.

Let's look at an example. Imagine that you are the personnel manager for a company, and it is your job to maintain records on the employees. Most of the data for an employee, such as home address and telephone number, is not particularly sensitive. However some, such as current salary, should be available only to authorized personnel. To maintain security of the sensitive information, you keep it in a separate table that is password protected. Consider the following pair of tables:

```
EMPLOYEE                    COMPENSATION
--------                    ------------
EMP_ID                      EMPLOY
F_NAME                      SALARY
L_NAME                      BONUS
CITY
PHONE
```

Fill the tables with some sample data:

```
EMP_ID F_NAME L_NAME    CITY     PHONE
------ ------ --------  -------  --------
     1 Whitey Ford      Orange   555-1001
     2 Don    Larson    Newark   555-3221
     3 Allie  Reynolds  Nutley   555-6905
     4 Bob    Turley    Passaic  555-8908

EMPLOY SALARY BONUS
------ ------ -----
     1  33000 10000
     2  18000  2000
     3  24000  5000
     4  22000  7000
```

Create a virtual result table with the following query:

```
SELECT *
   FROM EMPLOYEE, COMPENSATION ;
```

producing:

```
EMP_ID F_NAME L_NAME CITY     PHONE     EMPLOY SALARY BONUS
------ ------ ------ -------  --------  ------ ------ -----
     1 Whitey Ford   Orange   555-1001       1  33000 10000
     1 Whitey Ford   Orange   555-1001       2  18000  2000
     1 Whitey Ford   Orange   555-1001       3  24000  5000
     1 Whitey Ford   Orange   555-1001       4  22000  7000
     2 Don    Larson Newark   555-3221       1  33000 10000
     2 Don    Larson Newark   555-3221       2  18000  2000
     2 Don    Larson Newark   555-3221       3  24000  5000
     2 Don    Larson Newark   555-3221       4  22000  7000
     3 Sal    Maglie Nutley   555-6905       1  33000 10000
     3 Sal    Maglie Nutley   555-6905       2  18000  2000
     3 Sal    Maglie Nutley   555-6905       3  24000  5000
     3 Sal    Maglie Nutley   555-6905       4  22000  7000
     4 Bob    Turley Passaic  555-8908       1  33000 10000
     4 Bob    Turley Passaic  555-8908       2  18000  2000
     4 Bob    Turley Passaic  555-8908       3  24000  5000
     4 Bob    Turley Passaic  555-8908       4  22000  7000
```

The result table, which is the Cartesian product of the EMPLOYEE and the COMPENSATION tables, contains considerable redundancy. Furthermore, it doesn't make much sense. It combines every row of EMPLOYEE with every row of COMPENSATION. Of these, the only rows that convey meaningful information are those in which the EMP_ID number that came from EMPLOYEE matches the EMPLOY number that came from COMPENSATION. In those rows an employee's name and address are associated with that same employee's compensation.

When you are trying to get useful information out of a multitable database, the Cartesian product produced by a basic join is almost never what you want. However, it is almost always the first step toward what you want. By applying constraints to the join with a WHERE clause, you can filter out the unwanted rows. The most common join that uses the WHERE clause filter is the equi-join.

Equi-join

An *equi-join* is a basic join with a WHERE clause containing a condition specifying that the value in one column in the first table must be equal to the value of a corresponding column in the second table. If we apply an equi-join to the example tables from the previous section, we get a much more meaningful result,

```
SELECT *
  FROM EMPLOYEE, COMPENSATION
  WHERE EMPLOYEE.EMP_ID = COMPENSATION.EMPLOY ;
```

producing:

```
EMP_ID F_NAME L_NAME  CITY     PHONE     EMPLOY SALARY BONUS
------ ------ ------  -------  --------  ------ ------ -----
     1 Whitey Ford    Orange   555-1001       1  33000 10000
     2 Don    Larson  Newark   555-3221       2  18000  2000
     3 Sal    Maglie  Nutley   555-6905       3  24000  5000
     4 Bob    Turley  Passaic  555-8908       4  22000  7000
```

In this result table, the salaries and bonuses on the right apply to the employees named on the left. There is still some redundancy in the table however, since the EMP_ID column duplicates the EMPLOY column. We can fix this problem with a slight reformulation of the query.

```
SELECT EMPLOYEE.*,COMPENSATION.SALARY,COMPENSATION.BONUS
    FROM EMPLOYEE, COMPENSATION
    WHERE EMPLOYEE.EMP_ID = COMPENSATION.EMPLOY ;
```

This will produce:

```
EMP_ID F_NAME L_NAME  CITY     PHONE     SALARY BONUS
------ ------ ------  -------  --------  ------ -----
     1 Whitey Ford    Orange   555-1001   33000 10000
     2 Don    Larson  Newark   555-3221   18000  2000
     3 Sal    Maglie  Nutley   555-6905   24000  5000
     4 Bob    Turley  Passaic  555-8908   22000  7000
```

This table tells us what we want to know, and doesn't burden us with any extraneous data. However the query was somewhat tedious to write. To avoid ambiguity it is good practice to *qualify* the column names with the names of the tables they came from. Writing those table names repeatedly provides good exercise for the fingers, but otherwise has no merit.

We can cut down on the amount of typing by using aliases (or correlation names). An *alias* is a short name that stands for a table name. If we had used aliases in the preceding query, it would have looked like:

```
SELECT E.*, C.SALARY, C.BONUS
    FROM EMPLOYEE E, COMPENSATION C
    WHERE E.EMP_ID = C.EMPLOY ;
```

In this example, E is the alias for EMPLOYEE and C is the alias for COMPENSATION. The alias is local to the statement it is in. Once you have declared an alias (in the FROM clause), you must use it throughout the statement. You can't use both the alias and the long form of the table name. ■

The reason for not mixing the long form of table names with aliases is to avoid confusion. Consider the following very confusing example:

```
SELECT T1.C, T2.C
    FROM T1 T2, T2 T1
    WHERE T1.C > T2.C ;
```

In this example the alias for T1 is T2 and the alias for T2 is T1. Admittedly, this is not a very smart selection of aliases, but it is not forbidden by the rules. If it were possible to mix aliases with long form table names, you couldn't tell which table was which.

The preceding example with aliases is equivalent to the following SELECT with no aliases:

```
SELECT T2.C, T1.C
    FROM T1 , T2
    WHERE T2.C > T1.C ;
```

SQL-92 allows you to join more than two tables; the maximum number varies from one implementation to another. The syntax is analogous to the two-table case:

```
SELECT E.*, C.SALARY, C.BONUS, Y.TOTAL_SALES
    FROM EMPLOYEE E, COMPENSATION C, YTD_SALES Y
    WHERE E.EMP_ID = C.EMPLOY
        AND C.EMPLOY = Y.EMPNO ;
```

This statement performs an equi-join on three tables, pulling data from corresponding rows of each one to produce a result table showing the salespeople's names, the amount of sales they are responsible for, and their compensation. The sales manager can quickly see whether compensation is in line with production.

You may wonder why it is desirable to store a salesperson's year-to-date sales in a separate YTD_SALES table rather than keeping them in the EMPLOYEE table. There are performance and reliability reasons for doing this. The data in the EMPLOYEE table is relatively static. A person's name, address, and telephone number do not change very often. In contrast, one hopes that year-to-date sales would change very frequently indeed. Since YTD_SALES has fewer columns than EMPLOYEE, it can be updated more quickly. If in the course of updating sales totals you do not touch the EMPLOYEE table, there is less chance of accidentally modifying EMPLOYEE information that should stay the same. ■

Cross join

SQL-92 introduces the new keyword CROSS JOIN for the basic join without a WHERE clause that previous versions of SQL supported. Thus,

```
SELECT *
FROM EMPLOYEE, COMPENSATION ;
```

can now also be written:

```
SELECT *
FROM EMPLOYEE CROSS JOIN COMPENSATION ;
```

The result is the Cartesian product (also called cross product) of the two source tables. As I said when discussing the basic join, the cross join will rarely give you the final result you want, but it can be useful as the first step in a chain of data manipulation operations that ultimately produce the desired result.

Natural join

The natural join is a special case of an equi-join. In the WHERE clause of an equi-join, a column from one source table is compared with a column of a second source table for equality. The two columns must be of the same type and length. This is all true of a natural join, but in addition the columns being compared must have the same name. In fact, in a natural join, *all* columns in one table that have the same names as corresponding columns in the second table are compared for equality.

Let's imagine that the COMPENSATION table from the preceding example has columns EMP_ID, SALARY, and BONUS rather than EMPLOY, SALARY, and BONUS. If that were the case, then you could perform a natural join of the COMPENSATION table with the EMPLOYEE table. The traditional join syntax would look like this:

```
SELECT E.*, C.SALARY, C.BONUS
   FROM EMPLOYEE E, COMPENSATION C
   WHERE E.EMP_ID = C.EMP_ID ;
```

This is a natural join. SQL-92 introduces a new syntax for the same operation:

```
SELECT E.*, C.SALARY, C.BONUS
   FROM EMPLOYEE E NATURAL JOIN COMPENSATION C ;
```

Implementations that do not yet support the new syntax will still successfully perform a natural join the old-fashioned way.

Condition join

A *condition join* is like an equi-join, except the condition being tested does not have to be equality (although it could be). It can be any well-formed predicate. If the condition is satisfied, the corresponding row becomes part of the result table. The syntax is a little different from what you have seen so far, in that the condition is contained in an ON clause rather than a WHERE clause.

As an example, let's say our baseball statistician wants to know what National League pitchers have pitched exactly the same number of complete games as at least one American League pitcher. This is a job for an equi-join, which can also be expressed with condition join syntax.

```
SELECT *
   FROM NATIONAL JOIN AMERICAN
   ON NATIONAL.COMPLETE_GAMES = AMERICAN.COMPLETE_GAMES ;
```

The question now arises, "What National League pitchers have pitched a number of complete games that no American League pitcher has pitched? Inquiring minds want to know." The condition join that does the job is similar to the preceding one:

```
SELECT *
   FROM NATIONAL JOIN AMERICAN
   ON NATIONAL.COMPLETE_GAMES <> AMERICAN.COMPLETE_GAMES ;
```

Column-name join

The *column-name join* is like a natural join, but it is more flexible. In a natural join, all columns in the source tables that have the same name are compared against each other for equality. With the column-name join, you select which same name columns are to be compared and which are not. You can choose them all if you wish, making the column-name join effectively a natural join. Or you may choose fewer than all same-name columns. In this way you have a great degree of control over which cross product rows qualify to be placed into your result table.

Let's look at an everyday example. Say you are a chess set manufacturer and you have one inventory table to keep track of your stock of white pieces and another table to keep track of black pieces. The tables contain data as follows:

```
WHITE                              BLACK
-----                              -----

Piece   Quant   Wood               Piece   Quant   Wood
-----   -----   -----              -----   -----   -----
King      502   Oak                King      502   Ebony
Queen     398   Oak                Queen     397   Ebony
Rook     1020   Oak                Rook     1020   Ebony
Bishop    985   Oak                Bishop    985   Ebony
Knight    950   Oak                Knight    950   Ebony
Pawn      431   Oak                Pawn      453   Ebony
```

For each type of piece, the number of white pieces should match the number of black pieces. If they do not match, some chessmen are being lost or stolen and you will need to tighten up security measures. A natural join would compare all columns with the same name for equality. In this case a result table with no rows would be produced since no rows in the WOOD column in the WHITE table match any of the rows in the WOOD column in the BLACK table. This would not help us determine whether any merchandise is missing. Instead, do a column-name join which excludes the WOOD column from consideration. It could take the following form:

```
SELECT *
    FROM WHITE JOIN BLACK
    USING (PIECE, QUANT) ;
```

The result table shows only the rows for which the number of white pieces in stock equals the number of black pieces.

```
Piece   Quant   Wood    Piece   Quant   Wood
------  -----   -----   ------  -----   -----
King      502   Oak     King      502   Ebony
Rook     1020   Oak     Rook     1020   Ebony
Bishop    985   Oak     Bishop    985   Ebony
Knight    950   Oak     Knight    950   Ebony
```

The shrewd person can deduce that Queen and Pawn are missing from the list and thus there is a shortage somewhere for those piece types.

Inner join

By now you are probably getting the idea that joins are pretty esoteric, and that it takes an uncommon level of spiritual discernment to be able to deal with them adequately. You may have even heard of the mysterious inner join, and speculated that it probably represents the very core or essence of relational operations. Well, ha! The joke is on you. There is nothing mysterious about inner joins at all. In fact, all the joins we have covered so far in this chapter are inner joins. We could have formulated the column-name join in the last example as an inner join by using the following syntax:

```
SELECT *
  FROM WHITE INNER JOIN BLACK
  USING (PIECE, QUANT) ;
```

The result is exactly the same.

The *inner join* is so named to distinguish it from the outer join. An inner join discards all rows from the result table that do not have corresponding rows in both source tables. An *outer join* preserves unmatched rows. That is the difference. There is nothing metaphysical about it.

Outer join

When you are joining two tables, the first one (call it the one on the left) may have rows that do not have matching counterparts in the second table (the one on the right). Conversely, the table on the right may have rows that do not have matching counterparts in the table on the left. If you perform an inner join on those tables, all the unmatched rows are excluded from the output. Outer joins do not exclude them. Actually, there are three different kinds of outer joins: the left outer join, the right outer join, and the full outer join.

Left outer join

In a query that includes a join, the left table is the one that precedes the keyword JOIN and the right table is the one that follows it. The left outer join preserves unmatched rows from the left table, but discards unmatched rows from the right table.

To illustrate outer joins, let's consider a corporate database that maintains records of the company's employees, departments, and locations. The following tables contain the database's example data.

LOCATION	
LOCATION_ID	**CITY**
1	Boston
3	Tampa
5	Chicago

DEPT		
DEPT_ID	**LOCATION_ID**	**NAME**
21	1	Sales
24	1	Admin
27	5	Repair
29	5	Stock

EMPLOYEE		
EMP_ID	**DEPT_ID**	**NAME**
61	24	Kirk
63	27	McCoy

Now suppose you want to see all the data for all employees, including department and location. You can get this with an equi-join:

```
SELECT *
   FROM LOCATION L, DEPT D, EMPLOYEE E
   WHERE L.LOCATION_ID = D.LOCATION_ID
     AND D.DEPT_ID = E.DEPT_ID ;
```

This statement will produce the following result:

```
1    Boston    24   1   Admin    61   24   Kirk
5    Chicago   27   5   Repair   63   27   McCoy
```

This gives all the data for all the employees, including their location and department. The equi-join works because every employee has a location and a department.

Suppose now that you want the data on the locations, with the related department and employee data. This is a different problem, because there might be a location without any associated departments. To get what you want, you'll have to use an outer join, as in the following example:

```
SELECT *
   FROM LOCATION L LEFT OUTER JOIN DEPT D
      ON (L.LOCATION_ID = D.LOCATION_ID)
   LEFT OUTER JOIN EMPLOYEE E
      ON (D.DEPT_ID = E.DEPT_ID);
```

This join pulls data from three tables. First the LOCATION table is joined to the DEPT table. The resulting table is then joined to the EMPLOYEE table. Rows from the table on the left of the LEFT OUTER JOIN operator that have no corresponding row in the table on the right are included in the result. Thus, in the first join, all locations are included, even if there is no department associated with them. In the second join, all departments are included, even if there is no employee associated with them. The result is

```
1    Boston    24    1    Admin    61    24    Kirk
5    Chicago   27    5    Repair   63    27    McCoy
3    Tampa     NULL  NULL NULL     NULL  NULL  NULL
5    Chicago   29    5    Stock    NULL  NULL  NULL
1    Boston    21    1    Sales    NULL  NULL  NULL
```

The first two rows are the same as the two result rows in the previous example. The third row (3 Tampa) has nulls in the department and employee columns because there are no departments defined for Tampa, and there are no employees stationed there. The fourth and fifth rows (5 Chicago and 1 Boston) have data about the Stock and the Sales departments, but the employee columns for these rows contain nulls, because there are no employees in these two departments. This outer join tells us everything that the equi-join told us, plus the following:

- ✔ All the company's locations, whether they have any departments or not

- ✔ All the company's departments, whether they have any employees or not

The rows returned in the preceding example are not guaranteed to be in the order you want. The order may vary from one implementation to the next. To make sure the rows returned are in the order you want, add an ORDER BY clause to your SELECT statement, like this:

```
SELECT *
   FROM LOCATION L LEFT OUTER JOIN DEPT D
      ON (L.LOCATION_ID = D.LOCATION_ID)
   LEFT OUTER JOIN EMPLOYEE E
      ON (D.DEPT_ID = E.DEPT_ID)
   ORDER BY L.LOCATION_ID, D.DEPT_ID, E.EMP_ID;
```

The left outer join may be abbreviated as LEFT JOIN, since there is no such thing as a left inner join. ■

Right outer join

I bet you have figured out how the right outer join will behave. Right! The right outer join preserves unmatched rows from the right table, but discards unmatched rows from the left table. We can use it on the same tables and get the same result, by reversing the order in which we present tables to the join:

```
SELECT *
    FROM EMPLOYEE E RIGHT OUTER JOIN DEPT D
        ON (D.DEPT_ID = E.DEPT_ID)
    RIGHT OUTER JOIN LOCATION L
        ON (L.LOCATION_ID = D.LOCATION_ID) ;
```

In this formulation, the first join produces a table that contains all departments, whether they have an associated employee or not. The second join produces a table that contains all locations, whether they have an associated department or not.

The right outer join can be abbreviated as RIGHT JOIN, since there is no such thing as a right inner join. ■

Full outer join

The full outer join combines the functions of the left outer join and the right outer join. It retains the unmatched rows from both the left and the right tables. Consider the most general case of the company database used in the preceding examples. It could have:

- ✔ Locations that have no departments
- ✔ Departments with no locations
- ✔ Departments with no employees
- ✔ Employees with no departments

To show all locations, departments, and employees, regardless of whether they have corresponding rows in the other tables, use a full outer join. It would have the following form:

```
SELECT *
    FROM LOCATION L FULL JOIN DEPT D
```

```
        ON (L.LOCATION_ID = D.LOCATION_ID)
    FULL JOIN EMPLOYEE E
        ON (D.DEPT_ID = E.DEPT_ID) ;
```

Full outer join can be abbreviated as FULL JOIN, since there is no such thing as a full inner join. ■

Union join

Unlike the other kinds of join, the union join makes no attempt to match a row from the left source table with any of the rows in the right source table. It creates a new virtual table that contains the union of all the columns in both source tables. In the virtual result table the columns that came from the left source table contain all the rows that were in the left source table. For those rows, the columns that came from the right source table all have the null value. Similarly, the columns that came from the right source table contain all the rows that were in the right source table. For those rows, the columns that came from the left source table all have the null value. Thus the table resulting from a union join contains all the columns of both source tables, and a number of rows that is the sum of the number of rows in the two source tables.

The result of a union join by itself is not immediately useful in most cases. It produces a result table with a lot of nulls in it. We can use it, however, in conjunction with the COALESCE expression discussed in Chapter 9, to give us useful information. Let's look at an example.

Suppose you work for a company that designs and builds experimental rockets. You have several projects in the works. You also have several design engineers who have skills in multiple areas. As a manager, you want to know which employees, having which skills, have worked on which projects. Currently, this data is scattered among the EMPLOYEE table, the PROJECTS table, and the SKILLS table.

The EMPLOYEE table carries data about employees, and EMPLOYEE.EMP_ID is its primary key. The PROJECTS table has a row for each project than an employee has worked on. PROJECTS.EMP_ID is a foreign key referencing the EMPLOYEE table. The SKILLS table shows the expertise of each employee. SKILLS.EMP_ID is a foreign key referencing the EMPLOYEE table.

For each employee, there is exactly one row in the EMPLOYEE table, and zero or more rows in the PROJECTS table and the SKILLS table.

Tables 11-1, 11-2, and 11-3 show example data in the three tables.

Table 11-1: EMPLOYEE Table

EMP_ID	NAME
1	Ferguson
2	Frost
3	Toyon

Table 11-2: PROJECTS Table

PROJECT_NAME	EMP_ID
X-63 Structure	1
X-64 Structure	1
X-63 Guidance	2
X-64 Guidance	2
X-63 Telemetry	3
X-64 Telemetry	3

Table 11-3: SKILLS Table

SKILL	EMP_ID
Mechanical Design	1
Aerodynamics	1
Analog Design	2
Gyroscope Design	2
Digital Design	3
R/F Design	3

From the tables you can see that Ferguson has worked on X-63 and X-64 structure design and has expertise in mechanical design and aerodynamic loading.

Now suppose that as a manager, you want to see all the information about all the employees. You decide to apply an equi-join to the EMPLOYEE, PRO-JECTS, and SKILLS tables:

```
SELECT *
   FROM EMPLOYEE E, PROJECTS P, SKILLS S
   WHERE E.EMP_ID = P.EMP_ID
      AND E.EMP_ID = S.EMP_ID ;
```

This same operation can be expressed as an inner join, using the following syntax:

```
SELECT *
   FROM EMPLOYEE E INNER JOIN PROJECTS P
      ON (E.EMP_ID = P.EMP_ID)
   INNER JOIN SKILLS S
      ON (E.EMP_ID = S.EMP_ID ;
```

Both formulations give the same result, shown in Table 11-4.

Table 11-4: Result of INNER JOIN

E.EMP_ID	E.NAME	P.EMP_ID	PROJECT_NAME	S.EMP_ID	S.SKILL
1	Ferguson	1	X-63 Structure	1	Mechanical Design
1	Ferguson	1	X-63 Structure	1	Aerodynamic Loading
1	Ferguson	1	X-64 Structure	1	Mechanical Design
1	Ferguson	1	X-64 Structure	1	Aerodynamic Loading
2	Frost	2	X-63 Guidance	2	Analog Design
2	Frost	2	X-63 Guidance	2	Gyroscope Design
2	Frost	2	X-64 Guidance	2	Analog Design
2	Frost	2	X-64 Guidance	2	Gyroscope Design
3	Toyon	3	X-63 Telemetry	3	Digital Design
3	Toyon	3	X-63 Telemetry	3	R/F Design
3	Toyon	3	X-64 Telemetry	3	Digital Design
3	Toyon	3	X-64 Telemetry	3	R/F Design

This arrangement of the data is not particularly enlightening. The employee ID numbers are triplicated and the projects and skills are duplicated for each employee. The inner joins are not well suited to answering this type of question. We can put the union join to work here, along with some strategically chosen SELECT statements, to produce a more suitable result. Let's begin with the basic union join:

```
SELECT *
    FROM EMPLOYEE E UNION JOIN PROJECTS P
        UNION JOIN SKILLS S ;
```

Notice that the union join has no ON clause. It does no filtering of the data, and so does not need an ON clause. This statement produces the result shown in Table 11-5.

Table 11-5: Result of UNION JOIN

E.EMP_ID	E.NAME	P.EMP_ID	P.PROJECT_NAME	S.EMP_ID	S.SKILL
1	Ferguson	NULL	NULL	NULL	NULL
NULL	NULL	1	X-63 Structure	NULL	NULL
NULL	NULL	1	X-64 Structure	NULL	NULL
NULL	NULL	NULL	NULL	1	Mechanical Design
NULL	NULL	NULL	NULL	1	Aerodynamic Loading
2	Frost	NULL	NULL	NULL	NULL
NULL	NULL	2	X-63 Guidance	NULL	NULL
NULL	NULL	2	X-64 Guidance	NULL	NULL
NULL	NULL	NULL	NULL	2	Analog Design
NULL	NULL	NULL	NULL	2	Gyroscope Design
3	Toyon	NULL	NULL	NULL	NULL
NULL	NULL	3	X-63 Telemetry	NULL	NULL
NULL	NULL	3	X-64 Telemetry	NULL	NULL
NULL	NULL	NULL	NULL	3	Digital Design
NULL	NULL	NULL	NULL		R/F Design

Each table has been extended to the right or left with nulls, and those "null-extended" rows have been unioned. The order of the rows is arbitrary, and depends on the implementation. Now you can "massage" the data to put it in a more useful form.

First notice that there are three ID columns, only one of which is non-null in any row. You can improve the display by *coalescing* the ID columns. Recall from Chapter 9 that the COALESCE expression takes on the value of the first non-null value in a list of values. In the present case, it will take on the value of the only non-null value in a column list.

```
SELECT COALESCE (E.EMP_ID, P.EMP_ID, S.EMP_ID) AS ID,
    E.NAME, P.PROJECT_NAME, S.SKILL
  FROM EMPLOYEE E UNION JOIN PROJECTS P
    UNION JOIN SKILLS S
  ORDER BY ID ;
```

The FROM clause is the same as in the previous example, but now we are coalescing the three EMP_ID columns into a single column named ID. We are also ordering the result by ID. Table 11-6 shows the result.

Table 11-6: Result of UNION JOIN with COALESCE Expression

ID	E.NAME	P.PROJECT_NAME	S.SKILL
1	Ferguson	X-63 Structure	NULL
1	Ferguson	X-64 Structure	NULL
1	Ferguson	NULL	Mechanical Design
1	Ferguson	NULL	Aerodynamic Loading
2	Frost	X-63 Guidance	NULL
2	Frost	X-64 Guidance	NULL
2	Frost	NULL	Analog Design
2	Frost	NULL	Gyroscope Design
3	Toyon	X-63 Telemetry	NULL
3	Toyon	X-64 Telemetry	NULL
3	Toyon	NULL	Digital Design
3	Toyon	NULL	R/F Design

Each row in this result has data about a project or a skill, but not both. When you read the result, you have to first determine what type of information is in each row (project or skill). If the PROJECT_NAME column has a non-null value, the row names a project the employee has worked on. If the SKILL column is non-null, the row names one of the employee's skills.

You can make the result a little clearer by adding another COALESCE to the SELECT statement, as follows:

```
SELECT COALESCE (E.EMP_ID, P.EMP_ID, S.EMP_ID) AS ID,
    E.NAME, COALESCE (P.TYPE, S.TYPE) AS TYPE,
    PROJECT_NAME, S.SKILL
  FROM EMPLOYEE E
```

```
     UNION JOIN (SELECT "Project" AS TYPE, P.*
                     FROM PROJECTS) P
     UNION JOIN (SELECT "Skill" AS TYPE, S.*
                     FROM SKILLS) S
   ORDER BY ID, TYPE ;
```

In the union join the PROJECTS table has been replaced with a nested SELECT that appends a column named P.TYPE, with a constant value "Project", to the columns coming from the PROJECTS table. Similarly, the SKILLS table has been replaced with a nested SELECT that appends a column named S.TYPE, with a constant value "Skill", to the columns coming from the SKILLS table. In each row, P.TYPE will either be null or will be "Project", and S.TYPE will either be null or "Skill".

The outer SELECT list specifies a COALESCE of those two TYPE columns into a single column named TYPE. We then specify TYPE in the ORDER BY clause, which sorts the rows that all have the same ID so that all projects are first, followed by all the skills. The result is shown in Table 11-7.

Table 11-7: Refined Result of UNION JOIN with COALESCE Expressions

ID	E.NAME	TYPE	PROJECT_NAME	SKILL
1	Ferguson	Project	X-63 Structure	NULL
1	Ferguson	Project	X-64 Structure	NULL
1	Ferguson	Skill	NULL	Mechanical Design
1	Ferguson	Skill	NULL	Aerodynamic Loading
2	Frost	Project	X-63 Guidance	NULL
2	Frost	Project	X-64 Guidance	NULL
2	Frost	Skill	NULL	Analog Design
2	Frost	Skill	NULL	Gyroscope Design
3	Toyon	Project	X-63 Telemetry	NULL
3	Toyon	Project	X-64 Telemetry	NULL
3	Toyon	Skill	NULL	Digital Design
3	Toyon	Skill	NULL	R/F Design

The result table now presents a very readable account of the project experience and the skill sets of all the employees in the EMPLOYEE table.

Considering the number of different JOIN operations available, relating data from different tables should not be a problem, regardless of the structure of those tables. Have faith that if the raw data exists in your database, SQL-92 has the means to get it out and display it in a meaningful form.

ON versus WHERE

The function of the ON and WHERE clauses in the various types of joins is potentially confusing. Here are some facts that may help you keep things straight.

- ✔ The ON clause is part of the inner, left, right, and full joins. The cross join and union join don't have an ON clause, because neither of them does any filtering of the data.

- ✔ The ON clause in an inner join is logically equivalent to a WHERE clause: The same condition could be specified either in the ON clause or a WHERE clause.

- ✔ The ON clauses in outer joins (left, right, and full joins) are very different from WHERE clauses. The WHERE clause simply filters the rows that are returned by the FROM clause. Rows that are rejected by the filter are simply not included in the result. The ON clause in an outer join first filters the rows of a cross product, and then includes the rejected rows, extended with nulls.

Chapter 12

Delving Deep with Nested Queries

· ·

In This Chapter

▶ Pulling data from multiple tables with a single SQL statement

▶ Finding data items by comparing a value taken from one table with a set of values taken from another table

▶ Finding data items by comparing a value taken from one table with a single value SELECTed from another table

▶ Finding data items by comparing a value taken from one table with all the corresponding values in another table

▶ Making queries that correlate rows in one table with corresponding rows in another table

▶ Determining which rows to update, delete, or insert through use of a subquery

· ·

*I*n Chapter 6 I said that one of the best ways to protect the integrity of your data is to avoid modification anomalies by normalizing your database. Normalization involves breaking up a single table into multiple tables, each of which has a single theme. You don't want product information in the same table with customer information, even if the customers have bought products.

If you normalize a database properly, the data is scattered across multiple tables. Most queries that you would want to make will need to pull data from two or more tables. One way to do this, as we saw in Chapter 11, is to use a JOIN operator, or one of the other relational operators (UNION, INTERSECT, EXCEPT). The relational operators, recall, take information from multiple tables and combine it all into a single table. Different operators combine the data in different ways. Another way to pull data from two or more tables is to use a nested query.

In SQL, a *nested query* is one in which an outer enclosing statement contains within it a subquery. That subquery may itself serve as an enclosing statement for a lower level subquery that is nested within it. There is no theoretical limit to the number of nesting levels that a nested query may have, although there are implementation-dependent practical limits. ■

Subqueries are invariably SELECT statements, but the outermost enclosing statement could also be an INSERT, UPDATE, or DELETE.

Since a subquery can operate on a different table than the table operated on by its enclosing statement, nested queries give us another way to extract information from multiple tables.

For example, suppose you want to query your corporate database to find all departments whose managers are over 50 years old. With the joins that you've learned, you might use a query like this:

```
SELECT D.DEPTNO, D.NAME, E.NAME, E.AGE
   FROM DEPT D, EMPLOYEE E
   WHERE D.MANAGER_ID = E.ID AND E.AGE > 50 ;
```

D is the alias for the DEPT table and E is the alias for the EMPLOYEE table. The EMPLOYEE table has an ID column that is the primary key, and the DEPT table has a column MANAGER_ID that is the ID value of the employee who is the manager of the department. We use a simple join (the list of tables in the FROM clause) to pair related tables, and a WHERE clause to filter all rows except those that meet our criterion. Note that the select list includes the DEPTNO and NAME columns from the DEPT table, and the NAME and AGE columns from the EMPLOYEE table.

Next, suppose that you are interested in the same set of DEPT rows, but you only want the columns from the DEPT table — in other words, you are interested in the departments whose manager is 50 or older, but you don't care who that manager is or exactly how old she is. You could then write the query with a subquery, rather than a join:

```
SELECT D.DEPTNO, D.NAME
   FROM DEPT D
   WHERE EXISTS (SELECT * FROM EMPLOYEE E
            WHERE E.ID = D.MANAGERID AND E.AGE > 50) ;
```

This query has two new elements: the EXISTS keyword, and the "SELECT *" in the WHERE clause of the first SELECT. The second SELECT is a subquery (or subselect), and the EXISTS keyword is one of several ways of using a subquery that I'll describe in this chapter.

What Subqueries Do

Subqueries are located within the WHERE clause of their enclosing statement. Their function is to set the search conditions for the WHERE clause. Different kinds of subqueries produce different results. Some subqueries produce a list of values that is then used as input by the enclosing statement. Other subqueries produce a single value that the enclosing statement then evaluates with a comparison operator. A third kind of subquery returns a value of True or False.

Why Use One?

In many instances you can accomplish the same result with a subquery that you can with a join. In most cases the complexity of the subquery syntax is comparable to the complexity of the corresponding JOIN operation. It comes down to a matter of personal preference. Some people find it easier to formulate a retrieval in terms of joins and others prefer nested queries. There may be times, however, when it is not possible to get the results you want with a join. In those cases you will either have to use a nested query or break the problem up into multiple SQL statements and execute them one at a time.

Nested Queries that Return Sets of Rows

To illustrate how a nested query returns a set of rows, let's create an example database. Suppose you work for a system integrator of computer equipment. Your company, Zetec Corporation, assembles systems from components that you buy, then sells them to companies and government agencies. You keep track of your business with a relational database. The database consists of many tables, but right now we are only concerned with three of them: the PRODUCT table, the COMP_USED table, and the COMPONENT table. The PRODUCT table (shown in Table 12-1) contains a list of all your standard products. The COMPONENT table (shown in Table 12-2) lists components that go into your products, and the COMP_USED table (shown in Table 12-3) tracks which components go into each product. The tables are defined as follows:

Table 12-1: PRODUCT Table

Column	Type	Constraints
MODEL	Char (6)	NOT NULL, Primary Key
PRODNAME	Char (35)	
PRODDESC	Char (31)	
LISTPRICE	Numeric (9,2)	

Table 12-2: COMPONENT Table

Column	Type	Constraints
COMPID	Char (6)	NOT NULL, Primary Key
COMPTYPE	Char (10)	
COMPDESC	Char (31)	

Table 12-3: COMP_USED Table

Column	Type	Constraints
MODEL	Char (6)	Foreign Key for PRODUCT
COMPID	Char (6)	Foreign Key for COMPONENT

A component may be used in multiple products, and a product can contain multiple components (a many-to-many relationship). This situation could potentially cause integrity problems. To circumvent the problems the *linking table* COMP_USED has been created to relate COMPONENT to PRODUCT. A component may appear in many COMP_USED rows, but each COMP_USED row references only one component (a one-to-many relationship). Similarly, a product may appear in many COMP_USED rows, but each COMP_USED row references only one product (another one-to-many relationship). By adding the linking table, a troublesome many-to-many relationship has been transformed into two relatively simple one-to-many relationships. This process of reducing the complexity of relationships is one example of normalization.

Subqueries introduced by the keyword IN

One form of a nested query compares a single value with the set of values returned by a SELECT. It uses the IN predicate, with the following syntax:

```
SELECT column_list
    FROM table
    WHERE expression IN (subquery) ;
```

The expression in the WHERE clause evaluates to a value. If that value is IN the list returned by the subquery, then the WHERE clause returns a True value and the specified columns from the table row being processed are added to the result table. The subquery may reference the same table referenced by the outer query, or it may reference a different table.

Let's use Zetec's database to demonstrate this type of query. Assume there is a shortage of computer monitors. When you run out of monitors, you will no longer be able to deliver products that include them. You want to know which products will be affected. Enter the following query:

```
SELECT MODEL
    FROM COMP_USED
    WHERE COMPID IN
        (SELECT COMPID
            FROM COMPONENT
            WHERE COMPTYPE = 'Monitor') ;
```

SQL processes the innermost query first, so it processes the COMPONENT table, returning the value of COMPID for every row where COMPTYPE is 'Monitor'. The result is a list of the ID numbers of all monitors. The outer query then compares the value of COMPID in every row in the COMP_USED table against the list. If the comparison is successful, the value of the MODEL column for that row is added to the result table. The result is a list of all product models that include a monitor. Let's actually run the query and see what we get.

```
MODEL
------
CX3000
CX3010
CX3020
MB3030
MX3020
MX3030
```

We now know which products will soon be out of stock. It's time to go to the sales force and tell them to slow down on promoting these particular products.

When you use this form of nested query, the subquery must specify a single column, and the data type of that column must match the data type of the argument preceding the IN keyword. ■

Subqueries introduced by the keyword NOT IN

Just as you can introduce a subquery with the IN keyword, you can do the opposite and introduce it with the NOT IN keyword. In fact, now would be a great time for the management of Zetec to make such a query. By using the query in the preceding section, Zetec management learned what products *not* to sell. That is valuable information, but it doesn't pay the rent. What Zetec management really wants to know is what products *to* sell. They want to emphasize the sale of products that do not contain monitors. A nested query featuring a subquery introduced by the NOT IN keyword will give them the information they want.

```
SELECT MODEL
   FROM COMP_USED
   WHERE MODEL NOT IN
      (SELECT MODEL
          FROM COMP_USED
          WHERE COMPID IN
             (SELECT COMPID
                 FROM COMPONENT
                 WHERE COMPTYPE = 'Monitor')) ;
```

This query produces the following result:

```
MODEL
------
PX3040
PB3050
PX3040
PB3050
```

There are a couple of things worth noting here. First, there are two levels of nesting in this query. The two subqueries are identical to the previous query statement. The only difference is that a new enclosing statement has been wrapped around them. The enclosing statement takes the list of products that contain monitors, and applies to it a SELECT introduced by the NOT IN keyword. The result is a list of all product models except those that contain monitors.

The second thing to notice is that there are duplicates in the result table. This is because a product containing several components that are not monitors will have a row in the COMP_USED table for each of them. The query will create an entry in the result table for each of those rows.

In our example this is not much of a problem, because the result table is short. In the real world, however, such a result table may have hundreds or thousands of rows. To avoid confusion, we need to eliminate the duplicates. This can be easily done by adding the DISTINCT keyword to the query. Only rows that are distinct (different) from all previously retrieved rows will be added to the result table. ■

```
SELECT DISTINCT MODEL
   FROM COMP_USED
   WHERE MODEL NOT IN
      (SELECT MODEL
          FROM COMP_USED
          WHERE COMPID IN
             (SELECT COMPID
                 FROM COMPONENT
                 WHERE COMPTYPE = 'Monitor')) ;
```

As expected, the result is:

```
MODEL
------
PX3040
PB3050
```

Nested Queries that Return a Single Value

It is possible, and often useful, to introduce a subquery with one of the six comparison operators (=, <>, <, <=, >, >=). In such a case, the expression preceding the operator evaluates to a single value and the subquery following the operator must also evaluate to a single value. An exception to this is the case of the *quantified comparison operator*, which is a comparison operator followed by a quantifier (ANY, SOME, or ALL).

To illustrate a case where a subquery returns a single value, let's look at another piece of Zetec Corporation's database. It contains a CUSTOMER table that holds information about the companies that buy Zetec products. It also contains a CONTACT table that holds personal data about individuals at each of Zetec's customer organizations. The tables are structured as shown in tables 12-4 and 12-5.

Table 12-4: CUSTOMER Table

Column	Type	Constraints
CUSTID	Integer	NOT NULL, PRIMARY KEY
COMPANY	Char (40)	
CUSTADDRESS	Char (30)	
CUSTCITY	Char (20)	
CUSTSTATE	Char (2)	
CUSTZIP	Char (10)	
CUSTPHONE	Char (12)	
MODLEVEL	Integer	

Table 12-5: CONTACT Table

Column	Type	Constraints
CUSTID	Integer	Foreign Key
CONTFNAME	Char (10)	
CONTLNAME	Char (16)	
CONTPHONE	Char (12)	
CONTINFO	Char (50)	

Say you want to look at the contact information for Olympic Sales, but you don't remember that company's CUSTID. Use a nested query like this one to recover the information you want:

```
SELECT *
    FROM CONTACT
        WHERE CONTID =
            (SELECT CONTID
                FROM CUSTOMER
                    WHERE COMPANY = 'Olympic Sales') ;
```

The result will look something like this:

```
CUSTID CONTFNAME  CONTLNAME    CONTPHONE      CONTINFO
------ ---------- ------------ -------------- -------------
   118 Jerry      Attwater     505-876-3456   Will play
                                              major role in
                                              coordinating
                                              the
                                              information
                                              superhighway.
```

You can now call Jerry at Olympic and tell him about this month's special sale on fax/modems.

When you use a subquery in an "=" comparison, the SELECT list of the subquery must specify a single column (CONTID in the example). When the subquery is executed, it must return a single row, so that there is a single value for the comparison. ▪

In this example, we are assuming that there is only one row of the CUSTOMER table with a COMPANY value of 'Olympic Sales'. If the CREATE TABLE statement for CUSTOMER specified a UNIQUE constraint for COMPANY, this would guarantee that the subquery in the preceding example would return a single value (or no value). However, subqueries like the one in the example are commonly used on columns that are not specified to be UNIQUE. In such cases, you are relying on some other reasons for believing that the column has no duplicates.

If it turns out that there is more than one CUSTOMER with a COMPANY of 'Olympic Sales' (perhaps in different states), then the subquery will raise an error.

And if there is no CUSTOMER with such a company name, then the subquery is treated as if it were null, and the comparison will be "unknown". In this case, the WHERE clause will return no row (since it returns only rows with the condition True, and filters rows with condition False or "unknown"). This would probably happen, for example, if someone misspelled the COMPANY as 'Olumpic Sales'.

Although the equals operator (=) may be the most common, you could just as well use any of the other five comparison operators in a similar structure. For every row in the table specified in the enclosing statement's FROM clause, the single value returned by the subquery will be compared to the expression in the enclosing statement's WHERE clause. If the comparison gives a True value, a row will be added to the result table.

You can guarantee that a subquery will return a single value if you include an aggregate function in it. Aggregate functions always return a single value. (Aggregate functions are described in Chapter 4.) Of course, this is only helpful if you want the *result* of an aggregate function. Let's look at an example.

Say you are a Zetec salesperson and, because of bills coming due, you need to earn a big commission check this week. You decide that the best way to do that is to concentrate on selling Zetec's most expensive product. You can find out what that product is with a nested query.

```
SELECT MODEL, PRODNAME, LISTPRICE
    FROM PRODUCT
        WHERE LISTPRICE =
            (SELECT MAX(LISTPRICE)
                FROM PRODUCT) ;
```

This is an example of a nested query where both the subquery and the enclosing statement operate on the same table. The subquery returns a single value: the maximum list price in the PRODUCT table. The outer query retrieves all rows from the PRODUCT table that have that list price.

The next example shows a comparison subquery that uses a comparison operator other than =.

```
SELECT MODEL, PRODNAME, LISTPRICE
    FROM PRODUCT
        WHERE LISTPRICE <
            (SELECT AVG(LISTPRICE)
                FROM PRODUCT) ;
```

The subquery returns a single value: the average list price in the PRODUCT table. The outer query retrieves all rows from the PRODUCT table that have a list price less than the average list price.

In the original SQL standard and in most current products, a comparison could have only one subquery, and it had to be on the right-hand side of the comparison. SQL-92 allows either or both operands of the comparison to be subqueries. ∎

The ALL, SOME, and ANY Quantifiers

Another way to make sure that a subquery returns a single value is to introduce it with a quantified comparison operator. The universal quantifier ALL and the existential quantifiers SOME and ANY, when combined with a comparison operator, process the list returned by a subquery, reducing it to a single value.

How these quantifiers affect a comparison is best described through examples. Let's look again at the baseball pitchers complete game database that we used in Chapter 11.

The contents of the two tables are given by the following two queries:

```
SELECT * FROM NATIONAL

FIRST_NAME   LAST_NAME   COMPLETE_GAMES
----------   ---------   --------------
Sal          Maglie                  11
Don          Newcombe                 9
Sandy        Koufax                  13
Don          Drysdale                12
Bob          Turley                   8

SELECT * FROM AMERICAN

FIRST_NAME   LAST_NAME   COMPLETE_GAMES
----------   ---------   --------------
Whitey       Ford                    12
Don          Larson                  10
Bob          Turley                   8
Allie        Reynolds                14
```

Our theory is that the pitchers with the most complete games should be in the American league, because of the presence of designated hitters in that league. One way to verify our theory is to build a query that returns all American League pitchers who have thrown more complete games than all the National League pitchers. The query could be formulated as follows:

```
SELECT *
   FROM AMERICAN
   WHERE COMPLETE_GAMES > ALL
      (SELECT COMPLETE_GAMES FROM NATIONAL) ;
```

The result is:

```
FIRST_NAME   LAST_NAME   COMPLETE_GAMES
----------   ---------   --------------
Allie        Reynolds                14
```

The subquery (SELECT COMPLETE_GAMES FROM NATIONAL) returns the values in the COMPLETE_GAMES column for all National League pitchers.

The > ALL quantifier says to return only those values of COMPLETE_GAMES in the AMERICAN table that are greater than each of the values returned by the subquery. This translates into "greater than the highest value returned by the subquery." In this case the highest value returned by the subquery is 13 (Sandy Koufax). The only row in the AMERICAN table higher than that is Allie Reynolds' record, with 14 complete games.

There is a great temptation to formulate this query in the following way:

```
SELECT *
   FROM AMERICAN
   WHERE COMPLETE_GAMES > ANY
      (SELECT COMPLETE_GAMES FROM NATIONAL) ;
```

To do so would be wrong, however. There is an ambiguity in the English language regarding the use of the words "all" and "any." If you say "Return the names of all the American League pitchers who have pitched more complete games than any pitcher in the National League," you probably intend to get the preceding result. Instead, you get a list of all American League pitchers who have pitched more complete games than the National League pitcher who has pitched the least complete games. The result will be:

```
FIRST_NAME   LAST_NAME   COMPLETE_GAMES
----------   ---------   --------------
Whitey       Ford                    12
Don          Larson                  10
Allie        Reynolds                14
```

This may be easier to understand if we use the equivalent keyword SOME instead of ANY.

```
SELECT *
   FROM AMERICAN
   WHERE COMPLETE_GAMES > SOME
      (SELECT COMPLETE_GAMES FROM NATIONAL) ;
```

In this case we are looking for American League pitchers who have pitched more complete games than SOME National League pitcher. Bob Turley, with eight complete games (in the National League) is SOME National League pitcher. All American League pitchers who have hurled more than eight complete games qualify for the list resulting from this query.

What if your initial assumption was wrong? What if the major league leader in complete games was a National League pitcher, in spite of the fact that the NL has no designated hitter? If that were the case, the query

```
SELECT *
  FROM AMERICAN
  WHERE COMPLETE_GAMES > ALL
    (SELECT COMPLETE_GAMES FROM NATIONAL) ;
```

would return a warning stating that no rows satisfy the conditions of the query. This means that no American League pitcher has thrown more complete games than the pitcher who has thrown the most complete games in the National League.

Nested Queries that Are an Existence Test

A query will return data from all table rows that satisfy the conditions of the query. Sometimes many rows will be returned; sometimes only one. Sometimes none of the rows in the table will satisfy the conditions and no rows will be returned. You can use the EXISTS and NOT EXISTS predicates to introduce a subquery. That structure will tell you whether or not there are any rows in the table located in the subquery's FROM clause that meet the conditions in its WHERE clause.

Subqueries introduced with EXISTS and NOT EXISTS are fundamentally different from the subqueries we have looked at so far in this chapter. In all the previous cases, SQL first executes the subquery, then applies the result of that operation to the enclosing statement. EXISTS and NOT EXISTS subqueries are examples of correlated subqueries.

A *correlated subquery* first finds the table and row specified by the enclosing statement, then executes the subquery on the row in the subquery's table that correlates with the current row of the enclosing statement's table. ■

The subquery either returns one or more rows or it returns none. If it returns at least one row, the EXISTS predicate succeeds, and the action of the enclosing statement is performed. In the same circumstances the NOT EXISTS predicate fails, and the action of the enclosing statement is not performed. After one row of the enclosing statement's table is processed, the same operation is performed on the next row. This action is repeated until every row in the enclosing statement's table has been processed.

EXISTS

Say you are a salesperson for Zetec Corporation and you want to call your primary contact people at all the customers in California. Try the following query:

```
SELECT *
   FROM CONTACT
   WHERE EXISTS
      (SELECT *
          FROM CUSTOMER
          WHERE CUSTSTATE = 'CA'
             AND CONTACT.CUSTID = CUSTOMER.CUSTID) ;
```

Notice the reference to CONTACT.CUSTID, which is referencing a column from the outer query, and comparing it with a column, CUSTOMER.CUSTID from the inner query. That's the way such queries are defined and evaluated: For each candidate row of the outer query, you evaluate the inner query, using the CUSTID value from the current CONTACT row of the outer query for the evaluation of the inner query.

The CUSTID column links the CONTACT table to the CUSTOMER table. SQL looks at the first record in the CONTACT table, finds the row in the CUSTOMER table that has the same CUSTID, and checks that row's CUSTSTATE field. If CUSTOMER.CUSTSTATE = 'CA', the current CONTACT row is added to the result table. The next CONTACT record is then processed in the same way, and so on until the entire CONTACT table has been processed.

NOT EXISTS

In the previous example, the Zetec salesperson wanted to know the names and numbers of the contact people of all the customers located in California. Imagine a second salesperson is responsible for all of the USA except California. She can retrieve her contact people by using NOT EXISTS in a query similar to the preceding one:

```
SELECT *
   FROM CONTACT
   WHERE NOT EXISTS
      (SELECT *
          FROM CUSTOMER
          WHERE CUSTSTATE = 'CA'
             AND CONTACT.CUSTID = CUSTOMER.CUSTID) ;
```

Every row in CONTACT for which the subquery does *not* return a row is added to the result table.

Other Correlated Subqueries

As you saw in a previous section of this chapter, subqueries introduced by IN or by a comparison operator need not be correlated queries, but they can be.

Subqueries introduced with IN

Earlier in this chapter, you saw how a noncorrelated subquery can be used with the IN predicate. To show how a correlated subquery might use the IN predicate, let's ask the same question we asked when discussing the EXISTS predicate. "What are the names and phone numbers of the contacts at all of Zetec's customers in California?" You can answer this question with a correlated IN subquery:

```
SELECT *
   FROM CONTACT
   WHERE 'CA' IN
      (SELECT CUSTSTATE
         FROM CUSTOMER
         WHERE CONTACT.CUSTID = CUSTOMER.CUSTID) ;
```

The statement is evaluated for each record in the CONTACT table. If for that record, the CUSTID numbers in CONTACT and CUSTOMER match, the value of CUSTOMER.CUSTSTATE is compared to 'CA'. The result of the subquery is a list that contains at most one element. If that one element is 'CA', the WHERE clause of the enclosing statement is satisfied and a row is added to the query's result table.

Subqueries introduced with comparison operators

A correlated subquery can also be introduced by one of the six comparison operators. Let's look at another aspect of Zetec's database system to illustrate how.

Zetec pays bonuses to its salespeople based on their total monthly sales volume. The higher the volume, the higher the bonus percentage. The bonus percentage list is kept in a table named BONUSRATE:

MIN_AMOUNT	MAX_AMOUNT	BONUS_PCT
0.00	24999.99	0.
25000.00	49999.99	0.001
50000.00	99999.99	0.002
100000.00	249999.99	0.003
250000.00	499999.99	0.004
500000.00	749999.99	0.005
750000.00	999999.99	0.006

If a person's monthly sales are between $100,000.00 and $249,999.99 the bonus is 0.3% of sales.

Sales are recorded in a transaction master table named TRANSMASTER:

TRANSMASTER

Column	Type	Constraints
TRANSID	INTEGER	NOT NULL, PRIMARY KEY
CUSTID	INTEGER	FOREIGN KEY
EMPID	INTEGER	FOREIGN KEY
TRANSDATE	DATE	
NET_AMOUNT	NUMERIC	
FREIGHT	NUMERIC	
TAX	NUMERIC	
INVOICETOTAL	NUMERIC	

Sales bonuses are based on the sum of the NET_AMOUNT field for all of a person's transactions in the month. You can find any particular person's bonus rate with a correlated subquery that uses comparison operators:

```
SELECT BONUS_PCT
   FROM BONUSRATE
      WHERE MIN_AMOUNT <
         (SELECT SUM (NET_AMOUNT)
            FROM TRANSMASTER
               WHERE EMPID = 133)
      AND MAX_AMOUNT >
         (SELECT SUM (NET_AMOUNT)
            FROM TRANSMASTER
               WHERE EMPID = 133) ;
```

This query is interesting in that it contains two subqueries, making use of the logical connective AND. The subqueries use the SUM aggregate operator, which returns a single value: the total monthly sales of employee number 133. That value is then compared against the MIN_AMOUNT and the

MAX_AMOUNT columns in the BONUSRATE table, producing the bonus rate for that employee.

If you had not known the EMPID, but had known the name of the person in question, you could have arrived at the same answer with a slightly more complex query:

```
SELECT BONUS_PCT
    FROM BONUSRATE
        WHERE MIN_AMOUNT <
            (SELECT SUM (NET_AMOUNT)
                FROM TRANSMASTER
                    WHERE EMPID =
                        (SELECT EMPID
                            FROM EMPLOYEE
                                WHERE EMPLNAME = 'Coffin'))
        AND MAX_AMOUNT >
            (SELECT SUM (NET_AMOUNT)
                FROM TRANSMASTER
                    WHERE EMPID =
                        (SELECT EMPID
                            FROM EMPLOYEE
                                WHERE EMPLNAME = 'Coffin'));
```

This examples uses subqueries nested within subqueries that are in turn nested within an enclosing query, to arrive at the bonus rate for the employee named Coffin. This structure will only work if you know for sure that there is one and only one employee whose last name is Coffin. If there is more than one employee named Coffin, all of their sales will be added together, and the BONUS_PCT calculated will be too high. If you know there is more than one employee named Coffin, you can add terms to the WHERE clause of the innermost subquery until you are sure that only one row of the EMPLOYEE table will be selected.

Subqueries in a HAVING clause

You can have a correlated subquery in a HAVING clause, just as you can in a WHERE clause. As I mentioned in Chapter 10, a HAVING clause is normally preceded by a GROUP BY clause. The HAVING clause acts as a filter to restrict the groups created by the GROUP BY clause. Groups that do not satisfy the condition of the HAVING clause are not included in the result. When used in this way, the HAVING clause is evaluated for each group created by the GROUP BY clause. If there is no GROUP BY clause, the HAVING clause is evaluated for the set of rows passed by the WHERE clause, which is considered to be a single group. If there is neither a WHERE clause nor a GROUP BY clause, the HAVING clause is evaluated for the entire table:

```
SELECT TM1.EMPID
   FROM TRANSMASTER TM1
      GROUP BY TM1.EMPID
      HAVING MAX (TM1.NET_AMOUNT) >= ALL
         (SELECT 2 * AVG (TM2.NET_AMOUNT)
            FROM TRANSMASTER TM2
            WHERE TM1.EMPID <> TM2.EMPID) ;
```

This query uses two aliases for the same table, allowing you to retrieve the employee ID number of all salespeople who had a sale at least twice the average sale of all the other salespeople.

The query works as follows:

1. The outer query groups TRANSMASTER rows by the EMPID. This is done with the SELECT, FROM, and GROUP BY clauses.

2. The HAVING clause will filter these groups. For each group, it calculates the MAX of the NET_AMOUNT column for the rows in that group.

3. The inner query evaluates twice the average NET_AMOUNT from all rows of TRANSMASTER whose EMPID is different from the EMPID of the current group of the outer query. Note that in the last line we need to reference two different EMPID values, so in the FROM clauses of the outer and inner queries we use different aliases for TRANSMASTER.

4. We then use those aliases in the comparison of the last line of the query, to indicate that we are referencing both the EMPID from the current row of the inner subquery (TM2.EMPID) and the EMPID from the current group of the outer subquery (TM1.EMPID).

UPDATE, DELETE, and INSERT Statements

In addition to SELECT statements, UPDATE, DELETE, and INSERT statements can also include WHERE clauses. Those WHERE clauses can contain subqueries in the same way that SELECT statement WHERE clauses do.

For example, Zetec has just signed a volume purchase agreement with Olympic Sales and wants to retroactively provide a 10-percent credit to Olympic for all their purchases in the last month. You can do this with a single UPDATE statement:

```
UPDATE TRANSMASTER
   SET NET_AMOUNT = NET_AMOUNT * 0.9
```

```
WHERE CUSTID =
   (SELECT CUSTID
       FROM CUSTOMER
       WHERE COMPANY = 'Olympic Sales') ;
```

You can also have a correlated subquery within an UPDATE statement. Suppose that the CUSTOMER table has a column LAST_MONTHS_MAX, and that Zetec wants to give such a credit for all purchases that exceed LAST_MONTHS_MAX for the customer:

```
UPDATE TRANSMASTER TM
   SET NET_AMOUNT = NET_AMOUNT * 0.9
   WHERE NET_AMOUNT >
      (SELECT LAST_MONTHS_MAX
          FROM CUSTOMER C
          WHERE C.CUSTID = TM.CUSTID) ;
```

Note that this subquery is correlated: The WHERE clause in the last line references both the CUSTID of the CUSTOMER row from the subquery, and also the CUSTID of the current TRANSMASTER row that is a candidate for being updated.

It is also possible for a subquery in an UPDATE statement to reference the table that is being updated. Suppose that Zetec wants to give a 10-percent credit to customers whose purchases have exceeded $10,000:

```
UPDATE TRANSMASTER TM1
   SET NET_AMOUNT = NET_AMOUNT * 0.9
   WHERE 10000 < SELECT SUM(NET_AMOUNT)
      FROM TRANSMASTER TM2
          WHERE TM1.CUSTID = TM2.CUSTID;
```

The inner subquery is calculating the SUM of the NET_AMOUNT column for all TRANSMASTER rows for the same customer. But what does this mean? Suppose that customer with CUSTID 37 has four rows in TRANSMASTER with the following values for NET_AMOUNT: 3000, 5000, 2000, and 1000. The SUM of NET_AMOUNT for this CUSTID is 11000.

Note that the order that the UPDATE statement processes the rows is implementation-defined, and is generally not predictable. It may be the same each day, or it may differ depending on the way that the rows are actually arranged on the disk. Assume that the implementation processes the rows for this CUSTID in this order: first the TRANSMASTER with NET_AMOUNT 3000, then the one with NET_AMOUNT 5000, and so on. After the first three rows for CUSTID 37 have been updated, their NET_AMOUNT values will be 2700, 4500, 1800. Then, when we process the last TRANSMASTER row for CUSTID 37, whose NET_AMOUNT is 1000, the SUM returned by the subquery would *seem* to be 10000, that is, the SUM of the new NET_AMOUNT values of the first three rows for CUSTID 37, and the old NET_AMOUNT value of the last row for CUSTID 37. Thus it would *seem* that last row for CUSTID 37 will not be updated, since the comparison with that SUM is not True (10000 is not less than SELECT SUM (NET_AMOUNT)). But that is not the way the UPDATE statement is defined when a subquery references the table that is being updated. The rule is that all evaluations of subqueries in an UPDATE statement reference the *old* values of the table that is being updated. Thus, in the preceding UPDATE, for CUSTID 37, the subquery will return 11000, that is, the original SUM.

As you can see, the subquery in a WHERE clause operates exactly the same, whether it is in a SELECT statement or an UPDATE statement. The same holds true for DELETE and INSERT. To delete all of Olympic's transactions, you could use this statement:

```
DELETE TRANSMASTER
    WHERE CUSTID =
        (SELECT CUSTID
            FROM CUSTOMER
            WHERE COMPANY = 'Olympic Sales') ;
```

As with UPDATE, DELETE subqueries can also be correlated, and can also reference the table being deleted. The rules are similar to the rules for UPDATE subqueries. Consider a case where you want to delete all rows from TRANS-MASTER for customers whose total NET_AMOUNT is larger than $10,000:

```
DELETE TRANSMASTER TM1
    WHERE 10000 < SELECT SUM(NET_AMOUNT)
        FROM TRANSMASTER TM2
            WHERE TM1.CUSTID = TM2.CUSTID ;
```

This will delete all rows from TRANSMASTER that have CUSTID 37, as well as any other customers with purchases exceeding $10,000. All references to TRANSMASTER in the subquery denote the contents of TRANSMASTER before any deletes by the current statement. So even when you are deleting the last TRANSMASTER row for CUSTID 37, the subquery will be evaluated on the original TRANSMASTER table, and will return 11000.

Whenever you update, delete, or insert database records, there is a chance that you will change one table's data in such a way that it is no longer consistent with one or more other tables in the database. Such an inconsistency is called a modification anomaly, a problem discussed in Chapter 6. Specifically, if you delete TRANSMASTER records, and there is a TRANSDETAIL table that depends on TRANSMASTER, you must delete the corresponding records from TRANSDETAIL, too. This operation is called a cascading delete, because the deletion of a parent record must cascade to all of its associated child records. Otherwise, the undeleted child records become *orphans*. In this case, they would be invoice detail lines that are in limbo because they are no longer connected to an invoice record. ■

The INSERT command can include a SELECT clause. A typical use for this is in filling up "snapshot" tables. If you want to have a table with the contents of TRANSMASTER as of May 27, you can do it as follows:

```
CREATE TABLE TRANSMASTER_0527
   (TRANSID INTEGER,
        ...)
INSERT INTO TRANSMASTER_0527
   (SELECT * FROM TRANSMASTER) ;
```

Or you may only want to save rows for large NET_AMOUNTs:

```
INSERT INTO TRANSMASTER_0527
   (SELECT * FROM TRANSMASTER TM
   WHERE TM.NET_AMOUNT > 10000) ;
```

Part IV
Controlling Operations

The 5th Wave   By Rich Tennant

"C'MON BRICKMAN, YOU KNOW AS WELL AS I DO THAT 'NOSE-SCANNING' IS OUR BEST DEFENSE AGAINST UNAUTHORIZED ACCESS TO PERSONAL FILES."

In This Part ...

Once you've created a database and filled it with data, you will want to protect it from harm or misuse. In this part I'll discuss in detail SQL's tools for maintaining the safety and integrity of your data. SQL's Data Control Language (DCL) lets you protect your data from misuse by selectively granting or denying access to the data. You can protect your database from other threats, such as interference from concurrent access by multiple users, with SQL's transaction processing facilities. You can use constraints to help keep bad data from being entered in the first place. Although SQL can't defend you against bad application design, it can, if you take full advantage of the tools provided, protect your data from most categories of problems.

Chapter 13

Providing Database Security

· ·

· ·

*I*n the preceding chapters I've discussed those parts of SQL that create databases and then manipulate the data in them. In Chapter 4 I briefly mentioned SQL's facilities for protecting databases from harm or misuse. In this chapter we will go into more depth on the subject of misuse. The person in charge of a database has the power to determine who will have access to it, and what level of access they will have. Access to selected aspects of the system can be selectively granted and revoked. Even the right to grant and revoke access privileges can be granted and revoked. When used properly, the security tools SQL provides are powerful protectors of important data. When used incorrectly, they can be frustrating impediments to the efforts of legitimate users trying to do their jobs.

Databases often contain sensitive information that should not be available to everyone. SQL provides different levels of access, from complete to none, with several levels in between. By controlling exactly which operations can be performed by each authorized user, the person in charge of a database can make sure that people have all the data they need to do their job, but do not have access to other parts of the database that they have no business seeing or changing.

The SQL Data Control Language (DCL)

Those SQL statements that are used to create databases form a group called the Data Definition Language (DDL). Once a database has been created, you can use another set of SQL statements, called collectively the Data Manipulation Language (DML), to add, change, and remove data from the database. SQL has additional statements that do not fall into either of these categories. These statements are sometimes collectively called the Data Control Language (DCL). They primarily serve to protect the database from unauthorized access, from harmful interaction among multiple database users, and from power failures and equipment malfunctions. In this chapter I'll discuss protection from unauthorized access. In Chapter 14 I'll look at the other DCL functions.

User Access Levels

SQL-92 provides controlled access to six database management functions: creating, seeing, modifying, deleting, referencing, and using. Creating, seeing, modifying, and deleting correspond to the INSERT, SELECT, UPDATE, and DELETE operations that were discussed in Chapter 7. Referencing, using the REFERENCES keyword (discussed in Chapters 4 and 6), has to do with applying referential integrity constraints to a table that depends on another table in the database. Using, specified by the USAGE keyword, pertains to domains, character sets, collations, and translations. (Domains, character sets, collations, and translations were defined in Chapter 6.)

The Database Administrator

The supreme authority for a database is the database administrator (DBA). The DBA has all rights and privileges to all aspects of the database. Being a DBA can give you a real feeling of power, but it is also a great responsibility. With all that power at your disposal, you could easily mess up your database, and destroy thousands of hours of work. The DBA must think clearly and carefully about the consequences of every action she performs.

Not only does the DBA have all rights to the database, she also has control over what rights are granted to other users. In this way highly trusted individuals can have access to more functions, and perhaps to more tables than are available to the majority of users.

It's a tough job, but...

You are probably wondering how you can become a DBA, and accrue for yourself all the status and admiration that goes along with the title. The obvious answer is to kiss up to the boss, in hopes of being awarded this plum assignment. It may even help to demonstrate competence, integrity, and reliability in the performance of your everyday duties. Actually though, the key requisite is that you be sucker enough to take the job. I was kidding when I said that stuff about status and admiration. Mostly the DBA gets blamed if anything goes wrong with the database, and invariably, sooner or later, something will.

The best way to become a DBA is to install the database management system yourself. When you do, the installation manual will give you an account or login and a password. That login identifies you as a specially privileged user. Sometimes this user is called the DBA, sometimes the system administrator, and sometimes the super user. In any case, your first official act after logging in should be to change your password. If you don't change the password, anyone who reads the manual will be able to log in with full DBA privileges. This may not be very healthy for the database. Once you change the password, only people who know the new password will be able to log in as DBA.

You should share the new DBA password with a small number of highly trusted people. After all, you could be struck by a falling meteorite tomorrow, win the lottery, or in some other way become unavailable to the company. Your colleagues must be able to carry on in your absence. Anyone who knows the DBA login and password becomes the DBA when he or she uses them to access the system.

 If you have DBA privileges it is a good idea to log in as DBA only when you have a specific task to perform that requires DBA privileges. When you are finished, log out. For routine work, log in with your own personal login ID and password. This may save you from making mistakes that will have serious consequences for other users' tables as well as your own. ∎

Database Object Owners

Besides the DBA, there is another class of privileged user — the database object owner. Tables and views are examples of database objects. Any user who creates an object is considered its owner. A table owner has every possible privilege associated with that table, including the privilege to grant access to other people. Views are based on underlying tables. It is possible for a person who is not a table's owner to create a view based on that table. If this is the case, the view owner has only those privileges for the view that she had for its underlying table. The bottom line is that a user cannot circumvent the protection on a table by creating a view based on that table.

The Public

All users who are not specially privileged users (either DBA or object owner), and who have not been specifically granted access rights by a privileged user, are considered to be the public. When a privileged user grants certain access rights to PUBLIC, everyone having access to the system gains those rights.

There is a hierarchy of user privilege, where the DBA is at the highest level and the public is at the lowest. Figure 13-1 illustrates the privilege hierarchy.

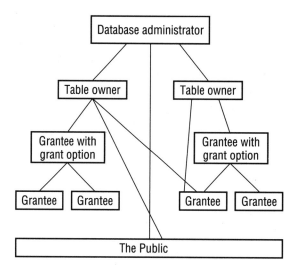

Figure 13-1:
The access privilege hierarchy.

Granting Privileges to Users

The DBA, by virtue of his position, has all privileges on all objects in the database. The owner of an object has all privileges with respect to that object. No one else has any privileges with respect to any object, unless they are specifically granted by someone who already has those privileges and the authority to pass them on. Privileges are granted using the GRANT statement, which has this syntax:

```
GRANT privilege-list
   ON object
   TO user-list
   [WITH GRANT OPTION]
```

where *privilege-list* is:

```
   privilege [, privilege] ...
 | ALL PRIVILEGES
```

where *privilege* is:

```
   SELECT
 | DELETE
 | INSERT [(column-name [, column-name]...)]
 | UPDATE [(column-name [, column-name]...)]
 | REFERENCES [(column-name [, column-name]...)]
 | USAGE
```

where *object* is:

```
   [TABLE] table-name
 | DOMAIN domain-name
 | CHARACTER SET character-set-name
 | COLLATION collation-name
 | TRANSLATION translation-name
```

and where *user-list* is:

```
   login-ID [, login-ID]...
 | PUBLIC
```

In this syntax, a view is considered to be a table. The SELECT, DELETE, INSERT, UPDATE, and REFERENCES privileges apply to tables and views only. The USAGE privilege applies to domains, character sets, collations, and translations. The following sections give examples of the various ways the GRANT statement can be used, and what the results are.

Inserting data

To grant someone the privilege of adding data to a table, follow this example:

```
GRANT INSERT
   ON CUSTOMER
   TO SALES_CLERK ;
```

This allows the clerk in the sales department to add new customer records to the CUSTOMER table.

Looking at data

To allow someone to view the data in a table:

```
GRANT SELECT
    ON PRODUCT
    TO PUBLIC ;
```

This allows anyone with access to the system (PUBLIC) to view the contents of the PRODUCT table.

 Actually, this statement could be dangerous. There may be columns in the PRODUCT table that contain information that should not be seen by everyone, such as COST_OF_GOODS. To provide access to most information while withholding access to sensitive information, define a view based on the table that does not include the sensitive columns. Then grant SELECT privileges on the view rather than on the underlying table:

```
CREATE VIEW MERCHANDISE AS
    SELECT MODEL, PRODNAME, PRODDESC, LISTPRICE
        FROM PRODUCT ;

GRANT SELECT
    ON MERCHANDISE
    TO PUBLIC ;
```

This way the public does not get to see the PRODUCT table's COST_OF_GOODS column, or any other column except the four listed in the CREATE VIEW statement. ■

Modifying table data

In any active organization, table data changes over time. Some people should have the right and power to make changes, and everyone else should be prevented from doing so. To grant change privileges, follow this example:

```
GRANT UPDATE (BONUSPCT)
    ON BONUSRATE
    TO SALES_MGR ;
```

The sales manager can adjust the bonus rate awarded for sales (the BONUS-PCT column), based on changes in market conditions. She cannot, however, modify the values in the MINAMOUNT and MAXAMOUNT columns that define the ranges for each step in the bonus schedule. To allow updates to all columns, either specify all column names, or do not specify any, as here:

```
GRANT UPDATE
    ON BONUSRATE
    TO VP_SALES ;
```

Deleting obsolete rows from a table

Customers go out of business, or stop buying for some other reason. Employees quit, retire, are laid off, or die. Products become obsolete. Life goes on, and things that we tracked in the past may no longer be of interest to us. Someone needs to remove obsolete records from their tables. On the other hand, you want to carefully control who can remove which records. This is another job for the GRANT statement.

```
GRANT DELETE
    ON EMPLOYEE
    TO PERSONNEL_MGR ;
```

The personnel manager can remove records from the EMPLOYEE table. So can the DBA and the person who created the EMPLOYEE table (who was probably the DBA also). No one else can remove personnel records (unless another GRANT statement gives him this power).

Referencing related tables

If one table includes a second table's primary key as a foreign key, information in the second table becomes available to users of the first table. This is potentially a dangerous "back door" through which confidential information can be extracted. A user does not have to have access rights to a table in order to learn something about its contents. If the user has access rights to a table that references the target table, that is often enough. Consider an example.

Suppose the table LAYOFF_LIST contains the names of the employees who will be laid off next month. Only authorized management people have SELECT access to the table. However, an unauthorized employee deduces that the table's primary key is EMPID and creates a new table SNOOP which has EMPID as a foreign key, referencing LAYOFF_LIST. (I describe how to create a foreign key with a REFERENCES clause in Chapter 6.)

```
CREATE TABLE SNOOP
    (EMPID INTEGER REFERENCES LAYOFF_LIST) ;
```

Now all the employee needs to do is try to INSERT rows corresponding to the employee ID numbers of all employees into SNOOP. The inserts that are allowed will be for the employees on the layoff list. All rejected inserts will be for employees not on the list.

SQL-92 prevents this kind of security breach by requiring that reference rights be explicitly granted:

```
GRANT REFERENCES (EMPID)
   ON LAYOFF_LIST
   TO PERSONNEL_CLERK ;
```

Using domains, character sets, collations, and translations

You can define a domain that encompasses a set of columns, all of which you want to have the same type, and to share the same constraints. The columns you create in your CREATE DOMAIN statement will inherit the type and constraints of the domain. For specific columns, these characteristics can be overridden, but domains provide a convenient way to apply numerous characteristics to multiple columns with a single declaration.

Domains come in handy when you have multiple tables that all have columns with similar characteristics. For example, your business database may have several tables, each of which has a PRICE column that should have a type of DECIMAL(10,2), and that should have values that are non-negative and no greater than 10,000. Before you create the tables holding these columns, create a domain that specifies the columns' characteristics:

```
CREATE DOMAIN PRICE_TYPE_DOMAIN  DECIMAL (10,2)
   CHECK (VALUE >= 0 AND VALUE <= 10000) ;
```

Perhaps your products are identified in multiple tables by PRODUCT_CODE, which is always of type CHAR (5), with a first character of "X", "C", or "H", and a last character of either "9" or "0". You can create a domain for these columns too:

```
CREATE DOMAIN PRODUCT_CODE_DOMAIN CHAR (5)
   CHECK (SUBSTR (VALUE, 1,1) IN ("X", "C", "H")
   AND SUBSTR (VALUE, 5, 1) IN ("9", "0") ) ;
```

With the domains in place, you can now proceed to create tables:

```
CREATE TABLE PRODUCT
   (PRODUCT_CODE PRODUCT_CODE_DOMAIN,
```

```
PRODUCT_NAME CHAR (30),
PRICE PRICE_TYPE_DOMAIN) ;
```

In the table definition, instead of giving the data type for PRODUCT_CODE and PRICE, specify the appropriate domain instead. This will give those columns the correct type and will also apply the constraints you specified in your CREATE DOMAIN statements.

There are security implications to the use of domains. What if someone else wants to use the domains you have created — might this cause problems? Yes, it might. What if someone creates a table with a column whose domain is PRICE_TYPE_DOMAIN. They can assign progressively larger values to that column until a value is rejected. By doing this they can determine the upper bound on PRICE_TYPE that you specified in the CHECK clause of your CRE-ATE DOMAIN statement. If you consider that upper bound to be private information, you won't want to allow others to use the PRICE_TYPE domain. To protect you in situations like this, SQL allows domains to be used only by those who are explicitly granted permission by the domain owner, the user who created the domain (and the DBA of course). You can grant such permission with a statement such as the following:

```
GRANT USAGE ON PRICE_TYPE DOMAIN TO SALES_MGR ;
```

Different security problems may arise when you DROP domains. Tables that have columns defined in terms of a domain will have problems if you try to DROP the domain. You may have to DROP all such tables first. Or you may be prevented from dropping the domain. Behavior may vary from one implementation to another. At any rate, you may want to restrict who can DROP domains. The same applies to character sets, collations, and translations. ∎

Granting the Power to Grant Privileges

The DBA can grant any privileges to anyone. An object owner can grant any privileges on that object to anyone. Users who have been granted privileges in this way, however, cannot in turn grant them to someone else. This helps the DBA or table owner retain a good measure of control. Only people empowered by the DBA or object owner gain access to the object in question.

From a security standpoint, limiting a person's ability to delegate access privileges makes a lot of sense. However, there are many occasions when such delegation is needed. Work cannot come to a screeching halt every time someone is ill, on vacation, or out to lunch. Some users can be trusted with the power to delegate their access rights to reliable designated alternates. To pass such a right of delegation to a user, the GRANT statement has the WITH GRANT OPTION clause. The following statement is one example of how it could be used:

```
GRANT UPDATE (BONUSPCT)
   ON BONUSRATE
   TO SALES_MGR
   WITH GRANT OPTION ;
```

Now the sales manager can delegate the UPDATE privilege by issuing the following statement:

```
GRANT UPDATE (BONUSPCT)
   ON BONUSRATE
   TO ASST_SALES_MGR ;
```

After the execution of this statement, the assistant sales manager can make changes to the BONUSRATE table — a power he didn't have before.

 There is a tradeoff here between security and convenience. The owner of the BONUSRATE table relinquished considerable control when she granted the UPDATE privilege to the sales manager WITH GRANT OPTION. One hopes that the sales manager takes his responsibility seriously and is careful about how the privilege is passed on. ■

Taking Privileges Away

If you have a way to give access privileges to people, you'd better have a way of taking them away, too. People's job functions change, and with the change their need for access to data changes. People may even leave the organization to join a competitor. Such people probably should have all their access privileges revoked. SQL provides for the removal of access privileges with the REVOKE statement. It acts just like the GRANT statement, except in reverse. The syntax is:

```
REVOKE [GRANT OPTION FOR] privilege-list
   ON object
   FROM user-list [RESTRICT|CASCADE] ;
```

You can use this structure to revoke specified privileges while leaving others intact. The principal difference between the REVOKE statement and the GRANT statement is the presence of the optional RESTRICT or CASCADE keyword in the REVOKE statement. If the privileges being revoked were granted WITH GRANT OPTION, using CASCADE in the REVOKE statement revokes privileges for the grantee and also for anyone who was granted those privileges as a result of the WITH GRANT OPTION clause. On the other hand, the REVOKE statement with the RESTRICT option works only if the specified privileges have not been delegated. In that case it revokes the grantee's privileges. If the grantee has passed on the specified privileges, the REVOKE statement with the RESTRICT option does not revoke anything, but instead returns an error.

You can use a REVOKE statement with the optional GRANT OPTION FOR clause to revoke only the grant option for specified privileges, while allowing the grantee to retain those privileges for himself. If the GRANT OPTION FOR clause and the CASCADE keyword are both present, all privileges granted by the grantee will be revoked along with the grantee's right to bestow such privileges. It will be as if the grant option had never been granted in the first place. If the GRANT OPTION FOR clause and the RESTRICT clause are both present, one of two things will happen. If the grantee has not granted any of the privileges being revoked, the REVOKE will be executed and her ability to grant privileges will be removed. If the grantee has already granted at least one of the privileges being revoked, the REVOKE will not be executed, but will return an error instead.

The fact that privileges can be granted WITH GRANT OPTION, combined with the fact that privileges can be selectively revoked, makes system security a whole lot more complicated than it appears at first glance. It is possible for a user to be granted a privilege by multiple grantors. When one of those then revokes the privilege, the user still retains it because of the still-existing grant from another grantor. When a privilege is passed from one user to another WITH GRANT OPTION, it creates a chain of dependency, where one user's privileges depend on those of another user. If you are a DBA or object owner, be aware that once you have granted a privilege WITH GRANT OPTION, that privilege might show up in unexpected places. Revoking it from unwanted users while letting legitimate users retain it may prove challenging. In general, there are numerous subtleties in the GRANT OPTION and CASCADE clauses. If you use them, check both the SQL-92 standard and your product documentation carefully. ■

Using GRANT and REVOKE Together Saves Time and Effort

Often you will want to grant multiple privileges to multiple users on selected columns only of a table. This could require a lot of typing. Consider the following example from Zetec Corporation. The vice president of sales wants everyone in the sales department to be able to see everything in the CUSTOMER table. However, only sales managers should be able to update, delete, or insert rows, and nobody should be able to update the CUSTID field. The sales managers are named Tyson, Keith, and David. You can grant appropriate privileges with a series of GRANT statements:

```
GRANT SELECT, INSERT, DELETE
    ON CUSTOMER
    TO TYSON, KEITH, DAVID ;

GRANT UPDATE
    ON CUSTOMER (COMPANY, CUSTADDRESS, CUSTCITY,
        CUSTSTATE, CUSTZIP, CUSTPHONE, MODLEVEL)
    TO TYSON, KEITH, DAVID ;

GRANT SELECT
    ON CUSTOMER
    TO JENNY, VALERIE, MELODY, NEIL, ROBERT, SAMMY,
        PRESTON, BRANDON, MICHELLE_T, ALLISON, ANDREW,
        SCOTT, MICHELLE_B, JAIME, LINLEIGH, MATT, AMANDA;
```

There. That should do it. Everyone has SELECT rights on the CUSTOMER table. The sales managers have full INSERT and DELETE rights on it, and they also have the right to update any column except the CUSTID column. This will work. However, there is an easier way. Try the following:

```
GRANT SELECT
    ON CUSTOMER
    TO PUBLIC ;

GRANT INSERT, DELETE, UPDATE
    ON CUSTOMER
    TO TYSON, KEITH, DAVID ;

REVOKE UPDATE
    ON CUSTOMER (CUSTID)
    FROM TYSON, KEITH, DAVID ;
```

It has still taken three statements to accomplish the same protection that was achieved in three statements up above. However, these three statements are significantly shorter, because we didn't have to name all the users in the sales department, and we did not have to name all the columns in the table.

Chapter 14

Protecting Data

● ●

In This Chapter

▶ Avoiding database damage

▶ Understanding the problems caused by concurrent operation

▶ SQL mechanisms for dealing with concurrency problems

▶ Tailoring protection to your needs with SET TRANSACTION

▶ Protecting your data without paralyzing operations

● ●

*E*veryone has heard of Murphy's Law, which is usually stated, "If anything *can* go wrong, it *will* go wrong." We joke about this pseudo-law because most of the time things go fine. At times it seems that we are among the lucky few who remain untouched by one of the basic laws of the universe. Usually, when unexpected problems arise, we recognize what has happened and deal with it.

However, in a very complex structure the potential for unanticipated problems rises approximately as the square of the complexity. This is why large software projects are almost always delivered late, and are often loaded with bugs. A nontrivial multiuser DBMS application is a large, complex structure. In the course of operation, there are a number of things that could potentially go wrong. Methods have been developed for minimizing the impact of these problems, but the problems will never be eliminated completely. This is good news for professional database maintenance and repair people, since it will probably never be possible to automate them out of a job.

Threats to Data Integrity

Data can be damaged or corrupted in a variety of ways. In Chapter 6 we discussed problems resulting from bad input data, operator error, deliberate destruction, and concurrent access. Poorly formulated SQL statements and improperly designed applications can also damage your data, and it doesn't take much imagination to figure out how. Two threats I haven't mentioned yet are platform instability and equipment failure. I'll discuss these briefly in this chapter, and give more extensive coverage to the problems that can be caused by concurrent access.

Platform instability

Platform instability is a category of problem that shouldn't even exist, but alas, it does. It is most prevalent when you are running one or more new and relatively untried components in your system. Problems could lurk in a new DBMS release, a new operating system version, or new hardware. Conditions or situations that have never arisen before come up while you are running a critical job. Your system locks up and your data is damaged. To remedy the problem you may direct a few choice words at your computer and the people who built it. Beyond that there is not much you can do, except hope that your latest backup was a good one.

Never put important production work on a system that has any unproven components. Resist the temptation to get the beta release of the newest, most function-laden version of your DBMS or operating system and put your bread and butter work on it. If you feel you must gain some hands-on experience with something new, make sure it is on a machine that is completely isolated from your production network. ▪

Equipment failure

Even well-proven, highly reliable equipment fails sometimes. Everything physical wears out eventually, even modern solid-state computers. If such a failure happens while your database is open and active, you could lose data. Even worse, you could lose data and not realize it. You can be sure that such a failure will happen sooner or later. If Murphy's Law is in operation that day, it will happen at the worst possible time.

One way to protect against equipment failure is redundancy. Keep extra copies of everything. For maximum safety, have duplicate hardware configured exactly the same as your production system. Have backups of your database and applications that can be loaded and run on your backup hardware when needed.

Cost constraints may keep you from duplicating everything (which effectively doubles your costs), but at least make sure your database and applications are backed up frequently enough that an unexpected failure does not require you to reenter a large amount of data.

Another way to avoid the worst consequences of equipment failure is to use transaction processing. I'll cover this important topic later in this chapter.

A *transaction* is an indivisible unit of work. Either the entire transaction is executed, or none of it is. The worst problems arise when only part of a series of database operations is processed. ■

Concurrent access

Assume you are running on proven hardware and software, your data is good, your application is bug-free, and your equipment is inherently reliable. Problems can still arise from *contention* when multiple people try to use the same database table at the same time. Multiple-user database systems must be able to handle concurrent access to data.

Consider an example of a case where interaction between concurrent users might cause problems. Suppose you are writing an order-processing application that involves four tables: ORDER_MASTER, CUSTOMER, LINE_ITEM, and INVENTORY. ORDER_MASTER has ORDER_NUMBER as a primary key, CUSTOMER_NUMBER as a foreign key referencing the CUSTOMER table, as well as other columns that do not concern us here. The LINE_ITEM table has LINE_NUMBER as a primary key, ITEM_NUMBER as a foreign key referencing the INVENTORY table, and QUANTITY. The INVENTORY table has ITEM_NUMBER as a primary key, QUANTITY_ON_HAND, and other columns.

Your company policy is to ship each order completely, or not at all. No partial shipments or back orders are allowed. The ORDER_PROCESSING application processes each order in ORDER_MASTER and determines whether it's possible to ship ALL of the line items. If so, it writes the order, decrements the QUANTITY_ON_HAND column of the INVENTORY table as required, and deletes the affected entries from the ORDER_MASTER and LINE_ITEM tables.

There is more than one way to perform the order processing function. One way (Method 1) would be to process the INVENTORY row corresponding to each row in the LINE_ITEM table. If QUANTITY_ON_HAND is large enough, decrement it. If QUANTITY_ON_HAND is not large enough, roll back the transaction to restore all of the inventory reductions made to other LINE_ITEMs in this order.

A second way of accomplishing the same result (Method 2) is to check the INVENTORY row corresponding to each row in an order's LINE_ITEMs. If they are ALL big enough, then process those items by decrementing them.

Method 1 is more efficient when you succeed in processing the order, and Method 2 is more efficient when you fail. Thus, if most orders can be filled most of the time, you are better off using Method 1. If most orders cannot be filled most of the time, you are better off with Method 2.

How would this example application be affected on a multiuser system, if there were not adequate concurrency control? Assume User 1 was processing an order using Method 1. There are ten pieces of Item 1 in stock, and User 1's order takes them all. The order processing is in progress and the quantity of Item 1 is decremented to zero. At this point, User 2 processes a small order for one piece of Item 1, and finds that there are not enough in stock to fill the order. User 2's order is rolled back because it cannot be filled. Meanwhile, User 1 tries to order five pieces of Item 37, but there are only four in stock. User 1's order is rolled back because it cannot be completely filled. The INVENTORY table is now back to the state it was in before either user started operating. Neither order has been filled, even though User 2's order could have been.

If a situation similar to this had occurred on a system using Method 2, there could still be a problem, although a different one. User 1 could check all the items ordered and decide that all the items ordered were available. However, if User 2 comes in and processes an order for one of those items before User 1 performs the decrement operation, User 1's transaction could fail.

There would be no conflict if transactions were executed serially rather than concurrently. In the first example, if User 1's transaction were completed before User 2's transaction started, the ROLLBACK after USER 1 failed to process all items would have made the item ordered by User 2 available during User 2's transaction. In the second example, User 2 would have no opportunity to change the quantity of any item until User 1's transaction was complete. User 1's transaction would complete successfully.

If transactions are executed serially, one after the other, there is no chance that they will interact destructively. Execution of concurrent transactions is termed *serializable* if the result is the same as it would be if the transactions were executed serially. ■

There are tradeoffs between performance and protection from harmful interactions. The higher the isolation level, the more time it takes to perform a function. You should be aware of what the tradeoffs are so you can configure your system for protection that is adequate, but not more than you need. Too strict control of concurrent access can kill overall system performance. ■

Reducing Vulnerability to Data Corruption

Precautions can be taken at several levels to reduce the chance that you will lose data through some mishap or unanticipated interaction. Some of these precautions are taken by your DBMS. Like guardian angels, they protect you from harm. Also like guardian angels, you don't see them, and probably don't even know they are helping you. Your database administrator (DBA) takes other precautions, and you may or may not be aware of these activities. Finally, there are precautions that you, the developer, can take yourself. Form the habit of doing these things automatically, so they are always included in your code or in your interactions with your database. You can avoid a lot of grief by adhering to a few simple principles whenever you interact with a database.

Using SQL transactions

The transaction is one of SQL's main tools for maintaining database integrity. An SQL transaction encapsulates all the SQL statements that could have an effect on the database. An SQL transaction is completed with either a COMMIT or a ROLLBACK statement. If the transaction is completed with a COMMIT, the effects of all the statements in the transaction are applied to the database at once. If it is completed with a ROLLBACK, the effects of all the statements are "rolled back" and the database is returned to the state it was in before the transaction began.

In this discussion I'm going to use the term *application* to mean either an execution of a program (in COBOL, C, or some other programming language), or a series of actions performed at a terminal during a single logon. An application can include a series of SQL transactions. The first SQL transaction begins when the application begins; the last SQL transaction ends when the application ends. Each COMMIT or ROLLBACK that the application performs ends one SQL transaction and begins the next SQL transaction. For example, an application with three SQL transactions would have the form:

```
Start of the application
    Various SQL statements (SQL transaction-1)
COMMIT or ROLLBACK
    Various SQL statements (SQL transaction-2)
COMMIT or ROLLBACK
    Various SQL statements  (SQL transaction-3)
End of the application
```

I refer to "SQL transaction," because the application could be using other facilities, such as for network access, that do other sorts of transactions. In the following discussion I'll simply say "transaction," to mean "SQL transaction."

A transaction has an access mode that is either READ-WRITE or READ-ONLY, and it has an isolation level that is either SERIALIZABLE, REPEATABLE READ, READ COMMITTED, or READ UNCOMMITTED. I'll describe these transaction characteristics shortly. The default characteristics are READ-WRITE and SERIALIZABLE. If you want any other characteristics, specify them with a SET TRANSACTION statement, such as

```
SET TRANSACTION READ ONLY ;
```

or

```
SET TRANSACTION READ ONLY REPEATABLE READ ;
```

or

```
SET TRANSACTION READ COMMITTED ;
```

You can have multiple SET TRANSACTION statements in an application, but you can only specify one of them in each transaction, and it must be the first SQL statement executed in the transaction. If you want to use a SET TRANS-ACTION statement, then execute it either at the beginning of the application, or after a COMMIT or ROLLBACK. You must perform a SET TRANSACTION at the beginning of every transaction for which you want nondefault properties, since each new transaction after a COMMIT or ROLLBACK is automatically given the default properties.

A SET TRANSACTION statement can also specify a DIAGNOSTICS SIZE, which determines the number of error conditions about which the implementation should be prepared to save information (since an implementation can detect more than one error during a statement). The default for this is implementor defined, and that default will almost always be adequate. ■

The default transaction

The default transaction has characteristics that are satisfactory for most users most of the time. On those few occasions when you require transaction characteristics other than those provided by the default transaction, you can specify different characteristics with a SET TRANSACTION statement, as described in the previous section. (I'll discuss this statement in more detail later in the chapter as well.)

The default transaction sets the mode to READ-WRITE, which, as you might expect, allows you to issue statements that change the database. It sets isolation level to SERIALIZABLE, which is the highest level of isolation possible, and thus the safest. The default diagnostics size is implementation dependent. You will have to look at your SQL's documentation to see what it is for your system.

Isolation levels

Ideally, you want the work that the system is performing for your transaction to be completely isolated from anything being done by other transactions that happen to be executing concurrently with yours. On a real-world multi-user system, however, complete isolation is not always feasible. It might exact too large a performance penalty. The question then arises, "How much isolation do you really want, and how much are you willing to pay for it in terms of performance?"

The weakest level of isolation is called READ UNCOMMITTED, which allows the sometimes problematic dirty read. A *dirty read* is a situation in which a change made by one user can be read by a second user before the first user COMMITs, or finalizes, the change. The problem arises when the first user aborts and rolls back his transaction. The second user's subsequent operations are now based on a wrong value. The classic example of this is in an inventory application, where the first user decrements inventory and the second user reads the new lower value. The first user then rolls back his transaction, restoring the inventory to its initial value. The second user, thinking inventory is low, orders more stock, possibly creating a severe overstock situation.

 You shouldn't use the READ UNCOMMITTED isolation level unless you don't care very much about the accuracy of your results, and performance is terrible because your system is loaded beyond its capacity.

You might use READ UNCOMMITTED when you want approximate statistical data, such as:

- ✔ The maximum delay in filling orders
- ✔ The average age of salespeople who don't make quota
- ✔ The average age of new employees

In many such cases approximate information is quite sufficient, and the extra (performance) cost of the concurrency control that would be required to give an exact result for some point in time isn't worthwhile. ■

The next highest level of isolation is READ COMMITTED, in which a change made by another transaction does not become visible to your transaction until the other user has COMMITted the other transaction. This is better than the previous case, but is still subject to a serious problem: the nonrepeatable read. To illustrate the *nonrepeatable read* phenomenon, let's return to our inventory example. User 1 queries the database to see how many of a particular product are in stock. There are ten. At almost the same time, User 2 starts and then COMMITs a transaction that records an order for ten units of that same product, decrementing the inventory, leaving none. Now User 1, having seen that there are ten available, tries to order five of them. However, there are no longer five left. User 1's initial read of the quantity available is not repeatable. The quantity has changed, so assumptions made on the basis of the initial read are not valid.

An isolation level of REPEATABLE READ guarantees that the nonrepeatable read problem will not happen. However, this isolation level is still subject to the *phantom read*, a problem that arises when a user issues a command whose search condition (the WHERE clause or HAVING clause) selects a set of rows. Immediately afterward, User 2 performs and commits an operation that changes data in some rows that used to meet the search condition, such that they no longer do. Other data that originally did not meet the search condition, now do. User 1, whose transaction is still active, issues another SQL statement with the same search conditions as her first one. She expects to retrieve the same rows. Instead, unknown to her, her second operation is performed on a different set of rows from those that her first operation used.

An isolation level of SERIALIZABLE is not subject to any of these problems. At this level, concurrent transactions could, in principle, be run serially, or one after the other, rather than in parallel, and the results would be the same. If you are running at this isolation level, hardware or software problems could still cause your transaction to fail, but at least you don't have to worry about the validity of your results if you know your system is functioning properly. Table 14-1 shows the four isolation levels and the problems they solve.

Table 14-1: Isolation Levels and Problems Solved

Isolation Level	Problems Solved
READ UNCOMMITTED	None
READ COMMITTED	Dirty read
REPEATABLE READ	Dirty read
	Nonrepeatable read
SERIALIZABLE	Dirty read
	Nonrepeatable read
	Phantom read

The implicit transaction-starting statement

Some implementations of SQL require that you signal the beginning of a transaction with an explicit statement, such as BEGIN or BEGIN TRAN. SQL-92 does not. If you don't have an active transaction and you issue a statement that calls for one, SQL-92 starts a default transaction for you. CREATE TABLE, SELECT, and UPDATE are examples of statements that require the context of a transaction. Issue one of these and SQL will start a transaction for you.

SET TRANSACTION

On occasion, you may want transaction characteristics that are different from those set by default. You can specify different characteristics with a SET TRANSACTION statement before you issue your first statement that requires a transaction. The SET TRANSACTION statement allows you to specify mode, isolation level, and diagnostics size.

You might issue the following statement:

```
SET TRANSACTION
    READ ONLY,
    ISOLATION LEVEL READ UNCOMMITTED,
    DIAGNOSTICS SIZE 4
```

With these settings you cannot issue any statements that change the database (READ ONLY), and you have the lowest and most hazardous isolation level (READ UNCOMMITTED). The diagnostics area has a size of 4. You are making minimal demands on system resources.

In contrast, you might issue:

```
SET TRANSACTION
    READ WRITE,
    ISOLATION LEVEL SERIALIZABLE,
    DIAGNOSTICS SIZE 8
```

These settings allow you to change the database, give you the highest level of isolation, and give you a larger diagnostics area. This makes larger demands on system resources. Depending on your implementation, these settings may be the same as those used by the default transaction. Naturally, you can issue SET TRANSACTION statements with other choices for isolation level and diagnostics size.

It may seem reasonable to always set your isolation level to SERIALIZABLE, just to be on the safe side. However, depending on your implementation and what you are doing, you may not need to, and performance could suffer significantly if you do. Set your transaction isolation level as high as you need to but no higher. If you don't intend to change the database in your transaction, set the mode to READ ONLY. Don't tie up any system resources that you do not need. ∎

COMMIT

Although SQL-92 does not have an explicit transaction-starting statement, it has two that terminate a transaction: COMMIT and ROLLBACK. Use COMMIT when you have come to the end of the transaction and you want to make permanent the changes you have made to the database (if any). You may include the optional keyword WORK (COMMIT WORK) if you wish. If an error is encountered or the system crashes while a COMMIT is in progress, you may have to roll the transaction back and try it again.

ROLLBACK

When you come to the end of a transaction, you may decide that you do not want to make permanent the changes that have occurred during the transaction. In fact, you want to restore the database to the state it was in before the transaction began. To do this, issue a ROLLBACK statement. ROLLBACK is a fail-safe mechanism. Even if the system crashes while a ROLLBACK is in progress, once the system is restored, the ROLLBACK can be restarted and it will restore the database to its pre-transaction state.

Locking

The isolation level set either by default or by a SET TRANSACTION statement tells the DBMS how zealous to be in protecting your work from interaction with the work of other users. The main thing the DBMS does to protect you from harmful interactions is to apply locks to the database objects you are using. Sometimes it will lock the table row you are accessing, preventing anyone else from accessing that record while you are using it. Sometimes it will lock an entire table, if you are performing an operation that could affect the whole table. Sometimes it will allow reading but not writing. Other times it will prevent both. Each implementation handles locking in its own way. Some implementations are more "bulletproof" than others, but most up-to-date systems will protect you from the worst problems that could arise in a concurrent access situation.

Backup

Backup is a protective action that your DBA should perform on a regular basis. All elements of your system should be backed up at intervals that depend on how frequently they are updated. If your database is updated daily it should be backed up daily. Your applications, forms, and reports may change too, although less frequently. Whenever you make changes to them, your DBA should back up the new versions.

Keep several generations of backups. Sometimes database damage does not become evident until some time has passed. To return to the last known good version, you may have to go back several backup versions. ■

There are several different ways to perform backups. One way is to use SQL to create backup tables and copy data into them. A second way is to use an implementation-defined mechanism that backs up the whole database or portions of it. This is generally much more convenient and efficient than using SQL. Finally, your installation may have a mechanism in place for backing up everything, including databases, programs, documents, spreadsheets, utilities, and computer games. If so, you may not have to do anything beyond assuring yourself that the backups are performed frequently enough to protect you.

Constraints within Transactions

To assure that the data in your database is valid, it is not enough just to make sure that it is of the right type. Some columns, for example, should never hold a null value. Others should perhaps hold values that fall within a certain range. These types of restrictions, called *constraints*, were discussed in Chapter 6.

Constraints are relevant to transactions because they could conceivably prevent you from doing what you want. For example, suppose you want to add data to a table that contains a column with a NOT NULL constraint. One common method of adding a record is to append a blank row to your table, then insert values into it later. However, the NOT NULL constraint on one column will cause the append operation to fail. SQL will not allow you to add a row that has a null value in a column with a NOT NULL constraint, even though you plan to add data to that column before your transaction is ended. To address this problem, SQL-92 allows you to designate constraints as either DEFERRABLE or NOT DEFERRABLE.

Constraints that are NOT DEFERRABLE are applied immediately. You can set deferrable constraints to be either initially DEFERRED or IMMEDIATE. If a deferrable constraint is set to IMMEDIATE, it acts like a not DEFERRABLE constraint. It is applied immediately. If a DEFERRABLE constraint is set to DEFERRED, it is not enforced.

To append blank records, or perform other operations that may violate DEFERRABLE constraints, you can use a statement similar to the following:

```
SET CONSTRAINTS ALL DEFERRED
```

This puts all DEFERRABLE constraints in the DEFERRED condition. It does not affect the NOT DEFERRABLE constraints. Once you have performed all operations that might violate constraints, and the table is now in a state that does not violate them, you can reapply them as follows:

```
SET CONSTRAINTS ALL IMMEDIATE
```

If you have made a mistake and one or more of your constraints is still being violated, you will find out now.

If you do not explicitly set your DEFERRED constraints to IMMEDIATE, SQL will do it for you when you attempt to COMMIT your transaction. If a violation is still present at that time, the transaction will not COMMIT, but instead SQL will give you an error message.

SQL's handling of constraints protects you from entering invalid data (or an invalid absence of data), while giving you the flexibility to temporarily violate constraints while a transaction is still active.

Let's consider a payroll example to illustrate why it is important to be able to defer the application of constraints.

Assume an EMPLOYEE table with columns EMP_NO, EMP_NAME, DEPT_NO, and SALARY. DEPT_NO is a foreign key referencing the DEPT table.

Assume a DEPT table with columns DEPT_NO and DEPT_NAME. DEPT_NO is a primary key.

Suppose that, in addition, we want to have a table like DEPT that also contains a PAYROLL column that holds the sum of the SALARY values for employees in each department.

We could create this with the following view:

```
CREATE VIEW DEPT2 AS
    SELECT D.*, SUM(E.SALARY) AS PAYROLL
        FROM DEPT D, EMPLOYEE E
        WHERE D.DEPT_NO = E.DEPT_NO
        GROUP BY D.DEPT_NO ;
```

We could also define this view equivalently as follows:

```
CREATE VIEW DEPT3 AS
    SELECT D.*,
        (SELECT SUM(E.SALARY)
            FROM EMPLOYEE E
            WHERE D.DEPT_NO = E.DEPT_NO) AS PAYROLL
        FROM DEPT D ;
```

But, suppose that for efficiency we don't want to calculate the SUM every time that we reference DEPT.PAYROLL. Instead, we want to store an actual PAYROLL column in the DEPT table. We will then update that column every time we change a SALARY.

And, to make sure that the SALARY column is accurate, we can include a CONSTRAINT in the table definition:

```
CREATE TABLE DEPT
    (DEPT_NO CHAR(5),
    DEPT_NAME CHAR(20),
    PAYROLL DECIMAL(15,2),
    CHECK (PAYROLL = SELECT SUM(SALARY)
                FROM EMPLOYEE E
                WHERE E.DEPT_NO = D.DEPT_NO));
```

Now, suppose that we want to increase the SALARY of employee 123 by 100. We can do it with the following update:

```
UPDATE EMPLOYEE
    SET SALARY = SALARY + 100
    WHERE EMP_NO = '123' ;
```

And you'll need to remember to do the following as well:

```
UPDATE DEPT D
SET PAYROLL = PAYROLL + 100
WHERE D.DEPT_NO = SELECT E.DEPT_NO
            FROM EMPLOYEE E
            WHERE E.EMP_NO = '123' ;
```

(We use the subquery to reference the DEPT_NO of employee 123.)

But we have a problem. Constraints are checked at the end of each statement. In principle, *all* constraints are checked. In practice, an implementation will only check those constraints that reference values that are modified by the statement.

So, after the first of the preceding UPDATE statements, the implementation will check all constraints that reference values that the statement modifies. This includes the constraint defined in the DEPT table, since that constraint references the SALARY column of the EMPLOYEE table, and the UPDATE statement is modifying that column. After the first UPDATE statement, that constraint will be violated. We assume that before we execute the UPDATE statement the database is correct, and each PAYROLL value in the DEPT table is equal to the sum of the SALARY values in the corresponding columns of the EMPLOYEE table. Then the first UPDATE statement increases a SALARY value, and this equality is no longer true. The second UPDATE statement corrects this state of affairs, and once again leaves the database values in a state for which the constraint is True. But in between the two updates, the constraint is False.

The purpose of the SET CONSTRAINTS DEFERRED statement is to let you temporarily disable or "suspend" all constraints, or only specified constraints. The constraints are deferred until either (1) you execute a SET CONSTRAINTS ON statement, or (2) you execute a COMMIT or ROLLBACK statement. Thus you would surround the previous two UPDATE statements with SET CONSTRAINTS statements:

```
SET CONSTRAINTS OFF ;
UPDATE EMPLOYEE
  SET SALARY = SALARY + 100
  WHERE EMP_NO = '123' ;
UPDATE DEPT D
  SET PAYROLL = PAYROLL + 100
  WHERE D.DEPT_NO = SELECT E.DEPT_NO
                      FROM EMPLOYEE E
          WHERE E.EMP_NO = '123' ;
SET CONSTRAINTS ON ;
```

Note that this defers all constraints, so if you are inserting new rows into DEPT, the primary keys won't be checked. You have removed protection that you might want to keep. It is therefore preferable to specify the particular constraint or constraints that you want to defer. To do this you must give the constraints names when you create them:

```
CREATE TABLE DEPT
  (DEPT_NO CHAR(5),
  DEPT_NAME CHAR(20),
  PAYROLL DECIMAL(15,2),
  CONSTRAINT PAY_EQ_SUMSAL
  CHECK (PAYROLL = SELECT SUM(SALARY)
              FROM EMPLOYEE E
              WHERE E.DEPT_NO = D.DEPT_NO)) ;
```

You can then reference the constraints individually:

```
SET CONSTRAINTS PAY_EQ_SUMSAL OFF;
UPDATE EMPLOYEE
   SET SALARY = SALARY + 100
   WHERE EMP_NO = '123' ;
UPDATE DEPT D
   SET PAYROLL = PAYROLL + 100
   WHERE D.DEPT_NO = SELECT E.DEPT_NO
               FROM EMPLOYEE E
               WHERE E.EMP_NO = '123' ;
SET CONSTRAINTS PAY_EQ_SUMSAL ON;
```

If you don't specify a constraint name in the CREATE statement, then SQL generates one implicitly, and that implicit name appears in the schema information tables (catalog tables). However, it is more straightforward to specify the names explicitly.

Now suppose that in the second UPDATE statement you mistakenly specified an increment value of 1000. This will be allowed during the UPDATE statement, since the constraint has been deferred. But, when you execute the SET CONSTRAINTS ON statement, the specified constraints are checked; and if they fail, the SET CONSTRAINTS statement raises an exception. If instead of a SET CONSTRAINTS ON statement you were to execute a COMMIT statement, and the constraints are found to be False, then the COMMIT will instead perform a ROLLBACK.

Thus it is only possible to defer the constraints within a transaction. When the transaction is terminated, either with a ROLLBACK or a COMMIT, the constraints will be both enabled and checked, and must be True. The ability to defer constraints is therefore only a convenience that can be used within a transaction, and not a mechanism that could in any way make data that violates a constraint available to any other transaction.

Part V
Using SQL Within Applications

I'VE BEEN ON THE PHONE ALL MORNING WITH YOU PEOPLE, AND THE SOFTWARE YOU SOLD ME STILL DOESN'T WORK! IN FACT, I WROTE EVERYTHING YOU TOLD ME TO TRY ON SCRAPS OF PAPER AND HAVE THEM ATTACHED TO MY COMPUTER RIGHT NOW WITH REFRIGERATOR MAGNETS, SO DON'T TELL ME I MUST BE DOING SOMETHING WRONG!

In This Part ...

Up to now we've looked at SQL in isolation, as if you could solve all your data handling problems with SQL alone. Alas, reality intrudes. There are many things you can't do with SQL, at least not with SQL by itself. However, by combining SQL with traditional procedural languages, such as COBOL, FORTRAN, or C, you can achieve results that you could not get with SQL alone. In this part I'll show you how to combine SQL with procedural languages.

Chapter 15

SQL in the Real World

*U*p until now in this book, I've mostly talked about SQL statements in isolation. I have, for example, asked questions about data, then built SQL queries that retrieved answers to the questions. This mode of operation, interactive SQL, is a fine way to learn what SQL can do, but it's not the way SQL is typically used.

Even though SQL syntax can be described as English-like, it is not an easy language to master. The overwhelming majority of computer users today are not fluent in SQL. It is reasonable to assume that the overwhelming majority of computer users will *never* be fluent in SQL, even if this book is wildly successful. When a database question comes up, Joe User will probably not sit down at his terminal and type in an SQL SELECT statement to find the answer. Systems analysts and application developers are the people who are likely to be comfortable with SQL, and they typically do not make a career of entering ad hoc queries into databases. They develop applications that make queries. If you are going to perform the same operation repeatedly, you shouldn't have to rebuild it every time from the console. Write an application to do the job, then run it as often as you like. SQL can be a part of an application, but when it is, it works a little differently than it does in interactive mode.

SQL in an Application

In Chapter 3 I mentioned that SQL was not a complete programming language, and that to use it in an application you need to combine it with a procedural language such as Pascal, FORTRAN, Ada, C, COBOL, PL/I, or dBASE. Because of the way it is structured, SQL has some strengths and some weaknesses. Procedural languages are structured differently, and have different strengths and different weaknesses. Happily, the strengths of SQL tend to make up for the weaknesses of the procedural languages, and the strengths of the procedural languages are in those areas where SQL is weak. By combining the two, you can build powerful applications with a broad range of capabilities. Recently, object-oriented rapid application development (RAD) tools such as Delphi have appeared, which incorporate SQL code into applications developed by manipulating objects rather than writing procedural code.

While discussing interactive SQL in previous chapters, I often used the asterisk (*) as a shorthand substitute for "all columns in the table." If there are numerous columns, the asterisk can save a lot of typing. However, there is a danger in using the asterisk this way when you are using SQL in an application program.

After your application is written, you or someone else may add new columns to a table, or delete old ones. Thus the meaning of "all columns" changes. Your application, when it specifies all columns with an asterisk, may retrieve different columns than it thinks it is getting.

Such a change to a table won't affect existing programs until they have to be recompiled to fix a bug or make some change. Then the "*" will be expanded to include all the now-current columns. This may cause the application to fail in a way totally unrelated to the bug fix or change that was made, causing a debugging nightmare.

To be safe, specify all column names explicitly in an application, rather than using the asterisk. ■

The strengths and weaknesses of SQL

SQL is strong in data retrieval. If important information is buried somewhere in a single-table or multitable database, SQL gives you the tools you need to retrieve it. You do not need to know the order of the rows or columns in a table, since SQL does not deal with the rows or columns individually. SQL's transaction processing facilities assure that your database operations will be unaffected by any other users that may be simultaneously accessing the same tables that you are.

A major weakness of SQL is its rudimentary user interface. It has no provision for formatting screens or reports. It accepts command lines from the keyboard, and sends retrieved values to the terminal, one row at a time.

Sometimes a strength in one context can be a weakness in another. One strength of SQL is its ability to operate on an entire table at once. It doesn't matter if the table has one row, a hundred rows, or a hundred thousand rows; a single SELECT statement can extract the data you want. However, SQL cannot operate on one row of a multirow table at a time, and there are times when you will want to deal with each row individually.

The strengths and weaknesses of procedural languages

In contrast to SQL, procedural languages are designed for one-row-at-a-time operation. This allows the application developer very precise control over the way a table is processed. This high level of control over exactly what is happening at every step is a great strength of procedural languages. However, there is a concomitant weakness. The application developer must have detailed knowledge of the way data is stored in the database tables. The order of the database's columns and rows is significant, and must be taken into account.

Because of the step-by-step nature of procedural languages, they have the flexibility to produce user-friendly screens for data entry and viewing. You can also produce printed reports of great sophistication, with any desired layout.

Problems in combining SQL with a procedural language

In view of the fact that the strengths of SQL complement the weaknesses of procedural languages, and vice versa, it makes sense to try to combine them in such a way that you can benefit from their strengths and not be penalized by their weaknesses. As valuable as such a combination would be, there are some challenges that must be overcome before it can be practically achieved.

Contrasting operating modes

A big problem in combining SQL with a procedural language is the very fact that SQL operates on tables a set at a time, while procedural languages work on them a row at a time. Sometimes this is not a big deal. You can separate set operations from row operations, doing each with the appropriate tool.

Other times, however, you may want to search a table for records meeting certain conditions, and perform different operations on the records depending on whether they meet the conditions or not. This requires both the retrieval power of SQL and the branching capability of a procedural language. Embedded SQL gives you this combination of capabilities by allowing you to "embed" SQL statements at strategic locations within a program you have written in a conventional procedural language.

Data type incompatibilities

Another hurdle to the smooth integration of SQL with any procedural language is the fact that SQL's data types are different from those of all major procedural languages. This should not be surprising, since the data types defined for any procedural language are different from the types for the other procedural languages. There is no standardization of data types across languages. In releases of SQL prior to SQL-92, data type incompatibility was a major concern. In SQL-92 however, the CAST statement addresses the problem. As we discussed in Chapter 9, you can use CAST to convert a data item from the procedural language's data type to one recognized by SQL, as long as the data item itself is compatible with the new data type.

Embedded SQL

The most common method of mixing SQL with procedural languages is called *embedded SQL*. The name is descriptive: SQL statements are dropped right into the middle of a procedural program, wherever they are needed. As you might expect, an SQL statement that appears suddenly in the middle of, for instance, a C program, could present a challenge for a compiler that is not expecting it. For that reason, programs containing embedded SQL are usually passed through a preprocessor before being compiled or interpreted. The preprocessor is warned of the imminent appearance of SQL code by the EXEC SQL directive.

As an example of embedded SQL, let's look at a program written in Oracle's Pro*C version of the C language, that accesses a company employee table. The program prompts the user for an employee name, then displays that employee's salary and commission. It will then prompt the user for new salary and commission data and will update the employee table with it.

```
EXEC SQL BEGIN DECLARE SECTION;
    VARCHAR uid[20];
    VARCHAR pwd[20];
    VARCHAR ename[10];
    FLOAT salary, comm;
```

```
        SHORT salary_ind, comm_ind;
EXEC SQL END DECLARE SECTION;
EXEC SQL INCLUDE SQLCA;

main()
{
        int sret;               /* scanf return code */
        /* Log in */
        strcpy(uid.arr,"FRED");     /* copy the user name */
        uid.len=strlen(uid.arr);
        strcpy(pwd.arr,"TOWER");    /* copy the password */
        pwd.len=strlen(pwd.arr);

        EXEC SQL WHENEVER SQLERROR STOP;
        EXEC SQL WHENEVER NOT FOUND STOP;
EXEC SQL CONNECT :uid;
printf("Connected to user: %s \n",uid.arr);
        printf("Enter employee name to update:  ");
        scanf("%s",ename.arr);
        ename.len=strlen(ename.arr);

        EXEC SQL SELECT SALARY,COMM INTO :salary,:comm
                    FROM EMPLOY
                    WHERE ENAME=:ename;

        printf("Employee: %s salary: %6.2f comm: %6.2f \n",
                ename.arr, salary, comm);
        printf("Enter new salary:  ");
        sret=scanf("%f",&salary);
        salary_ind = 0;
        if (sret == EOF !! sret == 0)    /* set indicator */
            salary_ind =-1;    /* Set indicator for NULL */
        printf("Enter new commission:  ");
        sret=scanf("%f",&comm);
        comm_ind = 0;    /* set indicator */
        if (sret == EOF !! sret == 0)
            comm_ind=-1;       /* Set indicator for NULL */

        EXEC SQL UPDATE EMPLOY
                    SET SALARY=:salary:salary_ind
                    SET COMM=:comm:comm_ind
                    WHERE ENAME=:ename;
printf("Employee %s updated. \n",ename.arr);
        EXEC SQL COMMIT WORK;
        exit(0);
}
```

You don't have to be an expert in C to understand the essence of what this program is doing, and how. First SQL declares host variables. Next C code controls the user login procedure, then SQL sets up error handling and connects to the database. C code then solicits an employee name from the user and places it in a variable. An SQL SELECT statement retrieves the named employee's salary and commission data and stores them in the host variables *:salary* and *:comm*. C then takes over again and displays the employee's name, salary, and commission, then solicits new values for salary and commission. It also checks to see that an entry has been made, and if one has not, it sets an indicator. Next, SQL updates the database with the new values. C then displays an operation complete message. SQL commits the transaction, and C finally exits the program.

It is possible to intermix the commands of two languages like this because of the preprocessor. The preprocessor separates the SQL statements from the host language commands, placing the SQL statements in a separate external routine. Each SQL statement is replaced with a host language CALL of the corresponding external routine. The language compiler can now do its job. The way the SQL part is passed to the database is implementation dependent. You, as the application developer, don't have to worry about any of this. The preprocessor takes care of it. There are a few things, however, that you must be concerned about, which do not appear in interactive SQL. ▓

Declaring host variables

Some information must be passed between the host language program and the SQL segments. This is done with host variables. In order for SQL to recognize the host variables, you must *declare* them before you use them. Declarations are included in a declaration segment that precedes the program segment. The declaration segment is announced by the directive

```
EXEC SQL BEGIN DECLARE SECTION
```

The end of the declaration segment is signaled by

```
EXEC SQL END DECLARE SECTION
```

Every SQL statement must be preceded by an EXEC SQL directive. The end of an SQL segment may or may not be signaled by a terminator directive. In COBOL the terminator directive is "END-EXEC"; in FORTRAN it is the end of a line, and in Ada, C, Pascal, and PL/I it is a semicolon.

Converting data types

Depending on the compatibility of the data types supported by the host language and those supported by SQL, you may have to use CAST to convert certain types. You can use host variables that have been declared in the DECLARE SECTION. Remember to prefix host variable names with a colon (:) when you use them in SQL statements, as in the following example:

```
INSERT INTO FOODS
    (FOODNAME, CALORIES, PROTEIN, FAT, CARBOHYDRATE)
    VALUES
    (:foodname, :calories, :protein, :fat, :carbo)
```

Module Language

Module language provides another method of using SQL with a procedural programming language. With module language, you explicitly put all of the SQL statements into a separate SQL module.

An *SQL module* is simply a list of SQL statements. Each of the SQL statements is called an *SQL procedure*, and is preceded by a specification of the name of the procedure and the number and types of the parameters. ■

Each SQL procedure contains a single SQL statement (the next version of the SQL standard will support procedures with multiple SQL statements, with loops and conditional structures). In the host program, you explicitly call an SQL procedure at whatever point in the host program you wish to execute the SQL statement in that procedure. You call the SQL procedure as if it were a host language subprogram.

Thus, an SQL module and the associated host program are essentially a way of explicitly hand-coding the result of the SQL preprocessor for embedded syntax.

Embedded SQL is much more common than module language. Most vendors offer some form of module language, but few emphasize it in their documentation. Module language does have several advantages. First, since the SQL is completely separated from the procedural language, you can hire the best SQL programmers available to write your SQL modules, whether they have any experience with your procedural language or not. In fact, you can even defer deciding on which procedural language to use until after your SQL modules are written and debugged. Second, you can hire the best programmers in your procedural language, even if they know nothing about SQL. Third, and probably most important, since there is no SQL mixed in with the procedural code, your procedural language debugger will work. This could save you considerable development time.

Once again, what can be looked at as an advantage from one perspective may be a disadvantage from another. Since the SQL modules are separated from the procedural code, when you are trying to understand how the program works, it is not as easy to follow the flow of the logic as it is in embedded SQL.

The syntax for a module is as follows:

```
MODULE [module-name]
    [NAMES ARE character-set-name]
    LANGUAGE {ADA|C|COBOL|FORTRAN|MUMPS|PASCAL|PLI}
    [SCHEMA schema-name]
    [AUTHORIZATION authorization-id]
    [temporary-table-declarations...]
    [cursor-declarations...]
    [dynamic-cursor-declarations...]
    procedures...
```

As indicated by the square brackets, the module name is optional. It is probably a good idea to name it anyway, just to help keep things from getting too confusing. The optional NAMES ARE clause specifies a character set. If you do not include a NAMES ARE clause, the basic set of SQL characters will be used. The LANGUAGE clause tells the module which language it will be called from. The compiler must know what the calling language will be, because it is going to make the SQL statements appear to the calling program as if they are subprograms in that program's language.

Although the SCHEMA clause and the AUTHORIZATION clause are both optional, you must specify at least one of them. You could also specify both. The SCHEMA clause specifies the default schema, and the AUTHORIZATION clause specifies the authorization identifier. The authorization identifier establishes the privileges you will have. If you do not specify an authorization ID, the DBMS will use the authorization ID associated with your session to determine the privileges your module will be allowed. If you don't have the privilege to perform the operation your procedure calls for, it will not be executed.

If your procedure requires temporary tables, declare them with the temporary table declaration clause. Declare cursors and dynamic cursors before any procedures that use them. It is permissible to declare a cursor after a procedure, as long as that procedure does not use the cursor. It may make sense to do this for cursors used by later procedures. I'll discuss cursors in Chapter 16 and dynamic cursors in Chapter 17. ■

Finally, after all these declarations, the functional parts of the module are the procedures. An SQL module language procedure has a name, parameter declarations, and an executable SQL statement. The procedural language program calls the procedure by its name, and passes values to it through the parameters that are declared. A procedure can contain only one SQL statement, which performs the function of the procedure. Procedure syntax is:

```
PROCEDURE procedure-name
    (parameter-declaration [, parameter-declaration ]... )
    SQL statement ;
```

The parameter declaration is of the form:

```
parameter-name data-type
```

or

```
SQLCODE
```

or

```
SQLSTATE
```

Parameters may be either input parameters, output parameters, or both. SQLCODE and SQLSTATE are status parameters through which errors are reported. I'll discuss them in detail in Chapter 18.

Object-Oriented RAD Tools

With state-of-the-art RAD tools, it is possible to develop sophisticated applications without knowing how to write a single line of code in C, Pascal, COBOL or FORTRAN. Instead, you choose objects from a library and place them in appropriate spots on the screen.

Objects of different standard types have characteristic *properties*, and selected *events* are appropriate for each object type. You can also associate a *method* with an object. The method is a procedure written in a procedural language. It is possible, however, to build very useful applications without writing any methods. ■

Although it is quite possible to build complex applications without using a procedural language, sooner or later you will probably need SQL. SQL has a richness of expression that is difficult, if not impossible, to duplicate with the object paradigm. As a result, full-feature RAD tools offer you a mechanism for injecting SQL statements into your object-oriented applications. Borland's

Delphi is an example of an object-oriented development environment that offers SQL capability.

In Chapter 5 I showed how to create database tables with Delphi. That operation, of course, represents only a small fraction of Delphi's capabilities. Its primary purpose is the development of applications that process the data in database tables. The developer places objects on forms, then customizes the objects by giving them properties, events, and possibly methods as well. Out of sight of the developer, Delphi converts the graphic representation of the application into an Object Pascal program, which can then be compiled and run.

Although RAD tools like Delphi are able to deliver high-quality applications in short amounts of time, they are usually specific to one or a small number of platforms. Delphi, for instance, runs only under Microsoft Windows. Keep that in mind if there is a possibility you might want to migrate your application to a different platform. ▪

One of the objects that you can place onto an application form is a *query object*. One of the query object's properties is the SQL property. Figure 15-1 shows the Delphi development environment, with a simple query application in the workspace.

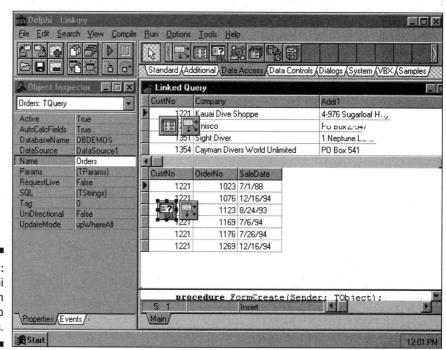

Figure 15-1:
Delphi application linking two tables.

This application displays data from two tables, CUSTOMER and ORDERS, one atop the other. When a line in the CUSTOMER table is selected, all the orders associated with that customer are displayed below it. This display is generated by the SQL statement shown in Figure 15-2.

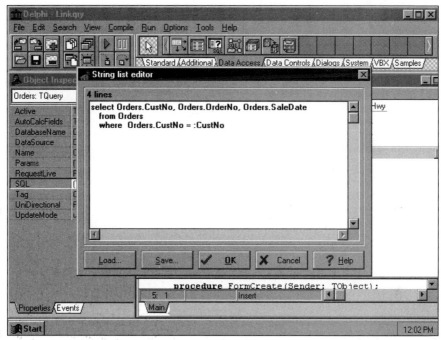

Figure 15-2:
SQL code that pulls desired data from the ORDERS table.

You can put SQL into an application by selecting a query object, such as the one in the selection box near the center of Figure 15-1, from the Data Access tab of the toolbar at the top of the screen. After placing the query object where you want it on your form, you can specify its properties in the Object Inspector on the left edge of Figure 15-1.

When you select the SQL property in the Object Inspector, the String List Editor dialog appears, allowing you to enter SQL code, as in Figure 15-2. The code shown in the example will display all rows for which ORDERS.CUSTNO is equal to the variable :CUSTNO. This query is an example of dynamic SQL, which will be covered in Chapter 17.

RAD tools like Delphi represent the beginning of the eventual merger of relational and object-oriented database design. The structural strengths of relational design and SQL will both survive. They will be augmented by the rapid and comparatively bug-free development that comes from object-oriented programming.

R:BASE

R:BASE is a relational DBMS developed by Microrim, Inc. of Redmond, Washington. It is unusual in that SQL is seamlessly integrated into its full-capability development language. This stems from its history. R:BASE is an evolutionary descendant of RIM, an early mainframe relational database management system. In its earliest incarnation it performed set-at-a-time operations using a data language very similar to SQL. Later, procedural facilities were added, but the core of the product retained the set-at-a-time orientation. As SQL became a de facto standard, R:BASE syntax migrated to become consistent with it.

You can develop an R:BASE application, taking advantage of SQL, without having to switch from a procedural language to SQL and back again, as you have to with either embedded SQL or module language. R:BASE demonstrates that it is possible to make SQL an integral part of a procedural application. Most established vendors, however, have too large an investment in their existing technology to consider starting from scratch and implementing the smoothly integrated technology of R:BASE. They also have an obligation to provide a migration path for their existing customers to any future versions of their products. Although revolutionary products such as Delphi and R:BASE will appear, and some of them will do well, embedded SQL and module language promise to be around for a long time.

Chapter 16

Cursors

In This Chapter

▶ Using a cursor to operate on SQL table data, one row at a time

▶ Specifying cursor scope with the DECLARE statement

▶ Specifying a processing sequence with the ORDER BY clause

▶ Shielding a table from the unwanted side effects of changes you are making to it, until all the changes are made

▶ Opening a cursor affects the way variables are treated

▶ Fetching data one row at a time

▶ Deleting rows accessed with a cursor

▶ Updating rows accessed with a cursor

▶ Closing a cursor

As I've mentioned before, a major incompatibility between SQL and the most popular application development languages is that SQL operates on data a set at a time, while the procedural languages operate on only a single table row at a time. The concept of a cursor was introduced to allow SQL to retrieve (or update, or delete) a single row at a time, so that SQL could be used in combination with an application written in any of the popular languages.

A *cursor* acts like a pointer that locates a specific table row. When a cursor is active, you can perform a SELECT, UPDATE, or DELETE operation on the row pointed to by the cursor. ■

Cursors are valuable when you want to retrieve selected rows from a table, check their contents, and perform different operations based on those contents. This is a sequence of operations that SQL cannot perform by itself. SQL can retrieve the rows, but procedural languages are better at making decisions based on field contents. Cursors enable SQL to retrieve rows from a table one at a time, then feed the result to procedural code for processing.

By placing the SQL code in a loop, you can process the entire table one row at a time.

In embedded SQL, the most common flow of execution will look like this:

```
EXEC SQL DECLARE CURSOR statement
EXEC SQL OPEN statement
Procedural code
Start loop
   Procedural code
   EXEC SQL FETCH
   Procedural code
   Test for end of table
End loop
EXEC SQL CLOSE statement
Procedural code
```

The SQL statements in this listing are DECLARE, OPEN, FETCH, and CLOSE. In the following sections I'll discuss each of these statements in detail.

If it is at all possible to perform the operation you want with normal SQL (set-at-a-time) statements, do so. You should declare a cursor, retrieve table rows one at a time, and use your system's host language only in those instances when normal SQL is incapable of giving you the results you want. ∎

Declaring a Cursor

To use a cursor, you first have to declare its existence to the DBMS. Do this with a DECLARE CURSOR statement. The DECLARE CURSOR statement does not actually cause anything to happen. It just announces the name of the cursor to the DBMS and specifies what query the cursor is going to operate on. An SQL-92 DECLARE CURSOR statement has the following syntax:

```
DECLARE cursor-name [INSENSITIVE][SCROLL] CURSOR FOR
    query expression
    [ORDER BY order-by expression]
    [FOR updatability expression] ;
```

The cursor name uniquely identifies a particular cursor, so it must be different from that of any other cursor name in the current module or compilation unit. ∎

To make your application more readable, give the cursor a meaningful name. Relate it to the data requested by the query expression, or to the operation that your procedural code will perform on the data. ■

The query expression

The *query expression* can be any legal SELECT statement. The rows that the SELECT statement retrieves are the ones that the cursor will step through one at a time. These rows are the *scope* of the cursor. ■

The query is not actually performed when the DECLARE CURSOR statement is read. The data is not retrieved until the OPEN statement is executed. The row-by-row examination of the data doesn't start until you enter the loop that encloses the FETCH statement.

The ORDER BY clause

You may want to process your retrieved data in a particular order, depending on what your procedural code is going to do with the data. You can sort the retrieved rows before processing them, using the optional ORDER BY clause. The clause has the following syntax:

```
ORDER BY sort-specification [ , sort-specification ]...
```

You can have multiple sort specifications, each of which has the following syntax:

```
( column-name | unsigned-integer )
  [ COLLATE BY collation-name ] [ ASC | DESC ]
```

In all cases you are sorting by a column, but you can specify the column either by its name, or by using an integer to designate the column. If you sort by column name, the column must be one of those in the SELECT list of the query expression. Columns that are in the table, but not in the query SELECT list, will not work as sort specifications. If you sort by unsigned integer, the integer represents the position of the column in the query SELECT list. The number 1 would represent the first column specified in the query's SELECT list, 2 would specify the second, and so on.

As an example, suppose you wanted to perform some operation not supported by SQL on selected rows of the CUSTOMER table. You could write a DECLARE CURSOR statement similar to this:

Unsigned integers as sort specifications have been deprecated

The use of an unsigned integer in a sort specification has been deprecated in SQL-92. When a feature is *deprecated* in an ANSI standard, the feature is considered either obsolete or undesirable. Its use is discouraged, and it will probably be dropped in the next release of the standard. Deprecating a feature in one version of a standard gives people time to eliminate the feature from their products before the next version of the standard comes out.

The use of integers in the ORDER BY clause was originally included in SQL as a way to reference SELECT list elements that were expressions (and therefore didn't have column names):

```
SELECT E_NM, SALARY+COMMISSION
    FROM EMPLOYEE ORDER BY 2 ;
```

There was originally no other way to reference that second column. SQL-92 then introduced the AS clause as a way to give names to SELECT list elements:

```
SELECT E_NM AS EMP_NAME,
    SALARY+COMMISSION AS PAY
    FROM EMPLOYEE ORDER BY PAY ;
```

The AS clause provides more readable names, and gives identifying names to expression columns. The latter use makes integers in ORDER BY unnecessary, so the feature was deprecated.

```
DECLARE cust1 CURSOR FOR
    SELECT CUST_ID, F_NAME, L_NAME, CITY, STATE, PHONE
        FROM CUSTOMER
    ORDER BY STATE, L_NAME, F_NAME ;
```

In this example, the SELECT statement retrieves rows sorted first by state, then by last name, and finally by first name. All customers in Alaska (AK) will be retrieved before the first customer from Alabama (AL) is retrieved. The customer records from Alaska will be sorted by customer last name. Aaron will come before Abbott. In cases where the last name is the same, the tie will be broken by looking at and sorting by first name. George Aaron will come before Henry Aaron. We could obtain the same result with the alternate syntax:

```
DECLARE cust1 CURSOR FOR
    SELECT CUST_ID, F_NAME, L_NAME, CITY, STATE, PHONE
        FROM CUSTOMER
    ORDER BY 5, 3, 2 ;
```

In this formulation we order the rows first by the fifth column in the query SELECT list (STATE), then by the third column (L_NAME), and finally by the second column (F_NAME).

Have you ever had to make 40 copies of a 20-page document on a photocopy machine that did not have a collater attached? What a drag! You had to make 20 stacks on tables, desks, and any other flat surfaces in sight, then walk by the stacks 40 times, placing a sheet on each stack as you went by. This ordering process is called *collation*. A similar process plays a role in SQL. In Chapter 6 I defined a collation as a set of rules that determine how strings in a character set compare with each other. A character set has a default collation sequence that defines the order in which things will be sorted. However, it is possible to apply a collation sequence other than the default to a column. To do so, use the optional COLLATE BY clause. Your implementation probably supports several common collations. You can pick one, then make the collation either ascending or descending by appending an ASC or DESC keyword to the clause.

In a DECLARE CURSOR statement, it is possible to specify a calculated column that does not exist in the underlying table. In such a case, the calculated column would not have a name that you could use in the ORDER BY clause. You can give it a name in the DECLARE CURSOR's query expression, which allows you to identify the column later. Consider the example:

```
DECLARE revenue CURSOR FOR
    SELECT model, units, price,
           units * price AS extprice
        FROM TRANSDETAIL
    ORDER BY model, extprice DESC ;
```

It this example, since there is no COLLATE BY clause in the ORDER BY clause, the default collation sequence is used. Note that the fourth column in the SELECT list is calculated from the data in the second and third columns. It is an extended price and is given the name *extprice*. In the ORDER BY clause, we first sort by model name and then by *extprice*. The sort on *extprice* is descending, as specified by the DESC keyword. This means that the transactions with the highest dollar value will be processed first. The default sort order is ascending (ASC), and sorts will be in ascending order if no sort order is specified.

Once you specify a sort order in an ORDER BY clause, that sort order remains in effect until it is explicitly changed. Thus if you have a sort specification list that includes a DESC sort, and you want the next sort to be in ascending order, you must explicitly specify ASC for that next sort. For example:

```
ORDER BY A, B DESC, C, D, E ASC, F
```

is equivalent to

```
ORDER BY A ASC, B DESC, C DESC, D DESC, E ASC, F ASC
```

The rule is to default to the first explicit ASC or DESC to the left, otherwise to ASC if there is no explicit ASC or DESC to the left. ■

The updatability clause

On some occasions you may want to update or delete table rows that you access via a cursor. At other times, you will probably want to guarantee that such updates or deletions cannot be made. SQL-92 gives you considerable control over this issue with the updatability clause of the DECLARE CURSOR statement. If you want to prevent updates and deletions within the scope of the cursor, use the clause:

```
FOR READ ONLY
```

To allow updates of specified columns only, leaving all others protected from changes, use:

```
FOR UPDATE OF column-name [ , column-name ]...
```

Of course, any columns listed must appear in the DECLARE CURSOR's query expression. If you don't include an updatability clause, the default assumption is that all columns listed in the query expression are updatable. In that case an UPDATE statement can update all the columns in the row to which the cursor is pointing, and a DELETE statement can delete that row.

Sensitivity

The rows that fall within the scope of a cursor are determined by the query expression in the DECLARE CURSOR statement. Consider a possible problem: What if a statement in your program, located between the OPEN and the CLOSE statements, changes the contents of some of those rows in such a way that they no longer satisfy the query? What if such a statement deletes some of those rows entirely? Does the cursor continue to process all the rows that originally qualified, or does it recognize the new situation and ignore rows that no longer qualify or that have been deleted?

If you change the data in columns that are part of a DECLARE CURSOR's query expression, after some but not all of the query's rows have been processed, you clearly have a mess on your hands. Your results will likely be inconsistent and misleading. To avoid this problem, you want to make your cursor *insensitive* to any changes that statements within its scope might make. You can do this by adding the INSENSITIVE keyword to your DECLARE CURSOR statement. If you do, as long as your cursor is open it will be insensitive to table changes that would otherwise affect rows qualified to be included in the cursor's scope. A cursor cannot be both insensitive and updatable. An insensitive cursor must be read-only.

Think of it this way. A normal SQL statement, such as UPDATE, INSERT, or DELETE, operates on a set of rows in a database table (perhaps the entire table). While such a statement is active, SQL's transaction mechanism protects it from interference by other statements acting concurrently on the same data. When you are using a cursor, however, your "window of vulnerability" to harmful interaction is wide open. From the moment that you OPEN a cursor until you CLOSE it you are at risk. If you open one cursor and start processing through a table, then open a second cursor while the first is still active, the actions you perform with the second cursor could affect what the statement controlled by the first cursor sees. For example:

```
DECLARE C1 CURSOR FOR SELECT * FROM EMPLOYEE
    ORDER BY SALARY ;
DECLARE C2 CURSOR FOR SELECT * FROM EMPLOYEE
    FOR UPDATE OF SALARY ;
```

Now let's say you open both cursors and FETCH a few rows with C1, and then UPDATE a salary with C2 to increase its value. This can cause a row that you have already fetched with C1 to appear again on a later FETCH of C1.

The peculiar interactions possible with multiple open cursors, or opened cursors and set operations, are the sort of concurrency problems that transaction isolation is designed to avoid. When you operate this way you are asking for trouble. So remember:

Don't operate with multiple open cursors. ■

Scrollability

Scrollability is a capacity that cursors did not have prior to SQL-92. In implementations adhering to SQL-86 or SQL-89, the only allowed movement of the cursor was sequential, starting at the first row retrieved by the query expression and ending with the last row. SQL-92's inclusion of the SCROLL keyword in the DECLARE CURSOR statement gives you the ability to access rows in any order you want. The movement of the cursor is controlled by the syntax of the FETCH statement, described later in this chapter.

One limitation to SQL-92's scrollability is that a scrollable cursor must be read-only. You cannot perform updates or deletes within the scope of a scrolled cursor.

Opening a Cursor

Although the DECLARE CURSOR statement specifies which rows to include in the cursor, it doesn't actually cause anything to happen, because DECLARE is a declaration and not an executable statement. The OPEN statement actually brings the cursor into existence. It has the following form:

```
OPEN cursor-name ;
```

To open the cursor used as an example in the previous discussion of the ORDER BY clause, use

```
DECLARE revenue CURSOR FOR
   SELECT model, units, price,
          units * price AS extprice
      FROM TRANSDETAIL
   ORDER BY model, extprice DESC ;
OPEN revenue ;
```

You can't FETCH rows from a cursor until the cursor has been opened. The moment you open a cursor, the values of variables referenced in the DECLARE CURSOR statement become fixed, as do all CURRENT date-time functions. Consider the following example:

```
DECLARE CURSOR C1 FOR SELECT * FROM ORDERS
WHERE ORDERS.CUSTOMER = :NAME
AND DUE_DATE < CURRENT_DATE ;

NAME := 'Acme Co';    --A host language statement
OPEN C1;
NAME := 'Omega Inc.';  --Another host statement
...
UPDATE ORDERS SET DUE_DATE = CURRENT_DATE;
```

The OPEN statement fixes the value of all variables referenced in the declare cursor, and also fixes a value for all CURRENT date-time functions. Thus, the second assignment to the NAME variable (NAME := 'Omega Inc.') has no effect on the rows that will be fetched by the cursor. (That value of NAME will be used the next time that you open C1.) And, even if the OPEN statement is executed a minute before midnight, and the UPDATE statement is executed a minute after midnight, the value of CURRENT_DATE in the UPDATE statement will be the value of that function at the time the OPEN was executed. This is true even if the DECLARE cursor doesn't reference the date-time function.

The fix is in (for date-times)

There is a similar "fixing" of date-time values in set operations. Consider:

```
UPDATE ORDERS
    SET RECHECK_DATE = CURRENT_DATE
    WHERE....;
```

Now suppose that there are a lot of orders. We begin executing this statement at a minute before midnight. At midnight the statement is still running, and it doesn't finish executing until five minutes after midnight. It doesn't matter, because if a statement has any reference to CURRENT_DATE (or TIME or TIMESTAMP), then the value is fixed when the statement begins, so all of the ORDERS rows in the statement will get the same RECHECK_DATE. Similarly, if a statement references TIMESTAMP, then only one time stamp value will be used for the whole statement, no matter how long the statement runs.

Here's an interesting example of an implication of this rule:

```
UPDATE EMPLOYEE SET
    KEY=CURRENT_TIMESTAMP;
```

You might expect that statement to set a unique value in the key column of each EMPLOYEE. You'd be disappointed: It will set the same value in every row.

So when the OPEN statement fixes date-time values for all statements referencing the cursor, it is treating all of those statements as something like an extended statement.

Fetching Data from a Single Row

While the DECLARE CURSOR statement specifies the name of the cursor and its scope, and the OPEN statement collects the table rows selected by the DECLARE CURSOR's query expression, the FETCH statement actually retrieves the data. The cursor will always be pointing either to one of the rows in the scope of the cursor or to the empty space between two rows. You can specify where the cursor points with the FETCH statement's *orientation* clause.

Syntax

The syntax for the FETCH command is:

```
FETCH [[orientation] FROM] cursor-name
    INTO target-specification [, target-specification ]...
```

There are six orientation options: NEXT, PRIOR, FIRST, LAST, ABSOLUTE, and RELATIVE. The default option is NEXT, which was the only orientation available in versions of SQL prior to SQL-92. It moves the cursor from wherever it is to the next row in the set specified by the query expression. If the cursor is located before the first record, it moves to the first. If it is pointing to record n, it moves to record $n+1$. If it is pointing to the last record in the set, it moves beyond that record and notification of a *no data* condition is returned in the SQLCODE system variable. (SQLCODE and the rest of SQL's error handling facilities are explained in Chapter 18.)

The target specifications are either host variables or parameters respectively, depending on whether the cursor is being used by embedded SQL or by module language. The number and types of the target specifications must match the number and types of the columns specified by the DECLARE CURSOR's query expression. So, in the case of embedded SQL, when you fetch a list of five values from a row of a table, there must be five host variables to receive those values, and they must be of the right types.

Orientation of a scrollable cursor

Since the SQL-92 cursor is scrollable, there are other choices besides NEXT. When you specify PRIOR, the pointer moves to the row immediately preceding its current location. When you specify FIRST, it points to the first record in the set, and when you specify LAST, it points to the last record.

ABSOLUTE and RELATIVE must be accompanied by an integer value specification. For example, FETCH ABSOLUTE 7 would move the cursor to the seventh row from the beginning of the set. FETCH RELATIVE 7 would move the cursor seven rows beyond its current position. FETCH RELATIVE 0 leaves the cursor at its current location.

FETCH RELATIVE 1 has the same effect as FETCH NEXT. FETCH RELATIVE -1 has the same effect as FETCH PRIOR. FETCH ABSOLUTE 1 gives you the first record in the set, and interestingly, FETCH ABSOLUTE -1 gives you the last record in the set. Any other negative value specification will return the *no data* exception condition code (+100) in the SQLCODE variable. Specifying FETCH ABSOLUTE 0 will also return the *no data* exception condition code, as will FETCH ABSOLUTE 17 when there are only sixteen rows in the set.

Positioned DELETE and UPDATE statements

You can perform delete and update operations on the row that the cursor is currently pointing to. The syntax of the DELETE statement is

```
DELETE FROM table-name WHERE CURRENT OF cursor-name ;
```

If the cursor is not currently pointing to a row, this statement will generate an error condition and no deletion will be performed.

The syntax of the UPDATE statement is

```
UPDATE table-name
    SET column-name = value [,column-name = value]...
    WHERE CURRENT OF cursor-name ;
```

The value that is placed into each specified column must be either a value expression, the keyword NULL, or the keyword DEFAULT. If the cursor has an ORDER BY clause, the columns used in the ordering cannot be updated. If any error condition is returned by an attempted positioned update operation, the update will not be performed.

Closing a Cursor

Once you have finished with a cursor, it is good practice to close it. Leaving a cursor open as your application goes on to deal with other issues may cause no harm, but then again it might. Also, open cursors consume system resources. Make a habit of closing your cursors after they have served their purpose.

If you close a cursor that was INSENSITIVE to changes made while it was open, then reopen it, the reopened cursor will now reflect any such changes. ■

Chapter 17

Dynamic SQL

• •

In This Chapter

▶ Compiling an application when you don't know what tables or columns it will operate on

▶ Providing for entry of complete SQL statements at run time

▶ Capturing a description of entries made at run time

▶ Retrieving information about runtime entries

▶ Modifying runtime entries with the application program

▶ Using dynamic cursors to operate on table rows that are not identified until run time

• •

*I*n previous chapters I mentioned three different ways to run SQL: interactive SQL, embedded SQL, and module language. Embedded SQL and module language can collectively be called *static SQL*, since once the code is compiled, it does not change. Dynamic SQL is a fourth, although not frequently used, way to run SQL. It is employed mainly by SQL experts performing system programming, and is rarely needed in SQL applications. This chapter is a brief introduction to dynamic SQL, so that you will recognize it when you see it. One way to look at dynamic SQL is to think of it as a hybrid that possesses some of the attributes of interactive SQL and some of the attributes of either embedded SQL or module language.

Interactive SQL, as the name implies, is a real-time conversation with the database. The user and the programmer are the same person, and in fact there is no distinction between using and programming. Embedded SQL and module language are used in a very different way. The program is written, compiled, and debugged by the programmer long before the intended user first sets eyes on it. All decisions as to what the application will do have already been made. The user does not need to have nearly the level of skill and understanding of SQL that the programmer does.

There are advantages and disadvantages to both modes of operation. Interactive SQL is good because you may not know until you have actually started an interactive session what some of the subsequent SQL statements should be. Embedded SQL and module language cannot accommodate such a requirement because they must be cast in concrete (compiled) before they can start running. On the other hand, interactive SQL is bad, because it requires the user to be as knowledgeable as a programmer, and because every statement in a session must be entered by hand, even when it is the fiftieth repetition of a statement that has been entered before. Aside from the tedium induced by all this keyboarding, performance drops to a mere fraction of what it would be for an equivalent compiled application.

Dynamic SQL provides a way of building a compiled application even when you do not know everything you need to know at compile time. The unknown values, known as *dynamic parameters* or *parameter markers*, can be supplied at run time. Dynamic parameters are denoted by question marks (?) in a dynamic SQL statement. The following example shows one way in which they are used:

```
UPDATE NATIONAL_LEAGUER
    SET COMPLETE_GAMES = ? WHERE LAST_NAME = ? ;
```

In this example there are two dynamic parameters, neither of which is known until run time.

It is challenging to use dynamic SQL when more than just a couple of values may be unknown until run time. The entire SQL statement may be unknown. It is possible to write your application in such a way that the user enters all the data needed to construct the statement. Since the user could enter a previously unknown statement, with an unknown number of parameters, smoothly coordinating the dynamic SQL with the procedural code that surrounds it could be a problem. To address this issue, you can set up SQL item descriptor areas that document the characteristics of the material entered at run time. The procedural code can interrogate the descriptor areas to determine how to deal with that material.

If you know the number of dynamic parameters to expect, you can represent them with host variables or static parameters in your dynamic SQL statement. If you do not know how many dynamic parameters there are, you will have to extract that information from the descriptor areas, described later in this chapter.

Prepared and Unprepared Dynamic SQL

Dynamic SQL has two modes of execution. One is more like the static modes (embedded and module language) and the other is more like the interactive mode. The first uses the PREPARE/EXECUTE statement pair. The second uses the EXECUTE IMMEDIATE statement.

Be prepared (or how the Boy Scout motto applies to SQL)

When you use the PREPARE/EXECUTE statement pair, you break your dynamic SQL activity into two parts: preparation and execution. The preparation activity is analogous to the compilation of static SQL. The PREPARE statement analyzes the dynamic SQL statement for proper syntax, then determines the types of any dynamic parameters. The PREPARE statement also gives the dynamic SQL statement a name and sets it up so as to optimize its execution.

The main advantage of breaking a dynamic SQL activity into two parts comes about when you must execute the activity repeatedly. You can do the preparation part once, repeating only the execution part. This slashes overhead, allowing faster completion of the entire job. Another advantage is the ability to use dynamic parameters.

Just do it (the Nike approach)

EXECUTE IMMEDIATE is handy when you are only going to execute an SQL statement once (and therefore don't care about separating out the preparation part), and when your statement does not include any dynamic parameters. If your statement does include dynamic parameters, you cannot use EXECUTE IMMEDIATE.

Let's consider a pseudocode example that does not involve dynamic parameters, and does not produce any output:

```
DECLARE STMNT_VAR CHAR (200);
BEGIN
DO WHILE condition = true
    DISPLAY ('Enter an SQL statement') ;
    READ (STMNT_VAR) ;
    EXEC SQL EXECUTE IMMEDIATE STMNT_VAR ;
    ...
END DO ;
END BEGIN ;
```

This program will DISPLAY the prompt, "Enter an SQL statement," READ whatever the user enters, then EXECUTE the entry as an SQL statement. The user can enter any SQL statement that does not include host variables or dynamic parameters, and does not produce an output. For example:

```
UPDATE EMPLOYEE SET SALARY=SALARY+100 WHERE AGE>50 ;
```

or

```
INSERT INTO DEPT VALUES("Sales", 1200, 1450) ;
```

If the user enters anything other than a valid SQL statement, she'll get an error message, just like in static SQL.

The PREPARE statement

The format of the PREPARE statement is

```
PREPARE statement-name
FROM statement-variable ;
```

One example of its use might be:

```
PREPARE game_update
FROM 'UPDATE NATIONAL_LEAGUER
SET COMPLETE_GAMES = ?
WHERE LAST_NAME = ?' ;
```

This statement prepares an update of the NATIONAL_LEAGUER table, using dynamic parameters whose values are determined at run time.

Describing a dynamic SQL statement

Since important details of a dynamic SQL statement may not become known until run time, they cannot be coded into your application. This information must be captured and stored somewhere so that it will be available when needed.

An SQL *item descriptor area* is an area used by a DBMS to store information about the dynamic parameters in your dynamic SQL statements. ■

The DESCRIBE statement causes a dynamic parameter to be represented in the item descriptor area. When the user enters a value for a dynamic parameter, SQL analyzes the value and puts the result of its analysis in the item descriptor area. Table 17-1 shows information stored about a dynamic parameter.

Table 17-1: Dynamic Parameter Information Stored in SQL Item Descriptor Area

Field Name	Field Data Type	Comment
TYPE	Exact numeric, scale 0	Code for the data type
LENGTH	Exact numeric, scale 0	Length in characters or bits for string types
OCTET_LENGTH	Exact numeric, scale 0	Length in octets for strings
RETURNED_LENGTH	Exact numeric, scale 0	Length in characters or bits returned from DBMS for strings
RETURNED_OCTET_LENGTH	Exact numeric, scale 0	Length in octets returned from DBMS for strings
PRECISION	Exact numeric, scale 0	Precision for numeric types
SCALE	Exact numeric, scale 0	Scale for exact numeric types
DATETIME_INTERVAL_CODE	Exact numeric, scale 0	Code for datetime/interval subtype
DATETIME_INTERVAL_PRECISION	Exact numeric, scale 0	Precision of interval's leading field
NULLABLE	Exact numeric, scale 0	Is column nullable?
NAME	Character string, length <= 128	Name of associated database column
UNNAMED	Exact numeric, scale 0	Is name real, or supplied by DBMS?
COLLATION_CATALOG	Character string, length <= 128	Catalog name for column's collation
COLLATION_SCHEMA	Character string, length <= 128	Schema name for column's collation
COLLATION_NAME	Character string, length <= 128	Collation name for column's collation
CHARACTER_SET_CATALOG	Character string, length <= 128	Catalog name for column's character set
CHARACTER_SET_SCHEMA	Character string, length <= 128	Schema name for column's character set
CHARACTER_SET_NAME	Character string, length <= 128	Collation name for column's character set
DATA	Specified by code in TYPE field	The actual data itself
INDICATOR	Exact numeric, scale 0	Value for indicator parameter

Some fields in the descriptor area contain codes rather than actual data. One of these is the TYPE field, which holds a code representing the data type of the column or parameter being described. Table 17-2 displays the codes and the data types they represent.

Table 17-2: TYPE Codes

Code	Data Type
Negative	Implementor-defined data types
1	CHARACTER
2	NUMERIC
3	DECIMAL
4	INTEGER
5	SMALLINT
6	FLOAT
7	REAL
8	DOUBLE PRECISION
9	DATE, TIME, or TIMESTAMP
10	INTERVAL
11	Reserved for future use
12	CHARACTER VARYING
13	Reserved for future use
14	BIT
15	BIT VARYING
> 15	Reserved for future use

DATETIME_INTERVAL_CODE is another field in the descriptor area that contains a code. This code distinguishes between the various DATETIME types. Table 17-3 gives the five possibilities for non-INTERVAL types. (Type code = 9.)

Table 17-3: DATETIME Codes for DATE, TIME, or TIMESTAMP Data

Code	Data Type
1	DATE
2	TIME
3	TIMESTAMP
4	TIME WITH TIME ZONE
5	TIMESTAMP WITH TIME ZONE

Table 17-4 displays the codes in DATETIME_INTERVAL_CODE that apply to INTERVAL type data. (Type code = 10.)

Table 17-4: DATETIME Codes for INTERVAL Data

Code	Data Type
1	YEAR
2	MONTH
3	DAY
4	HOUR
5	MINUTE
6	SECOND
7	YEAR TO MONTH
8	DAY TO HOUR
9	DAY TO MINUTE
10	DAY TO SECOND
11	HOUR TO MINUTE
12	HOUR TO SECOND
13	MINUTE TO SECOND

The ALLOCATE DESCRIPTOR statement

If you want to pass data from your procedural code to your dynamic SQL code via a dynamic parameter, a DESCRIBE INPUT statement will place information about that parameter into the descriptor area. Conversely, if you want to pass data from a database column to your procedural code via a dynamic parameter, a DESCRIBE OUTPUT statement will place information about the parameter into the descriptor area.

Before you can put data into a descriptor, you must allocate space for it in the descriptor area. Do this with an ALLOCATE DESCRIPTOR statement, which has the following syntax:

```
ALLOCATE DESCRIPTOR descriptor-name
    [WITH MAX occurrences] ;
```

Once you establish a descriptor name, you can refer to it in subsequent DESCRIBE, SET DESCRIPTOR, GET DESCRIPTOR, and DEALLOCATE DESCRIP-TOR statements. The optional WITH MAX *occurrences* clause tells how many items to make space for. Occurrences is a positive integer. If you do not spec-ify a WITH MAX *occurrences* clause, your implementation will give you what-ever its default maximum number of occurrences is.

The DESCRIBE statement

The DESCRIBE statement puts information into the descriptor table, based on the data entered by the user. Let's look at an example to see dynamic SQL in action. Getting everything properly declared, allocated, and described is a lengthy process. When you see just how lengthy, you may be discouraged from ever using dynamic SQL, unless there is absolutely no other way to accomplish your objectives.

Suppose you want to update the values of a column in selected rows of a table. At compile time you do not know the name of the table, the primary keys of the rows, or the values to be placed in the column. This looks like a job for dynamic SQL.

The first thing you need to do is define variables to hold the quantities you are interested in. You'll need a variable for the name of the table, another for the name of its primary key column, and a third variable for the name of the column to update. Let's call these variables *table_name*, *col_name_1*, and *col_name_2*. That takes care of the *names* of the data items. The SQL state-ment that we want to construct will be of the following form:

```
UPDATE table_name
    SET col_name_2 = V2
    WHERE col_name_1 = V1 ;
```

The name of the column that serves as the primary key of the table will be captured into the *col_name_1* variable, and the name of the column to be updated will be captured into the *col_name_2* variable.

I'll use generic pseudocode with embedded SQL statements to show what must be done.

```
DECLARE table_name CHAR (18) ;
DECLARE col_name_1 CHAR (18) ;
DECLARE col_name_2 CHAR (18) ;
```

You will also need to declare variables to hold the data itself, and information about its type. Let's make the simplifying assumption that the data will be of either CHARACTER or INTEGER type, to keep the example from getting too tedious. (It's tedious enough as it is!)

```
DECLARE CHAR_V1 CHAR (100) ;
DECLARE INT_V1 INTEGER ;
DECLARE CHAR_V2 CHAR (100) ;
DECLARE INT_V2 INTEGER ;
DECLARE TYPE_VAR1 INTEGER ;
DECLARE TYPE_VAR2 INTEGER ;
DECLARE UPDATE_STMNT CHAR (100) ;
```

Next, you'll need to solicit the names of the table and the two columns of interest from the user.

```
DISPLAY ('Enter the table name, the key column name, '
    || 'and the data column name') ;
READ (table_name, col_name_1, col_name_2) ;
```

Now, with the variable data in hand, you can construct the UPDATE statement.

```
UPDATE_STMNT := 'UPDATE ' || table_name
                || ' SET ' || col_name_2 || '= ?'
                || 'WHERE ' || col_name_1 || '= ?' ;
```

This produces a dynamic SQL statement that looks like:

```
UPDATE table_name SET col_name_2 =? WHERE col_name_1 =?;
```

Now, at last, you get to some SQL, which prepares our dynamic UPDATE statement for execution:

```
EXEC SQL PREPARE S FROM UPDATE_STMT ;
```

Before executing the UPDATE, you have to determine the data types of the values being entered:

```
EXEC SQL ALLOCATE DESCRIPTOR 'D' ;
EXEC SQL DESCRIBE INPUT INTO SQL DESCRIPTOR 'D' ;
```

```
EXEC SQL GET DESCRIPTOR 'D' VALUE 1 TYPE_VAR1 = TYPE ;
EXEC SQL GET DESCRIPTOR 'D' VALUE 2 TYPE_VAR2 = TYPE ;
IF (TYPE_VAR1 <> 1 AND TYPEVAR1 <> 4)
      OR (TYPE_VAR2 <> 1 AND TYPE_VAR2 <> 4)
    THEN DISPLAY ('This program only handles '
        || 'character and integer data. ') ;
END IF ;
```

Recall from Table 17-2 that 1 is the TYPE code for CHARACTER data and 4 is the TYPE code for INTEGER data. At last you are ready to have the user start entering data, and to perform the updates:

```
DO WHILE condition = true
    DISPLAY ('Enter values for '
          || col_name_1 || ' AND ' || col_name_2) ;
    IF TYPE_VAR1 = 1 AND TYPE_VAR2 = 1
        THEN READ (CHAR_V1, CHAR_V2) ;
            EXEC SQL EXECUTE S USING (CHAR_V1, CHAR_V2) ;
    END IF ;
    IF TYPE_VAR1 = 1 AND TYPE_VAR2 = 4
        THEN READ (CHAR_V1, INT_V2) ;
            EXEC SQL EXECUTE S USING (CHAR_V1, INT_V2) ;
    END IF ;
    IF TYPE_VAR1 = 4 AND TYPE_VAR2 = 1
        THEN READ (INT_V1, CHAR_V2) ;
            EXEC SQL EXECUTE S USING (INT_V1, CHAR_V2) ;
    END IF ;
    IF TYPE_VAR1 = 4 AND TYPE_VAR2 = 4
        THEN READ (INT_V1, INT_V2) ;
            EXEC SQL EXECUTE S USING (INT_V1, INT_V2) ;
    END IF ;
    ...
  END DO WHILE ;
```

In this skeleton of a program, there is no error checking, loop termination condition, or other things that you would normally have in a real program. There is only enough to show a broad outline of what is involved in using dynamic SQL in an application.

It is fair to say that conceptually, dynamic SQL is simple. However, it is not easy to use in practice. Every line of code in the preceding examples is simple, performing rudimentary action. But such programs are not easy to write, because there are a lot of rudimentary actions. If you include error checking, null checking, and a full range of data types, as of course you should, the application will be even more difficult to write, although perhaps no more complex.

The DESCRIBE statement loads the allocated descriptor areas with information about the dynamic parameters. Assuming the primary key is of the CHARACTER type and the data to be updated is of INTEGER type, Table 17-5 shows the contents of the first descriptor area, and Table 17-6 shows the contents of the second descriptor area.

Table 17-5: Descriptor Area 1

Field Name	Field Contents
TYPE	1
LENGTH	100
OCTET_LENGTH	100 (assuming ASCII characters)
RETURNED_LENGTH	100
RETURNED_OCTET_LENGTH	100
PRECISION	n/a
SCALE	n/a
DATETIME_INTERVAL_CODE	n/a
DATETIME_INTERVAL_PRECISION	n/a
NULLABLE	1
NAME	EMPLOYEE_ID
UNNAMED	0
COLLATION_CATALOG	implementation dependent
COLLATION_SCHEMA	implementation dependent
COLLATION_NAME	implementation dependent
CHARACTER_SET_CATALOG	implementation dependent
CHARACTER_SET_SCHEMA	implementation dependent
CHARACTER_SET_NAME	implementation dependent
DATA	set when data is retrieved
INDICATOR	set when data is retrieved

Table 17-6: Descriptor Area 2

Field Name	Field Contents
TYPE	4
LENGTH	n/a
OCTET_LENGTH	n/a
RETURNED_LENGTH	n/a
RETURNED_OCTET_LENGTH	n/a
PRECISION	9
SCALE	0
DATETIME_INTERVAL_CODE	n/a
DATETIME_INTERVAL_PRECISION	n/a
NULLABLE	1
NAME	SALARY
UNNAMED	0
COLLATION_CATALOG	implementation dependent
COLLATION_SCHEMA	implementation dependent
COLLATION_NAME	implementation dependent
CHARACTER_SET_CATALOG	implementation dependent
CHARACTER_SET_SCHEMA	implementation dependent
CHARACTER_SET_NAME	implementation dependent
DATA	set when data is retrieved
INDICATOR	set when data is retrieved

The GET DESCRIPTOR statement

Once a dynamic parameter has been described, information about it is stored in a descriptor area. Your application can now access the information and take appropriate action. The GET DESCRIPTOR statement is the tool you use to do this.

You can use the GET DESCRIPTOR statement two ways, first to give you a count of how many parameters are described in the selected area, and second to find out the nature of those parameters. You may need the count if you don't know how many dynamic parameters are contained in the SQL statement that is entered or constructed at run time. Once you know the count, hopefully you will be able to deduce what each of the dynamic variables is.

To get a count of the number of dynamic parameters in an area, issue a statement in the form:

```
GET DESCRIPTOR  descriptor-name
number-of-parameters = COUNT ;
```

Follow up with statements that return information about the parameter of interest within the descriptor area. For example, if you wanted information about the first parameter stored in the descriptor area named 'D' you could issue the following statement:

```
GET DESCRIPTOR 'D' VALUE 1
:type = TYPE,
:length = LENGTH,
:name = NAME,
:nullable = NULLABLE,
:data = DATA,
:indicator = INDICATOR ;
```

In the previous example, we were only interested in retrieving the data types of the values to be entered, so we used the statements:

```
GET DESCRIPTOR 'D' VALUE 1 TYPE_VAR1 = TYPE ;
```

and

```
GET DESCRIPTOR 'D' VALUE 2 TYPE_VAR2 = TYPE ;
```

You can select whatever information you want from the descriptor table, retrieve it, then cause your program to take one action or another, based on what you retrieve.

The SET DESCRIPTOR statement

Once a descriptor area has been described, the natural course of events is for it to fill up with information based on the data coming to it at run time. However, it is also possible for you (the programmer/developer) to set values for fields of selected items in an area. The SET DESCRIPTOR statement, with syntax very similar to that of the GET DESCRIPTOR statement, does this. Here's its syntax:

```
SET DESCRIPTOR  descriptor-name
   COUNT = number-of-parameters ;
```

This statement sets the total number of items that you plan to use in a descriptor area. Of course COUNT cannot be greater than the maximum number of occurrences set in the preceding ALLOCATE DESCRIPTOR statement. If it is, an error will be returned.

To specify values for a item in the descriptor area, use this syntax:

```
SET DESCRIPTOR descriptor-name
   VALUE item-number
   item-field-name = value [,item-field-name = value]...
```

Here's an example:

```
SET DESCRIPTOR 'D'
   VALUE 1
   TYPE = :type,
   LENGTH = :length,
   NAME = :name,
   NULLABLE = :nullable,
   DATA = :data,
   INDICATOR = :indicator ;
```

You can set whatever fields you want to whatever values you want, as long as those values are valid for the field you are trying to put them in.

The EXECUTE statement

After a dynamic SQL statement is prepared, and its descriptor area is allocated and described, you can (at last!) execute it. The EXECUTE statement specifies the name of the statement being executed, the identity of input parameters (if any), and the identity of results (if any). The syntax is

```
EXECUTE statement-name
   USING input-parameter-list
   INTO result-list ;
```

SQLDAs

The dynamic SQL facility in the SQL-92 standard includes the statements ALLOCATE DESCRIPTOR, GET DESCRIPTOR, and SET DESCRIPTOR, all of which operate on the "encapsulated" descriptors. These statements, and encapsulated descriptors themselves, are new features of the SQL standard that many SQL products have not yet implemented. The more common technique in current SQL products is to use an "exposed" descriptor area, called the SQLDA. It is a host language data structure explicitly declared in the host program. With the SQLDA approach, the user declares or allocates the SQLDAs directly, rather than using ALLOCATE DESCRIPTOR. After an SQLDA has been filled with a DESCRIBE statement, the user accesses the fields directly, rather than using GET DESCRIPTOR and SET DESCRIPTOR statements. SQLDAs are then referenced in DESCRIBE and FETCH statements in the same manner that encapsulated descriptors are referenced.

Encapsulated descriptors have replaced the commonly used SQLDAs because:

✔ The detailed specifications of SQLDA structures vary from one implementation to the next. Thus, programs that use SQLDAs are not portable across platforms.

✔ SQLDAs include fields that the user must fill in with pointers to dynamically allocated storage. This means that SQLDAs cannot be used with host programming languages such as COBOL and FORTRAN, which don't have pointers or dynamic storage allocation.

✔ Storage for encapsulated descriptors and for the associated variables is allocated implicitly by SQL. Any required pointers to dynamically allocated storage are hidden within the encapsulated descriptor. This makes encapsulated descriptors much easier to use than SQLDAs.

The DEALLOCATE PREPARE and the DEALLOCATE DESCRIPTOR statements

Once you have finished with a dynamic SQL statement that you have prepared, and you are sure you will not need it again, you can free up the resources that it has been using with a DEALLOCATE PREPARE statement. Similarly, when you are finished with a descriptor area, DEALLOCATE DESCRIPTOR will release whatever system resources it was using.

If resources are tight, pay attention to your usage of descriptors and prepared dynamic SQL statements. Deallocate them as soon as they have served their purposes. ▪

If you are only going to execute a dynamic SQL statement once, and it has no dynamic parameters, there is no benefit to preparing it in advance. The processor is going to have to perform all the same actions anyway; so it might as well do them all at once. Not only that, but as you may have gathered from the previous discussion, using the PREPARE/EXECUTE approach can get pretty involved. If the statement you want to execute contains no host variables or dynamic parameters, and returns no output, it is much easier to use EXECUTE IMMEDIATE. ∎

Cursors and Dynamic SQL

The dynamic SQL we have discussed so far deals with non-SELECT statements and SELECT statements that are guaranteed to return no more than one row. To handle SELECT statements that return more than one row, you must invoke cursors, since your application's host language will probably not be able to handle data a set at a time.

The dynamic cursor is very similar to the static cursor described in Chapter 16. It is also set up by a DECLARE CURSOR statement, but there is a slight difference in syntax:

```
DECLARE cursor-name [INSENSITIVE][SCROLL] CURSOR
   FOR statement-name ;
```

In static SQL, the FOR clause holds a query expression. In dynamic SQL you probably don't know what the query is at compile time. Instead, the FOR clause argument is a statement name that will be equated to a character string at run time. This character string is the query expression.

The dynamic OPEN CURSOR statement is similar to the analogous static statement, but with one additional restriction: If one or more dynamic parameters appear in the cursor declaration, they must be listed in a USING clause. If there are no dynamic parameters involved, the USING clause is not needed:

```
OPEN cursor-name [USING dynamic-parameter-list] ;
```

The dynamic FETCH has the form:

```
FETCH [[orientation] FROM] cursor-name
   USING dynamic-parameter-list ;
```

Here the USING clause is mandatory. The FETCH must return at least one value, and the USING clause tells the DBMS where to put it.

When you are finished using a dynamic cursor, close it with:

```
CLOSE cursor-name ;
```

The dynamic OPEN, FETCH, and CLOSE statements are static statements, even though they operate on dynamic cursors. Thus there is no need to PREPARE them. The only fact about the operation that you need to know at compile time is whether you want the cursor to be insensitive or scrollable. All other aspects of the operation are determined at run time.

Dynamic Positioned Statements

In Chapter 16 I covered the static positioned DELETE and UPDATE statements. These statements let you delete or update selected rows in a table, accessed by a cursor. You can perform positioned deletes and updates with a dynamic cursor, too. The syntax is identical to the static DELETE and UPDATE statements:

```
DELETE FROM table-name WHERE CURRENT OF cursor-name ;

UPDATE table-name
   SET column-name = value [,column-name = value]...
   WHERE CURRENT OF cursor-name ;
```

One problem with this UPDATE statement is that in a dynamic situation, you may not know the column names at compile time. In that case you will have to prepare the dynamic positioned UPDATE statement. When the update has been prepared, the *table-name* becomes optional in the UPDATE statement, because it has already been specified in the PREPARE statement. The syntax becomes:

```
UPDATE [table-name]
   SET column-name = value [,column-name = value]...
   WHERE CURRENT OF cursor-name ;
```

To keep DELETE syntax consistent with UPDATE syntax, *table-name* is also optional in the dynamic positioned DELETE statement:

```
DELETE [FROM table-name] WHERE CURRENT OF cursor-name ;
```

A Final Word of Advice on Dynamic SQL

Dynamic SQL is not very common. It is used for writing utility programs that provide generalized access to data. Most SQL applications are intended to do specific things to specific tables, and thus can be written in static SQL. Many SQL sites have no programs that use dynamic SQL, and the rest have only a few such programs.

When you need to write a program using dynamic SQL, find some other program using dynamic SQL that has a function similar to the one you want to perform. Copy that other program and modify it as needed. You should be able to find such a program, because there are relatively few varieties of dynamic SQL programs. You may well find what you need in the programmer's manual for the DBMS you are using. ■

Chapter 18

Error Handling

In This Chapter

▶ Flagging error conditions

▶ Branching to error handling code

▶ Determining the exact nature of an error

▶ Determining which DBMS generated an error condition

*I*t would be great if every application you wrote worked perfectly every time. It would also be great to win $57 million in the Oregon state lottery. Both possibilities are about equally likely. Since error conditions of one sort or another are inevitable, it could be helpful to know what caused them. SQL-92 has two mechanisms for returning error information to you. They are the status parameters (or host variables) SQLCODE and SQLSTATE. Based on the contents of either of these parameters, you may want to take different actions. The WHENEVER clause allows you to take a predetermined action whenever a specified condition (such as SQLCODE having a negative value) is met. Detailed status information about the SQL statement just executed is stored in the *diagnostics area*. In this chapter, I'll explain these error handling facilities and how to use them.

SQLCODE

In versions of the SQL standard prior to SQL-92, there was only one mechanism for returning error information: SQLCODE. SQLCODE is an integer variable that is updated after the execution of every SQL statement. If the executed statement was successful, SQLCODE assumes a value of zero. If the statement did not produce an error, but encountered a *no data* condition, SQLCODE assumes a value of 100. A no data condition occurs, for example, when you execute a SELECT on a table that has no rows, or a FETCH on a table when the cursor is already located on the last record. A no data condition may or may not be an error, depending on the situation. Any result besides successful completion (0) or no data (100) is an error of some sort and returns a negative number. Table 18-1 shows the possibilities.

Table 18-1: SQLCODE Values

Execution State	SQLCODE
Successful completion	0
No data	100
Error	A negative number

The SQL standard has never specified which particular error conditions produce a particular value in SQLCODE. Consequently, implementors have all come up with their own specifications, which naturally do not agree with each other. This means that if you want to migrate an application from one DBMS to another, you will probably have to recode all of the error handling. This can amount to rewriting a major portion of the entire application. ■

Because so many applications had already been written that depended on the values of SQLCODE established by the various implementors, it was not practical for SQL-92 to try to establish standard meanings for the negative numbers that denote various error conditions. To do so would have been a retrofit nightmare for almost everyone who had already written an SQL application. Instead, SQL-92 standardizes a new status parameter, SQLSTATE. In the process SQLCODE has been deprecated. This does not mean that it is cursed in the literal sense. SQLCODE still works the way it has in the past, however its use is discouraged. All new applications should use SQLSTATE instead. Although SQL-92 still supports SQLCODE, it may be dropped from a future release of the standard. It is wise to switch to SQLSTATE wherever possible. ■

SQLSTATE

SQLSTATE does the same thing that SQLCODE does, but in a more standardized way. A large number of conditions have been specified, as opposed to two (successful completion and no data) for SQLCODE. This makes it much easier to migrate applications that use SQLSTATE from one DBMS platform to another.

Where SQLCODE is defined as an integer, SQLSTATE is a five-character string. Only the uppercase letters A through Z and the numerals 0 through 9 are valid characters. The five characters are divided into two groups: a two-character *class code* and a three-character *subclass code*. Figure 18-1 illustrates the SQLSTATE layout.

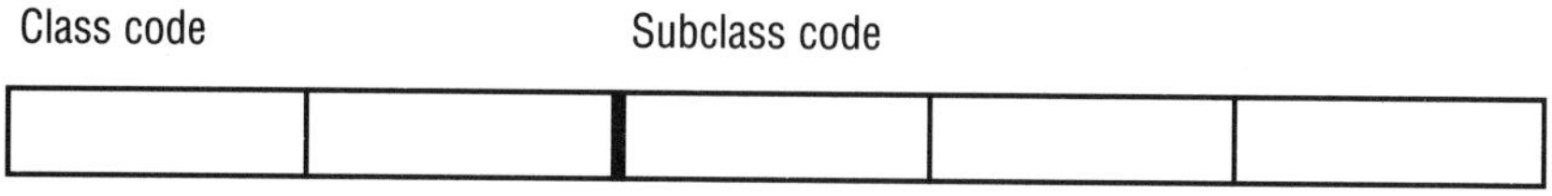

Class code   Subclass code

Figure 18-1: SQLSTATE status parameter layout.

Any class code starting with the letters A through H or the numerals 0 through 4 is defined by the SQL standard, and thus will mean the same thing in any implementation. Class codes starting with I through Z or 5 through 9 are left open for implementors to define. These codes are left to the implementors, because the SQL specification cannot anticipate every condition that might come up in every implementation. Clearly, however, implementors should use them as little as possible to avoid the migration problems that are unavoidable with SQLCODE. Ideally, they will use the standard codes most of the time and the nonstandard codes only under the most unusual circumstances.

A class code of 00 indicates successful completion. 01 means that statement executed successfully, but produced a warning. Class code 02 indicates the no data condition, and thus is equivalent to an SQLCODE of 100. Any class code other than 00, 01, or 02 indicates that the statement did not execute successfully.

Since SQLSTATE is updated after every SQL operation, you can check it after every statement executes. If it contains 00000 (successful completion), proceed with the next operation. If it contains anything else, you probably will want to branch out of the main line of your code to handle the situation. The specific class code and subclass code contained in SQLSTATE will determine which of several possible actions you should take.

To use SQLSTATE in a module language program, include a reference to it in your procedure definitions, as shown in the following example:

```
PROCEDURE NUTRIENT
    (SQLSTATE, :foodname CHAR (20), :calories SMALLINT,
       :protein DECIMAL (5,1), :fat DECIMAL (5,1),
       :carbo DECIMAL (5,1))

INSERT INTO FOODS
    (FOODNAME, CALORIES, PROTEIN, FAT, CARBOHYDRATE)
```

```
VALUES
(:foodname, :calories, :protein, :fat, :carbo) ;
```

At the appropriate spot in your procedural language program, you would make values available for the parameters (perhaps by soliciting them from the user), then call the procedure. The syntax of this will vary from one language to another, but will look something like:

```
foodname = "Okra, boiled" ;
calories = 29 ;
protein = 2.0 ;
fat = 0.3 ;
carbo = 6.0 ;
NUTRIENT(state, foodname, calories, protein, fat, carbo);
```

The status of SQLSTATE will be returned in the variable *state*. Your program can examine this variable, then take the appropriate action, based on its contents.

Older implementations of SQL will support only SQLCODE. Newer ones will support both SQLCODE and SQLSTATE. If your implementation supports SQLSTATE, use it instead of SQLCODE. SQLSTATE provides all the information that SQLCODE does, is more precisely specified, and is guaranteed to be supported in future releases of the SQL specification. ▪

The WHENEVER Clause

There is little point in knowing that an SQL operation has not executed successfully if you can't do anything about it. If an error occurs, you do not want your application to continue executing as if everything were fine. You want to acknowledge the error and do something to correct it if you can. If you can't correct it, at the very least you want to inform the user of the problem and bring the application to a graceful termination. The WHENEVER clause is SQL's mechanism for dealing with execution exceptions.

The WHENEVER clause is actually a declaration, and as such is located in your application's SQL Declare Section, ahead of the executable SQL code. The syntax is

```
WHENEVER condition action ;
```

The *condition* may be either SQLERROR or NOT FOUND. The *action* may be either CONTINUE or GOTO address. SQLERROR will be True if SQLCODE is negative or if SQLSTATE has a class code other than 00, 01, or 02. NOT FOUND will be True if SQLCODE is 100 or if SQLSTATE is 02000.

If the action is CONTINUE, then nothing special takes place. Execution continues normally. If the action is GOTO address (or GO TO address), then execution branches to the designated address in the program. At the branch address, you can put a conditional statement that examines SQLCODE or SQLSTATE and takes different actions based on what it finds. Some examples of this might be:

```
WHENEVER SQLERROR GO TO error_trap ;
```

or

```
WHENEVER NOT FOUND CONTINUE ;
```

The GO TO option is simply a macro: The implementation (that is, the embedded language precompiler) inserts the following test after every EXEC SQL statement:

```
IF SQLSTATE <> '00000' THEN GOTO error_trap;
```

The CONTINUE option is essentially a NO-OP, saying "ignore this." ∎

The Diagnostics Area

Although SQLSTATE can potentially give you more information than SQLCODE can about why a particular statement failed, it is still pretty brief. SQL-92 provides for the capture and retention of considerable additional status information in a *diagnostics area*. This can be particularly helpful in cases where the execution of a single SQL statement generates multiple errors. SQLCODE and SQLSTATE would only report the occurrence of one of them, while the diagnostics area has the capacity to report on multiple (hopefully all) errors.

The *diagnostics area* is a data structure managed by the DBMS, that has two components, a *header* and a *detail* area. The header contains general information about the last SQL statement to be executed. The detail area holds information about each code (either error, warning, or success) that is generated by the statement. ∎

In Chapter 14 I covered the SET TRANSACTION statement. In this statement you can specify DIAGNOSTICS SIZE. The SIZE you specify will be the number of detail areas allocated for status information. If you do not include a DIAGNOSTICS SIZE clause in your SET TRANSACTION statement, your DBMS will assign its default number of detail areas, whatever that happens to be.

The header area contains five items, listed in Table 18-2.

Table 18-2: The Diagnostics Header Area

Item	Data Type
NUMBER	Exact numeric, scale 0
MORE	Character string, length 1
COMMAND_FUNCTION	Character varying, length <= 128
DYNAMIC_FUNCTION	Character varying, length <= 128
ROW_COUNT	Exact numeric, scale 0

The NUMBER field tells the number of detail areas filled with data as a result of the execution of the statement. The MORE field will contain either 'Y' or 'N', 'Y' if the diagnostics area holds all the conditions detected by the DBMS, and 'N' if more conditions were detected than the detail area can hold. COMMAND_FUNCTION contains a character string that is the SQL statement that generated the diagnostic entry. If a dynamic SQL statement generated the entry, COMMAND_FUNCTION will contain either EXECUTE or EXECUTE IMMEDIATE, and DYNAMIC_FUNCTION will hold the dynamic SQL statement itself. ROW_COUNT holds the number of rows affected by the SQL statement.

The detail areas contain data on each individual error, warning, or success condition. Each detail area contains 17 items, as shown in Table 18-3.

CONDITION_NUMBER holds the sequence number of the detail area. If a statement generates five status items that fill up five detail areas, the CONDITION_NUMBER for the fifth one will be five. To retrieve a specific detail area for examination, use a GET DIAGNOSTICS statement with the desired CONDITION_NUMBER. RETURNED_SQLSTATE holds the SQLSTATE value that caused this detail area to be filled.

CLASS_ORIGIN tells you the source of the value returned in SQLSTATE. If it is defined by the SQL standard, CLASS_ORIGIN will be 'ISO 9075'. If the value was defined by your DBMS implementation, CLASS_ORIGIN will hold a string identifying the source of your DBMS. SUBCLASS_ORIGIN will act similarly.

CLASS_ORIGIN is important. If you get an SQLSTATE such as '22012', the values indicate that it is in the range of standard SQLSTATEs, so you know that it will mean the same thing in all SQL implementations. However, if the SQLSTATE is '22500', then the first two characters are in the standard range, and indicate "data exception," but the last three characters are in the implementation-defined range. And, if SQLSTATE is '900001', then it is completely in the implementation-defined range. So, how do you find out the detailed meaning of '22500', or the meaning of '900001'? You have to look in the implementor's documentation. Which implementor? If you are using CONNECT, you may be

Table 18-3: The Diagnostics Detail Area

Item	*Data Type*
CONDITION_NUMBER	Exact numeric, scale 0
RETURNED_SQLSTATE	Character string, length 5
CLASS_ORIGIN	Character varying, length <= maximum length of an identifier
SUBCLASS_ORIGIN	Character varying, length <= maximum length of an identifier
CONSTRAINT_CATALOG	Character varying, length <= maximum length of an identifier
CONSTRAINT_SCHEMA	Character varying, length <= maximum length of an identifier
CONSTRAINT_NAME	Character varying, length <= maximum length of an identifier
CONNECTION_NAME	Character varying, length <= maximum length of an identifier
ENVIRONMENT_NAME	Character varying, length <= maximum length of an identifier
CATALOG_NAME	Character varying, length <= maximum length of an identifier
SCHEMA_NAME	Character varying, length <= maximum length of an identifier
TABLE_NAME	Character varying, length <= maximum length of an identifier
COLUMN_NAME	Character varying, length <= maximum length of an identifier
CURSOR_NAME	Character varying, length <= maximum length of an identifier
MESSAGE_TEXT	Character varying, length <= maximum length of an identifier
MESSAGE_LENGTH	Exact numeric, scale 0
MESSAGE_OCTET_LENGTH	Exact numeric, scale 0

connecting to various products. To determine which one produced the error condition, look at CLASS_ORIGIN and SUBCLASS_ORIGIN: They have values that identify each implementation. You can test the CLASS_ORIGIN and SUBCLASS_ORIGIN to see if they identify implementors for which you have the SQLSTATE listings. The actual values placed in CLASS_ORIGIN and SUBCLASS_ORIGIN are implementor-defined, but are expected to be self-explanatory company names.

If the error reported is a constraint violation, the CONSTRAINT_CATALOG, CONSTRAINT_SCHEMA, and CONSTRAINT_NAME will identify the constraint being violated.

This is probably the most important information provided by GET DIAGNOS-TICS. Consider an EMPLOYEE table such as the following:

```
CREATE TABLE EMPLOYEE
(ID CHAR(5) CONSTRAINT EMP_PK PRIMARY KEY,
SALARY DEC(8,2) CONSTRAINT EMP_SAL CHECK SALARY > 0,
DEPT CHAR(5) CONSTRAINT EMP_DEPT
   REFERENCES DEPARTMENT) ;
```

And possibly a DEPARTMENT table such as:

```
CREATE TABLE DEPARTMENT
  (DEPTNO CHAR(5),
  BUDGET DEC(12,2) CONSTRAINT DEPT_BUDGET
  CHECK(BUDGET >= SELECT SUM(SALARY) FROM EMPLOYEE
        WHERE EMPLOYEE.DEPT=DEPARTMENT.DEPTNO),
  ...);
```

Now consider an INSERT:

```
INSERT INTO EMP VALUES(:ID_VAR, :SAL_VAR, :DEPT_VAR);
```

Now suppose you get an SQLSTATE of '23000'. You look it up, and it says "integrity constraint violation," Now what? That SQLSTATE value means that either:

- The value in ID_VAR is a duplicate of an existing ID value: You violated the PRIMARY KEY constraint.

- The value in SAL_VAR is negative: You violated the CHECK constraint on SALARY.

- The value in DEPT_VAR isn't a valid key value for any existing row of DEPARTMENT: You violated the REFERENCES constraint on DEPT.

✔ The value in SAL_VAR is large enough that the sum of the employees' salaries in this department exceeds the BUDGET: You violated the CHECK constraint in the BUDGET column of DEPARTMENT. (Recall that when you change the database, *all* constraints that may be affected are checked, not just those defined in the immediate table.)

Well, you would have to do a lot of testing to figure out what is wrong with that INSERT. But you can find out what you need to know with GET DIAGNOSTICS:

```
DECLARE CONST_NAME_VAR CHAR(18) ;
GET DIAGNOSTICS EXCEPTION 1
    CONST_NAME_VAR = CONSTRAINT_NAME ;
```

Assuming that SQLSTATE was '23000', this GET DIAGNOSTICS will set CONST_NAME_VAR to either 'EMP_PK', 'EMP_SAL', 'EMP_DEPT', or 'DEPT_BUDGET'. Note that in practice you would also want to obtain the CONSTRAINT_SCHEMA and CONSTRAINT_CATALOG, in order to uniquely identify the constraint given by CONSTRAINT_NAME.

This use of GET DIAGNOSTICS is particularly important in the case where ALTER TABLE was used to add constraints that did not exist when you wrote the program:

```
ALTER TABLE EMPLOYEE
    ADD CONSTRAINT SAL_LIMIT CHECK(SALARY < 100000) ;
```

Now when you insert into EMPLOYEE or update the SALARY column of an EMPLOYEE, you will get an SQLSTATE of '23000' if SALARY exceeds 100000. You can therefore program your INSERT statement so that if you get an SQL-STATE of '23000', and you don't recognize the particular constraint name returned by GET DIAGNOSTICS, then you can display a helpful message such as "Invalid INSERT: Violated constraint SAL_LIMIT."

CONNECTION_NAME and ENVIRONMENT_NAME identify the connection and environment to which you are connected at the time the SQL statement is executed.

If the report deals with a table operation, CATALOG_NAME, SCHEMA_NAME, and TABLE_NAME will identify the table. COLUMN_NAME will identify the column within the table that caused the report to be made. If the situation involves a cursor, CURSOR_NAME will give its name.

Sometimes a DBMS will produce a string of natural language text to explain a condition. The MESSAGE_TEXT item is for this kind of information. The contents of this item are up to the implementation; they are not explicitly defined by SQL-92. If you do have something in MESSAGE_TEXT, its length in characters is recorded in MESSAGE_LENGTH and its length in octets is recorded in MESSAGE_OCTET_LENGTH. If the message is in normal ASCII characters, MESSAGE_LENGTH will equal MESSAGE_OCTET_LENGTH. If on the other hand, the message is in Kanji, or some other language whose characters require more than an octet to express, MESSAGE_LENGTH will differ from MESSAGE_OCTET_LENGTH.

To retrieve diagnostic information from a diagnostics area header use:

```
GET DIAGNOSTICS status₁ = item₁ [, status₂ = item₂]...
```

Status$_n$ is a host variable or parameter. *Item$_n$* can be any of the keywords NUMBER, MORE, COMMAND_FUNCTION, DYNAMIC_FUNCTION, or ROW_COUNT.

To retrieve diagnostic information from a diagnostics detail area the syntax is:

```
GET DIAGNOSTICS EXCEPTION condition-number
     status₁ = item₁ [, status₂ = item₂]...
```

Once again, *status$_n$* is a host variable or parameter. *Item$_n$* is any of the 16 keywords for the detail items listed in Table 18-3. The *condition-number* is (surprise!) the detail area's CONDITION_NUMBER item.

The treatment of the SQL diagnostic area and the SQL descriptor areas (covered in Chapter 17) is similar: The approach in both cases is to encapsulate the information, and to provide a GET statement to extract the information (and for descriptor areas, the SET statement to modify the information). GET DIAGNOSTICS and GET DESCRIPTOR retrieve very different information, but the approach used is similar. ■

Part VI
The Part of Tens

In This Part ...

If you've read this far, you may now consider yourself an SQL weenie. To raise your status that final degree from weenie to wizard, you'll have to master a set of rules to live by. But don't make the mistake of just reading the section headings. All the tips in this part are short and to the point. You'll need to read them all in their entirety then put them into practice before you can be a true SQL wizard.

Chapter 19

Ten Common Mistakes

*I*f you are reading this book, you must be interested in building relational database systems. Nobody studies SQL for the fun of it. SQL is the language you use to build database applications. A necessary prelude to building a database application is creating a database for it to work on. Many projects go awry before the first line of the application is coded. If you don't get the database definition right, your application is doomed, no matter how well it is written. This chapter gives you ten helpful database creation suggestions that will virtually guarantee the failure of your development effort.

Believe Your Client Really Knows What He Needs When He Asks You to Design and Build a Database System

Generally, when you are called in to design a database system, someone has a problem and their current methods are not working. They believe they know what the problem is, and what needs to be done to solve it. They tell you what to do.

Giving the client exactly what he asks for is usually a sure-fire prescription for disaster. Most users (and their managers) are not trained in the analytical methods needed to find out what the problem really is, so they have no chance of determining the best solution.

What you must do is tactfully convince the client that you are the expert in systems analysis and design, and that you must do a proper analysis to uncover the real cause of the problem that has manifested itself. Usually the real cause is hidden from view.

Don't Bother to Get Agreement on the Scope of the Project at the Beginning

At the beginning of a development project, your client will tell you what they want the new application to accomplish. Unfortunately, there is always something they forget to tell you — usually several things. Somewhere along the way, these new requirements crop up and are tacked onto the project. If you are being paid on a project basis rather than an hourly basis, this kind of scope growth can change what was once a profitable project into a loser. Make sure everything you are obligated to deliver is specified in writing before you start.

Ignore All Factors Except the Technical Ones When Assessing Feasibility

Application developers tend to look at potential projects in terms of their technical feasibility, and base their estimates of effort and time on that determination. However, issues of cost maximums, resource availability, schedule requirements, and organization politics can have a major effect on the project. In fact, these issues may turn a project that is technically feasible into a nightmare. Make sure you understand all relevant factors before starting any development project. You may decide it makes no sense to proceed. It is better to come to that conclusion at the beginning than to realize it after you have expended considerable effort.

Don't Solicit Feedback from Users When Designing the Database

Listen to the managers. The users themselves don't have any clout. Better yet, ignore the managers too. They usually don't have a clue anyway. Although it may be true that data entry clerks don't have much organizational clout, and that many managers have only a dim understanding of some aspects of their areas of responsibility, isolating yourself from them is almost certain to result in a system that solves a problem that nobody has. Communication with your clients is critical.

Choose Your Favorite Development Environment, Whether It Is Appropriate for This Job or Not

Chances are you have spent months or even years becoming proficient in the use of a particular DBMS or application development environment. This environment, no matter what it is, has strengths and weaknesses. There will be occasions when a development task you are trying to perform makes heavy demands in an area where your preferred development environment is weak. Rather than kludge together something that is not really the best solution, bite the bullet. You should do one of two things: Either climb the learning curve of a more appropriate tool and then use it, or candidly tell your client that their job would best be done with a tool that you are not expert in using. Suggest that they hire someone who can become productive with that tool immediately. Professional conduct of this sort will raise your client's respect for you. It may also get you laid off or fired.

Choose Your Favorite System Architecture, Whether It Is Appropriate for This Job or Not

Nobody can be an expert at everything. Database management systems that work in a teleprocessing environment are different from those that work in client-server, resource sharing, and distributed database environments. The one or two that you are expert in may not be the best for the job at hand. Choose the best architecture anyway, even if it means passing on this job. Not getting the job is better than getting it but producing a system that does not serve the client's needs.

Define Database Tables and Don't Worry About How They Relate to Each Other

Improper identification of data objects and their relationships to each other leads to database tables that are prone to introducing errors into the data that can destroy the validity of any results. To design a sound database, you must consider the overall organization of the data objects and carefully determine how they relate to each other. Usually, there is no one "right" way. You must determine what is appropriate, considering the present and projected future needs of your client.

Skip the Design Review — Design Reviews are a Waste of Time That Could Be Spent Coding

Nobody's perfect. Even the best designer and developer can miss important points that are evident to someone looking at the situation from another perspective. Actually, if you have to present your work to a formal design review, it will make you more disciplined in your work, and you will probably avoid numerous problems that you would otherwise have experienced. Have a competent professional review your proposed design *before* you start development.

Put the New System into Production Right Away — Beta Testing Is for Wimps

Any database application complex enough to be truly useful is also complex enough to contain bugs. Even if you test it in every way you can think of, there are sure to be failure modes you will not uncover. Beta testing means giving the application to people who do not understand it as well as you do. Chances are, they will have all kinds of problems that you never encountered, because you knew too much. It is best to fix such things before the product goes officially into use.

Don't Waste Time Documenting Your System — It Is So Well Designed, No One Will Ever Want to Change It

Ha! The only thing we can be absolutely sure of in this world is change. Count on it. Six months from now you will not remember why you designed things the way you did, unless you carefully document what you did and why you did it that way. If, God forbid, you were to be transferred to a different department or win the lottery and retire, your replacement has almost no chance of modifying your work to meet new requirements. She will probably have to scrap the whole thing and start from scratch. Don't just document your work adequately — overdocument. Put in more detail than you think is reasonable. When you come back to this project after six or eight months away from it, you will be glad you did.

The 5th Wave   By Rich Tennant

WHILE SEEKING HER PC-BASED RECIPE INDEX, DEBBY INADVERTENTLY LOADS A CAD/CAM PROGRAM. INSTEAD OF MAKING CHERRIES JUBILEE, SHE BUILDS A SUBOCEANIC DIVING PROBE.

Chapter 20

Ten Retrieval Tips

A database can be a virtual treasure trove of information, but like the treasure of the Caribbean pirates of long ago, the stuff you really want is probably buried and hidden from view. The SQL SELECT statement is the tool you use to dig up this hidden information. Even if you have a very clear idea of what you want to retrieve, translating that idea into SQL can be a challenge. If your formulation is just a little off, you could end up with wrong results that are close enough to what you expect to mislead you. To reduce the chances of being misled, follow these ten principles.

Verify that the Database Is Structured Appropriately

If you retrieve data from a database and your results don't seem reasonable, check the database design. There are a lot of poorly designed databases in use, and if you are working with one, fix the design before you try any other remedies. Good design is a prerequisite of data integrity.

Perform Your Query on a Test Database First

Create a test database that has exactly the same structure as your production database, but with only a few representative rows in the tables. Choose the data so that you know in advance what the result of your query should be. Run the query on the test data and see if the result matches your expectations. If it doesn't, you may need to reformulate your query.

Build several sets of test data, and be sure to include odd cases, such as empty tables and extreme values at the very limit of allowable ranges. Try to think of very unlikely scenarios, and check for proper behavior when they occur. In the course of checking for unlikely cases, you may gain insight into problems that are more likely to happen.

Triple-Check Any Query that Contains a Join

Joins are notorious for being counterintuitive. If your query contains one, make sure it is doing what you expect before you add WHERE clauses or other complicating factors.

Triple-Check Any Query that Contains a Subselect

Because of the way subselects can entangle data taken from one table with data taken from another, they are frequently misapplied. You must make sure that the data retrieved by the inner SELECT is the data needed by the outer SELECT to produce the desired end result. If you have two or more levels of subselects, you need to be even more careful.

Use a GROUP BY Clause with the Set Functions to Summarize Data for Groups Within a Table or View

Say you have a table (NATIONAL) giving the name (PLAYER), team (TEAM) and number of home runs hit (HOMERS) by every player in the National League. You can retrieve the team homer total for all teams with a query like this:

```
SELECT TEAM, SUM (HOMERS)
   FROM NATIONAL
   GROUP BY TEAM ;
```

This query lists each team, followed by the total number of home runs hit by all the players on that team.

Be Aware of Restrictions on the Use of the GROUP BY Clause

Suppose you want a list of power hitters in the National League. Consider the following query:

```
SELECT PLAYER, TEAM, HOMERS
   FROM NATIONAL
   WHERE HOMERS >= 20
   GROUP BY TEAM ;
```

In most implementations, this query will return an error. Generally, only columns used for grouping or columns used in a set function may appear in the SELECT list. The following formulation will work:

```
SELECT PLAYER, TEAM, HOMERS
   FROM NATIONAL
   WHERE HOMERS >= 20
   GROUP BY TEAM, PLAYER, HOMERS ;
```

Since all the columns you want to display appear in the GROUP BY clause, the query will succeed, and deliver the results you want. This formulation has the effect of sorting the resulting list first by TEAM, then by PLAYER, and finally by HOMERS.

Use Parentheses with the Logical Connectives AND, OR, and NOT

Sometimes when you mix ANDs and ORs, SQL does not process the expression in the order you expect. Use parentheses in complex expressions to make sure the result you get is the one you intended to get. The few extra keystrokes are a small price to pay for better quality results.

Don't Grant Retrieval Privileges to People Who Shouldn't Have Them

Many people don't use the security features available on their DBMS, because they don't want to bother with them and because they consider misuse and misappropriation of data to be something that happens only to other people. Don't wait to get burned. Establish and maintain security for all databases that have any value.

Back Up Your Databases Regularly

Data is hard to retrieve after a power surge, fire, earthquake, or mortar attack has destroyed your hard disk. Make frequent backups and remove them to a safe place.

Handle Error Conditions Gracefully

Whether you are making ad hoc queries from the console or embedding queries in an application, on occasion SQL will return an error message rather than the desired results. At the console, you can decide what to do next, based on the message returned, then take appropriate action. In an application the situation is different. The application user probably would not know what action would be appropriate. Put extensive error handling into your applications to cover every conceivable error that might occur. This will take a lot of effort, but is better than having the user stare quizzically at a frozen screen.

Appendix A

SQL-92 Reserved Words

ABSOLUTE

ACTION

ADD

ALLOCATE

ALTER

ARE

ASSERTION

AT

BETWEEN

BIT

BIT_LENGTH

BOTH

CASCADE

CASCADED

CASE

CAST

CATALOG

CHAR_LENGTH

CHARACTER_LENGTH

COALESCE

COLLATE

COLLATION

COLUMN

CONNECT

CONNECTION

CONSTRAINT

CONSTRAINTS

CONVERT

CORRESPONDING

CROSS

CURRENT_DATE

CURRENT_TIME

CURRENT_TIME-STAMP

CURRENT_USER

DATE

DAY

DEALLOCATE

DEFERRABLE

DEFERRED

DESCRIBE

DESCRIPTOR

DIAGNOSTICS

DISCONNECT

DOMAIN

DROP

ELSE

END-EXEC

EXCEPT

EXCEPTION

EXECUTE

EXTERNAL

EXTRACT

FALSE

FIRST

FULL

GET

GLOBAL

HOUR

IDENTITY

IMMEDIATE

INITIALLY

INNER

INPUT

INSENSITIVE

INTERSECT

INTERVAL

ISOLATION

JOIN

LAST

LEADING

LEFT

LEVEL

LOCAL

LOWER

MATCH

MINUTE

MONTH

NAMES

NATIONAL

NATURAL

NCHAR

NEXT

NO

NULLIF

OCTET_LENGTH

ONLY

OUTER

OUTPUT

OVERLAPS

PAD

PARTIAL

POSITION

PREPARE

PRESERVE

PRIOR

READ

RELATIVE

RESTRICT

REVOKE

RIGHT	SUBSTRING	TRANSACTION	USING
ROWS	SYSTEM_USER	TRANSLATE	VALUE
SCROLL	TEMPORARY	TRANSLATION	VARCHAR
SECOND	THEN	TRIM	VARYING
SESSION	TIME	TRUE	WHEN
SESSION_USER	TIMESTAMP	UNKNOWN	WRITE
SIZE	TIMEZONE_HOUR	UPPER	YEAR
SPACE	TIMEZONE_MINUTE	USAGE	ZONE
SQLSTATE	TRAILING		

Appendix B

Entry, Intermediate, and Full Subsets of SQL-92

● ●

There are three levels of adherence to the SQL-92 specification: entry, intermediate, and full.

Entry SQL-92

Entry SQL-92 is very close to SQL-89, with just a few differences. The main differences are:

- ✔ The SQLSTATE status variable and parameter have been added.
- ✔ The AS clause has been added to allow naming of columns in a SELECT list.
- ✔ Interfaces to the Ada, C, and MUMPS languages have been added.
- ✔ Commas and parentheses are allowed in parameter lists.
- ✔ Colons are now required preceding parameter names in procedures in modules.
- ✔ Delimited identifiers, enclosed in double quotation marks, are now allowed. Within the quotes you can have any characters, including blanks and punctuation. A delimited identifier can even be the same as a reserved word, for example:

    "Rate-of-pay"

    "New Salary after adjustment"

    "select"

- ✔ The semantics of WITH CHECK OPTION has been clarified.
- ✔ Various errors in the SQL-89 specification have been corrected.

Intermediate SQL-92

Intermediate SQL-92 includes features that were already implemented by several vendors, features that should be relatively easy to implement, and features deemed to be of high value to users. The most significant are:

- ✔ Dynamic SQL (partial)
- ✔ CASCADE DELETE
- ✔ The FULL OUTER JOIN operator
- ✔ The INTERSECT and EXCEPT set operators
- ✔ The CASE expression
- ✔ CAST data type conversion capability
- ✔ Better handling of isolation levels in transactions
- ✔ Row and table value constructors (partial)
- ✔ Schema manipulation statements
- ✔ Character string operations and functions (SUBSTRING, TRIM, concatenation, and FOLD)
- ✔ Enhancements to the LIKE predicate
- ✔ The UNIQUE predicate
- ✔ User-defined constraint names
- ✔ The GET DIAGNOSTICS statement
- ✔ Support for multiple modules in one application
- ✔ Domain support
- ✔ Support for character sets beyond the default
- ✔ Variable length character strings
- ✔ Datetime and interval data types and some of their associated operations
- ✔ Scrolled cursors
- ✔ Explicit DEFAULT VALUES allowed in INSERT statements and row value constructors
- ✔ A flag for use when writing portable applications

Full SQL-92

Full SQL-92 includes everything defined by the standard. In addition to the features of entry and intermediate SQL-92, it also includes

- Full dynamic SQL
- Deferred constraint checking and named constraints
- Full row and table value constructor support
- A fuller implementation of subqueries
- UPDATEs and DELETEs that reference the table they are modifying
- Additional operations on datetime and interval data
- The UNION JOIN and CROSS JOIN operators
- CASCADE UPDATE
- BIT and BIT VARYING data types
- Assertions
- Temporary tables
- Internationalization features, including character translation

Glossary

● ●

Aggregate function A function that produces a single result based on the contents of an entire set of table rows. Also called a **set function**.

Alias A short substitute or "nickname" for a table name.

Assertion A constraint that is specified by a CREATE ASSERTION statement (rather than by a clause of a CREATE TABLE statement). Assertions commonly apply to more than one table.

Back end That part of a DBMS that interacts directly with the database.

Catalog A named collection of schemas.

Client That part of a DBMS that displays information on a screen and responds to user input (the front end).

Client-server system A multiuser system in which a central processor (the server) is connected to multiple intelligent user workstations (the clients).

CODASYL DBTG database model The network database model. Note: This use of the term "network" refers to the structuring of the data ("network" as opposed to "hierarchy"), rather than to network communications.

Collating sequence The ordering of characters in a character set. All collating sequences for character sets that have the Latin characters (a, b, c) define the

obvious ordering (a,b,c,...). But, they differ in the ordering of special characters (+, -, <, ?, etc.), and in the relative ordering of the digits and the letters.

Column A component of a table that holds a single attribute of the table.

Composite key A key made up of two or more table columns.

Conceptual view The schema of a database.

Concurrent access Two or more users operating on the same rows in a database table at the same time.

Constraint A restriction you specify on the data in a database.

Constraint, deferred A constraint that is not applied until you change its status to immediate or until you COMMIT the encapsulating transaction.

Cursor An SQL feature that specifies a set of rows, an ordering of those rows, and a current row within that ordering.

Data Control Language (DCL) That part of SQL that protects the database from harm.

Data Definition Language (DDL) That part of SQL used to define, modify, and eradicate database structures.

Data Manipulation Language (DML) That part of SQL that operates on database data.

Data redundancy Having the same data stored in more than one place in a database.

Data sublanguage A subset of a complete computer language that deals specifically with data handling. SQL is a data sublanguage.

Database A self-describing collection of integrated records.

Database, organizational A database containing information used by an entire organization.

Database, personal A database designed for use by a single person on a single computer.

Database, workgroup A database designed to be used by a department or workgroup within an organization.

Database administrator (DBA) The person ultimately responsible for the functionality, integrity, and safety of a database.

Database engine That part of a DBMS which directly interacts with the database (part of the back end).

Database server The server component of a client-server system.

DBMS A database management system.

Deletion anomaly An inconsistency in a multitable database that occurs when a row is deleted from one of its tables.

Descriptor An area in memory used to pass information between an application's procedural code and its dynamic SQL code.

Diagnostics area A data structure managed by the DBMS that contains detailed information about the last SQL statement executed, and any errors that occurred during its execution.

Distributed data processing A system in which data is distributed across multiple servers.

Domain The set of all values that a database item can assume.

Domain integrity A property of a database table column where all data items in that column fall within the domain of the column.

Entity integrity A property of a database table that is entirely consistent with the real-world object that it models.

File server The server component of a resource sharing system. It does not contain any database management software.

Flat file A collection of data records having minimal structure.

Foreign key A column or combination of columns in a database table that references the primary key of another table in the database.

Front end That part of a DBMS that interacts directly with the user.

Functional dependency A relationship between or among attributes of a relation.

Hierarchical database model A tree-structured model of data.

Host variable A variable within an application written using embedded SQL.

Implementation A particular relational DBMS running on a specific hardware platform.

Index A table of pointers used to rapidly locate rows in a data table.

Information schema The system tables, which hold the database's meta-data.

Insertion anomaly An inconsistency introduced into a multitable database when a new row is inserted into one of its tables.

Join A relational operator that combines data from multiple tables into a single result table.

Logical connectives Used to connect or change the truth value of predicates to produce more complex predicates.

Meta-data Data about the structure of the data in a database.

Modification anomaly A problem introduced into a database when a modification (insertion, deletion, or update) is made to one of the tables in the database.

Module language A form of SQL in which SQL statements are placed in modules, which are called by an application program written in a host language.

Nested query A statement that contains one or more subqueries.

Network database model A way of organizing a database so that redundancy of data items is minimized by allowing any data item (node) to be directly connected to any other.

Normalization A technique that reduces or eliminates the possibility that a database will be subject to modification anomalies.

Oracle A relational database management system marketed by Oracle Corporation.

Parameter A variable within an application written in SQL module language.

Precision The maximum number of digits allowed in a numeric data item.

Predicate A statement that may be either true or false.

Primary key A column or combination of columns in a database table that uniquely identifies each row in the table.

Procedural language A computer language that solves a problem by executing a procedure in the form of a sequence of steps.

Query A question you ask about the data in a database.

Rapid Application Development tool A proprietary graphically oriented alternative to SQL. There are a number of such tools on the market.

Record A representation of some physical or conceptual object.

Referential integrity A state in which all the tables in a database are consistent with each other.

Relation A two-dimensional array of rows and columns, containing single-valued entries and no duplicate rows.

Reserved words Words that have a special significance in SQL and cannot be used as variable names or in any other way that differs from their intended use.

Row value expression A list of value expressions enclosed in parentheses and separated by commas.

Scale The number of digits in the fractional part of a numeric data item.

Schema The structure of an entire database. The database's meta-data.

Schema owner The person who created the schema.

SEQUEL A data sublanguage created by IBM that was a precursor of SQL.

Set function A function that produces a single result based on the contents of an entire set of table rows. Also called an **aggregate function**.

SQL An industry standard data sublanguage, specifically designed to create, manipulate, and control relational databases. SQL-92 is the latest version of the standard.

SQL, dynamic A means of building compiled applications where all data items are not identifiable at compile time.

SQL, embedded An application structure in which SQL statements are embedded within programs written in a host language.

SQL, interactive A real-time conversation with a database.

SQL/DS A relational database management system marketed by IBM Corporation.

Subquery A query within a query.

Table A relation.

Teleprocessing system A powerful central processor connected to multiple dumb terminals.

Transaction A sequence of SQL statements whose effect is not accessible to other transactions until all of the statements are executed.

Transitive dependency One attribute of a relation depends on a second attribute, which in turn depends on a third attribute.

Translation table Tool for converting character strings from one character set to another.

Update anomaly A problem introduced into a database when a table row is updated.

Value expression An expression that combines two or more values.

Value expression, conditional A value expression that assigns different values to arguments, based on whether a condition is true.

Value expression, datetime A value expression that deals with DATE, TIME, TIMESTAMP, or INTERVAL data.

Value expression, numeric A value expression that combines numeric values using the addition, subtraction, multiplication, or division operators.

Value expression, string A value expression that combines character strings with the concatenation operator.

Value function A function that performs an operation on a single character string, number, or datetime.

View A database component that behaves exactly like a table, but has no independent existence of its own.

Virtual table A view.

Index

• •

• SYMBOLS •

* (asterisk), 121, 272
[] (brackets), 127, 146, 170
: (colon), 277, 337
, (comma), 337
> (greater-than sign), 62
< (less-than sign), 62
() (parentheses), 334, 337
% (percent sign), 176, 177
# (pound sign), 177
; (semicolon), 276
_ (underscore character), 176
| (vertical bar), 152

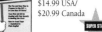

The Internet For Macs® For Dummies® 2nd Edition	by Charles Seiter	ISBN: 1-56884-371-2	$19.99 USA/$26.99 Canada
The Internet For Macs® For Dummies® Starter Kit	by Charles Seiter	ISBN: 1-56884-244-9	$29.99 USA/$39.99 Canada
The Internet For Macs® For Dummies® Starter Kit Bestseller Edition	by Charles Seiter	ISBN: 1-56884-245-7	$39.99 USA/$54.99 Canada
The Internet For Windows® For Dummies® Starter Kit	by John R. Levine & Margaret Levine Young	ISBN: 1-56884-237-6	$34.99 USA/$44.99 Canada
The Internet For Windows® For Dummies® Starter Kit, Bestseller Edition	by John R. Levine & Margaret Levine Young	ISBN: 1-56884-246-5	$39.99 USA/$54.99 Canada

MACINTOSH

Mac® Programming For Dummies®	by Dan Parks Sydow	ISBN: 1-56884-173-6	$19.95 USA/$26.95 Canada
Macintosh® System 7.5 For Dummies®	by Bob LeVitus	ISBN: 1-56884-197-3	$19.95 USA/$26.95 Canada
MORE Macs® For Dummies®	by David Pogue	ISBN: 1-56884-087-X	$19.95 USA/$26.95 Canada
PageMaker 5 For Macs® For Dummies®	by Galen Gruman & Deke McClelland	ISBN: 1-56884-178-7	$19.95 USA/$26.95 Canada
QuarkXPress 3.3 For Dummies®	by Galen Gruman & Barbara Assadi	ISBN: 1-56884-217-1	$19.99 USA/$26.99 Canada
Upgrading and Fixing Macs® For Dummies®	by Kearney Rietmann & Frank Higgins	ISBN: 1-56884-189-2	$19.95 USA/$26.95 Canada

MULTIMEDIA

Multimedia & CD-ROMs For Dummies® 2nd Edition	by Andy Rathbone	ISBN: 1-56884-907-9	$19.99 USA/$26.99 Canada
Multimedia & CD-ROMs For Dummies® Interactive Multimedia Value Pack, 2nd Edition	by Andy Rathbone	ISBN: 1-56884-909-5	$29.99 USA/$39.99 Canada

OPERATING SYSTEMS:

DOS

MORE DOS For Dummies®	by Dan Gookin	ISBN: 1-56884-046-2	$19.95 USA/$26.95 Canada
OS/2® Warp For Dummies® 2nd Edition	by Andy Rathbone	ISBN: 1-56884-205-8	$19.95 USA/$26.99 Canada

UNIX

MORE UNIX® For Dummies®	by John R. Levine & Margaret Levine Young	ISBN: 1-56884-361-5	$19.99 USA/$26.99 Canada
UNIX® For Dummies®	by John R. Levine & Margaret Levine Young	ISBN: 1-878058-58-4	$19.95 USA/$26.95 Canada

WINDOWS

MORE Windows® For Dummies® 2nd Edition	by Andy Rathbone	ISBN: 1-56884-048-9	$19.95 USA/$26.95 Canada
Windows® 95 For Dummies®	by Andy Rathbone	ISBN: 1-56884-240-6	$19.99 USA/$26.99 Canada

PCS/HARDWARE

Illustrated Computer Dictionary For Dummies® 2nd Edition	by Dan Gookin & Wallace Wang	ISBN: 1-56884-218-X	$12.95 USA/$16.95 Canada
Upgrading and Fixing PCs For Dummies® 2nd Edition	by Andy Rathbone	ISBN: 1-56884-903-6	$19.99 USA/$26.99 Canada

PRESENTATION/AUTOCAD

AutoCAD For Dummies®	by Bud Smith	ISBN: 1-56884-191-4	$19.95 USA/$26.95 Canada
PowerPoint 4 For Windows® For Dummies®	by Doug Lowe	ISBN: 1-56884-161-2	$16.99 USA/$22.99 Canada

PROGRAMMING

Borland C++ For Dummies®	by Michael Hyman	ISBN: 1-56884-162-0	$19.95 USA/$26.95 Canada
C For Dummies® Volume 1	by Dan Gookin	ISBN: 1-878058-78-9	$19.95 USA/$26.95 Canada
C++ For Dummies®	by Stephen R. Davis	ISBN: 1-56884-163-9	$19.95 USA/$26.95 Canada
Delphi Programming For Dummies®	by Neil Rubenking	ISBN: 1-56884-200-7	$19.99 USA/$26.99 Canada
Mac® Programming For Dummies®	by Dan Parks Sydow	ISBN: 1-56884-173-6	$19.95 USA/$26.95 Canada
PowerBuilder 4 Programming For Dummies®	by Ted Coombs & Jason Coombs	ISBN: 1-56884-325-9	$19.99 USA/$26.99 Canada
QBasic Programming For Dummies®	by Douglas Hergert	ISBN: 1-56884-093-4	$19.95 USA/$26.95 Canada
Visual Basic 3 For Dummies®	by Wallace Wang	ISBN: 1-56884-076-4	$19.95 USA/$26.95 Canada
Visual Basic "X" For Dummies®	by Wallace Wang	ISBN: 1-56884-230-9	$19.99 USA/$26.99 Canada
Visual C++ 2 For Dummies®	by Michael Hyman & Bob Arnson	ISBN: 1-56884-328-3	$19.99 USA/$26.99 Canada
Windows® 95 Programming For Dummies®	by S. Randy Davis	ISBN: 1-56884-327-5	$19.99 USA/$26.99 Canada

SPREADSHEET

1-2-3 For Dummies®	by Greg Harvey	ISBN: 1-878058-60-6	$16.95 USA/$22.95 Canada
1-2-3 For Windows® 5 For Dummies® 2nd Edition	by John Walkenbach	ISBN: 1-56884-216-3	$16.95 USA/$22.95 Canada
Excel 5 For Macs® For Dummies®	by Greg Harvey	ISBN: 1-56884-186-8	$19.95 USA/$26.95 Canada
Excel For Dummies® 2nd Edition	by Greg Harvey	ISBN: 1-56884-050-0	$16.95 USA/$22.95 Canada
MORE 1-2-3 For DOS For Dummies®	by John Weingarten	ISBN: 1-56884-224-4	$19.99 USA/$26.99 Canada
MORE Excel 5 For Windows® For Dummies®	by Greg Harvey	ISBN: 1-56884-207-4	$19.95 USA/$26.95 Canada
Quattro Pro 6 For Windows® For Dummies®	by John Walkenbach	ISBN: 1-56884-174-4	$19.95 USA/$26.95 Canada
Quattro Pro For DOS For Dummies®	by John Walkenbach	ISBN: 1-56884-023-3	$16.95 USA/$22.95 Canada

UTILITIES

Norton Utilities 8 For Dummies®	by Beth Slick	ISBN: 1-56884-166-3	$19.95 USA/$26.95 Canada

VCRS/CAMCORDERS

VCRs & Camcorders For Dummies™	by Gordon McComb & Andy Rathbone	ISBN: 1-56884-229-5	$14.99 USA/$20.99 Canada

WORD PROCESSING

Ami Pro For Dummies®	by Jim Meade	ISBN: 1-56884-049-7	$19.95 USA/$26.95 Canada
MORE Word For Windows® 6 For Dummies®	by Doug Lowe	ISBN: 1-56884-165-5	$19.95 USA/$26.95 Canada
MORE WordPerfect® 6 For Windows® For Dummies®	by Margaret Levine Young & David C. Kay	ISBN: 1-56884-206-6	$19.95 USA/$26.95 Canada
MORE WordPerfect® 6 For DOS For Dummies®	by Wallace Wang, edited by Dan Gookin	ISBN: 1-56884-047-0	$19.95 USA/$26.95 Canada
Word 6 For Macs® For Dummies®	by Dan Gookin	ISBN: 1-56884-190-6	$19.95 USA/$26.95 Canada
Word For Windows® 6 For Dummies®	by Dan Gookin	ISBN: 1-56884-075-6	$16.95 USA/$22.95 Canada
Word For Windows® For Dummies®	by Dan Gookin & Ray Werner	ISBN: 1-878058-86-X	$16.95 USA/$22.95 Canada
WordPerfect® 6 For DOS For Dummies®	by Dan Gookin	ISBN: 1-878058-77-0	$16.95 USA/$22.95 Canada
WordPerfect® 6.1 For Windows® For Dummies® 2nd Edition	by Margaret Levine Young & David Kay	ISBN: 1-56884-243-0	$16.95 USA/$22.95 Canada
WordPerfect® For Dummies®	by Dan Gookin	ISBN: 1-878058-52-5	$16.95 USA/$22.95 Canada

IDG BOOKS WORLDWIDE™

Order Center: **(800) 762-2974** *(8 a.m.–6 p.m., EST, weekdays)*

Quantity	ISBN	Title	Price	Total

Shipping & Handling Charges

	Description	First book	Each additional book	Total
Domestic	Normal	$4.50	$1.50	$
	Two Day Air	$8.50	$2.50	$
	Overnight	$18.00	$3.00	$
International	Surface	$8.00	$8.00	$
	Airmail	$16.00	$16.00	$
	DHL Air	$17.00	$17.00	$

*For large quantities call for shipping & handling charges.
**Prices are subject to change without notice.

Ship to:

Name _____

Company _____

Address _____

City/State/Zip _____

Daytime Phone _____

Payment: ☐ Check to IDG Books Worldwide (US Funds Only)

☐ VISA   ☐ MasterCard   ☐ American Express

Card # _____ Expires _____

Signature _____

Subtotal _____

CA residents add applicable sales tax _____

IN, MA, and MD residents add 5% sales tax _____

IL residents add 6.25% sales tax _____

RI residents add 7% sales tax _____

TX residents add 8.25% sales tax _____

Shipping _____

Total _____

Please send this order form to:

**IDG Books Worldwide, Inc.
7260 Shadeland Station, Suite 100
Indianapolis, IN 46256**

*Allow up to 3 weeks for delivery.
Thank you!*

IDG BOOKS WORLDWIDE REGISTRATION CARD

RETURN THIS REGISTRATION CARD FOR FREE CATALOG

Title of this book: SQL For Dummies

My overall rating of this book: ❑ Very good [1] ❑ Good [2] ❑ Satisfactory [3] ❑ Fair [4] ❑ Poor [5]

How I first heard about this book:

❑ Found in bookstore; name: [6]

❑ Advertisement: [8]

❑ Word of mouth; heard about book from friend, co-worker, etc.: [10]

❑ Book review: [7]

❑ Catalog: [9]

❑ Other: [11]

What I liked most about this book:

What I would change, add, delete, etc., in future editions of this book:

Other comments:

Number of computer books I purchase in a year: ❑ 1 [12] ❑ 2-5 [13] ❑ 6-10 [14] ❑ More than 10 [15]

I would characterize my computer skills as: ❑ Beginner [16] ❑ Intermediate [17] ❑ Advanced [18] ❑ Professional [19]

I use ❑ DOS [20] ❑ Windows [21] ❑ OS/2 [22] ❑ Unix [23] ❑ Macintosh [24] ❑ Other: [25]_____ (please specify)

I would be interested in new books on the following subjects:
(please check all that apply, and use the spaces provided to identify specific software)

❑ Word processing: [26]

❑ Data bases: [28]

❑ File Utilities: [30]

❑ Networking: [32]

❑ Other: [34]

❑ Spreadsheets: [27]

❑ Desktop publishing: [29]

❑ Money management: [31]

❑ Programming languages: [33]

I use a PC at (please check all that apply): ❑ home [35] ❑ work [36] ❑ school [37] ❑ other: [38] _____

The disks I prefer to use are ❑ 5.25 [39] ❑ 3.5 [40] ❑ other: [41]_____

I have a CD ROM: ❑ yes [42] ❑ no [43]

I plan to buy or upgrade computer hardware this year: ❑ yes [44] ❑ no [45]

I plan to buy or upgrade computer software this year: ❑ yes [46] ❑ no [47]

Name: _____ Business title: [48] Type of Business: [49]

Address (❑ home [50] ❑ work [51]/Company name: _____)

Street/Suite#

City [52]/State [53]/Zipcode [54]: _____ Country [55]

❑ **I liked this book!** You may quote me by name in future IDG Books Worldwide promotional materials.

My daytime phone number is _____

IDG BOOKS ®

THE WORLD OF
COMPUTER
KNOWLEDGE

❏ YES!

Please keep me informed about IDG's World of Computer Knowledge.
Send me the latest IDG Books catalog.